Integrated
Project Management

Integrated
Project Management

Bruce T. Barkley, Sr.
Senior Faculty
Keller Graduate School of Management
DeVry University
Cumming, Georgia

McGraw-Hill

New York   Chicago   San Francisco   Lisbon   London   Madrid
Mexico City   Milan   New Delhi   San Juan   Seoul
Singapore   Sydney   Toronto

The **McGraw·Hill** Companies

Cataloging-in-Publication Data is on file with the Library of Congress.

Copyright © 2006 by The McGraw-Hill Companies, Inc. All rights reserved. Printed in the United States of America. Except as permitted under the United States Copyright Act of 1976, no part of this publication may be reproduced or distributed in any form or by any means, or stored in a data base or retrieval system, without the prior written permission of the publisher.

1 2 3 4 5 6 7 8 9 0   DOC/DOC   0 1 3 2 1 0 9 8 7 6

ISBN 0-07-146626-6

The sponsoring editor for this book was Larry S. Hager and the production supervisor was Pamela A. Pelton. It was set in Century Schoolbook by International Typesetting and Composition. The art director for the cover was Margaret Webster-Shapiro.

Printed and bound by RR Donnelley.

This book was printed on acid-free paper.

McGraw-Hill books are available at special quantity discounts to use as premiums and sales promotions, or for use in corporate training programs. For more information, please write to the Director of Special Sales, McGraw-Hill Professional, Two Penn Plaza, New York, NY 10121-2298. Or contact your local bookstore.

To the over 3,000 hard working, adult graduate and undergraduate students at DeVry University/Keller Graduate School of Management—Atlanta, and at The University College, University of Maryland, who have provided me over the past 30 years with wonderful opportunities to learn from them—undoubtedly more than they learned from me.

Contents

Organization of the Book   xiii
Preface   xvii
Acknowledgements   xxv

Chapter 1. Project Integration   1

Introduction   1
Integration: Concepts and Models   1
Vertical and Horizontal Integration   4
Analysis, Selection, and Scheduling: Portfolio Integration   5
eProcurement: Example of Horizontal Integration   6
PMBOK and Project Planning   6
Strategic Planning   7
Ethics and Project Integration   8
Integration Model   8
Project Integration Management: Organizational Issues   9
Develop Project Charter   12
Develop Preliminary Project Scope Statement   19
Develop Project Management Plan   21
Direct and Manage Project Execution   23
Monitor and Control Project Work   26
Integrated Change Control   27
Close Project   30

Chapter 2. Case Study of PMBOK Implementation: Integrated Transportation System   33

Integration Gateway 1: Global Interface   39
Integration Gateway 2: Business Planning   40
Integration Gateway 3: Organizational Development   40
Integration Gateway 4: Global Team Composition and Development   41
Integration Gateway 5: Support Systems Audit   42
Integration Gateway 6: Portfolio Development and Management   43
Integration Gateway 7: Market and Customer Interface   44

Integration Gateway 8: Project Integration Management   44
Integration Gateway 9: Systems Safety and Reliability   45
Integration Gateway 10: Chassis, Mechanical, and Electronics
  Design and Development   46
Integration Gateway 11: Software Design and Development   46
Integration Gateway 12: Test Equipment and Testing   46
Integration Gateway 13: Integration of Software and Hardware   46

**Chapter 3. Case Application: Integration Issues in Portfolio
and Project Planning Life Cycles**   47

The Case: QuickTech Building Systems   48
The Portfolio: Integration Issues and Procedures
  in Development   49
Definition: Work Breakdown Structure   51
Plan Tasks for Earned Value   53
Network Diagram   54
Analysis of Early and Late Starts   55
Gantt Chart   56
Resource Integration   56
Scale and Integration   57
Integrated Monitoring   57
"Reading" the Project as an Integrated Whole   58
Integration of Cost, Schedule, Risk, and Quality   59
Steps in the Integration Process   60
Integration Skills of the Program and Project Manager   61
Single Project Management   61
Program (or Multiproject) Management   62
Buildlt: A Sample Integrated Program Structure   63
Organization   63
Strategic Statement   64
Program of Projects   64
PCAS   65

**Chapter 4. A Program Management Manual for Integrated
Project Management**   67

Program Management Principles   67
Integrated Program Management: Roles and Responsibilities   69
Program Management Office   70
Departmental Manager Roles in the Matrix   71
Role of the Program Administrator/Planner   71
Five-Step Scheduling Process   75
Integrated Resource Planning and Control   79
Integrated Tracking and Program Review   80
Schedule Update Procedures   80
Analyzing Variance   81
Program Closeout and Lessons Learned   82
Earned Value and Other Integrating Functions and Forces   82

Chapter 5. Rebuilding New Orleans: A Case in Integrated Program and Project Management   91

The Concept: Leased Land under Public Ownership   92
The Integration Challenge   92
Motivation   94
Contract Goals   94
Contract Objectives   94
Technical Requirements for Community Internet System   95
Security Systems   95
Structure   95
Fire Suppression Systems   95
Transportation   95
Management Approach   96
Project Reporting Requirements   96
Stage Gate Process and Payment Milestones   96
Affordability Requirements   96
The New Vision Program   97
Questions for New Visions in Setting Up Its Integrated Project
  Management Approach   97
Accurate Performance Assessment   98
Reliable Prediction of Future Performance   98
Timely Management Action   98
Schedule Categories   99

Chapter 6. Technical Program and Project Integration Tools   101

Project Management Integration Activities   101
Schedule Structures: WBS and IMP   106
Supplier Data Integration   106
Program Networks   106
Critical Path Methodology   107
Project Contract Integration: The Federal Government Model 107
Teamwork Difficult in Engineering Environment   110
IMP and IMS Relationships   110
Integration of the Business Plan, Product Development and Production 111
More on Stage Gate Process as an Integrating Function   114

Chapter 7. Quality and Project Integration   117

System Development/Improvement   118
Concurrent Engineering   118
Quality Function Deployment   119
Robust Design   120
Statistical Process Control   121
Cost of Poor Quality   121
Just-in-Time   122
Total Production Maintenance   122
Manufacturing Resource Planning   122

History of Project Integration Management and Quality   125
Generating Commitment and Purpose in the
  Integrated Project Team   131
Integration and Individual Involvement   132
Teams   134
Listening   144
Focus Setting   145
Rules of Conduct Examples   149
Brainstorming   153
Presentation   157

Chapter 8. Creating a Quality Organization in the New Millennium   165

Individual Work Ethic   165
Flexible Organization   166
Full Cycle Customer Involvement   166
Embedded and Integrated Quality   166
The Internet   167
Tracking Change and Integrating Midstream Correction   168
Traditional Project Teams   169
The Texture of Integration   170
Integration and Ethics and Internal Control Management   170
Vertical Integration of Businesses: Another Application of Integration   171
Project Integration Lessons Learned   171

Chapter 9. Risk and Project Integration   173

Earned Value: A Risk Integration Indicator   179
The Risk of "Unaccountability"   179
Project Manager Integration Roles   180
Integration Issues in Budgeting   181
Why Integrate Risk?   181
Integration and Sensitivity Analysis   182
Monte Carlo Risk Analysis : Quantitative Risk Integration   182
Special Challenges of the Integration Risk
  into a Software Project   183

Chapter 10. Strategic Integration: The Eastern Case   185

Commitment and Partnership   187
Stakeholder Relations   187
Eight Strategies   188
Overview on Integration Issues   189
Strengths, Weaknesses, Opportunities, and Threats   189
Eastern's Strategic Plan   192
Eight Key Strategies   194
Communicating Strategy and Risk   202
Postscript to the Strategic Plan   202
Acquisition and Merger   202

Integration in Global and International Projects   202
Postscript on Integration and the Eastern Case   203

Chapter 11. How to Use the Integration Tools in Microsoft Project   205

WBS and Task Outline   205
Integrating Projects in Microsoft Project   209
Summing up the MS Project Integration Function   210

Chapter 12. Tools in Building an Integrated Project Management System   213

Organization-Wide Project Management System   213
Program/Portfolio Planning and Development System   215
Resource Management System   216
Program Information Technology System   216
Product/Service Development Process   217
Interface Management   217
Portfolio Management   218
Program Monitoring and Control System   218
Change Management System   218
Program Evaluation System   219
Limitations of Integration Systems   219

Chapter 13. In Sum   221

Project Integration and Interface Points   221
Integration of Customer Requirements and Project Scope of Work   223
Achieving Alignment   223
Integrating Business Financial Goals with Project Selection   224
Project Planning Phase   224
WBS: New Product Project   225
Development of the Project Management System Framework
  with New Product Development   226
Project/Product Development Phase   228
Program, Multiproject Management Phase   229
Organizational and Accountability Phase   230
Project Monitoring Phase   231
The Project Management System Supports Integration   231
Integrated Project Review   234
Transition to Marketing Phase   245
New Concepts in Integration   245
Organizational and Technical Interfaces   252
Risk Reviews   253
General Responsibilities   254
Detailed Requirements   254
Critical Design Gate Review   255
Software Development "Points of Risk": A Function of Complexity   257
Integrating Risk Mitigation   258
Quality and Risk in Software Development   258

Appendix 1. Integrated Project Management—An Introduction   259

Introduction   259
Requirements and Features   259
Scope of Work   260
Project Life Cycle   260
Work Breakdown Structure   260
Scheduling   260
Resources and Costs   261
Risk Planning and Management   261
Monitoring and Tracking   261
Change Management Process   261
The Project Team and Organizational Structures   262
Microsoft Project   262
Contract Management Issues   262

Appendix 2. Nine Elements of Integrated Project Management   263

Appendix 3. Integrated Program Management Tools   265

Organization-Wide Project Management System   265
Program Management System   266
Resource Management System   266
Program Information Technology System   266
Product/Service Development Process   266
Interface Management   267
Portfolio Management   267
Program Monitoring and Control System   267
Change Management System   267
Program Evaluation and Audit   267

Appendix 4. Project Manager Challenges in Integration   269

Appendix 5. Graphs on Earned Value and Integration   271

Appendix 6. Notes on Project Integration   275

How to Fail in Project Management Without Really Trying   275
What You Don't Know About Making Decisions   275
Bringing Discipline to Project Management   276
Theory of Constraints Dictionary   276
What You Don't Know   276
Learning From Projects   276
The Successful Integrated Project   277
Selecting and Developing PMs   277
Synergistic Team Relations   277
Criteria for Competent PMs   278
Leadership   278
Leadership Impacts   278
Developing Core Teams   278
Project Team Competence   278
Assessing Team Competence   279

Motivation   279
Total Manager   279
Communication   280
Presentations   280
Motivation and Leadership   280
Project Management and Conflict   281
Steps in Conflict   281
Getting Unstuck   281
Negotiating   281
Conflicts   282
Meeting Skills   282
Personal Effectiveness   282

Appendix 7. Why Project Risk Management and Integration?   283

Introduction   283
Purpose of Project Risk Management   283
Risk and Decision Making   284
Risk Elements   284
Rewards of Taking Risks   284
Potential Project Risk Factors   284
Project Management Body of Knowledge (PMBOK)   285
PMBOK Section 11: Risk Management Processes   285

Appendix 8. Integrated Risk Planning   291

Introduction   291
Risk Planning: Inputs   291
Risk Planning: Tools   291
Risk Planning: Outputs   292
Risk Planning: Setting Up Company for Risk Management   292
Issues in Risk Planning   292
Scope Risks   292
Resource Risks   293
Quality Risks   293
Cost Risks   293
Time/Schedule Risks   293
Technology Risks   293
Risk Information   294
Risk Intensity in Project Life Cycle Phases   294

Appendix 9. Integrated Risk-Based Scheduling Using Microsoft Project 295

Introduction   295
Choose Risks for Three-Scenario Analysis   295
Generating Scenarios   295
Microsoft Project PERT Tool   296
PERT Is "What If" Analysis   296

Index   297

Organization of the Book

Chapter 1 addresses the new standard for project integration management in the Project Management Institute Body of Knowledge revised in 2005, so it will be of direct interest to those Project Management Professionals (PMPs) who are doing refresher work as well as those preparing for the PMP certification. Chapters 2 and 3 are case studies and Chap. 4 is a sample manual on integration. Chapter 5 applies integration principles to the national challenge of rebuilding the city of New Orleans. Chapters 6 and 7 cover technical issues on project integration and Chap. 8 targets the organization itself. Chapter 9 treats risk as an integrating function and Chap. 10 is a strategic planning case with integration implications. Chapter 11 shows how to integrate projects using Microsoft project tools and operations, Chap. 12 discusses the systems necessary to build the capacity for integrated project management, and Chap. 13 summarized the essential points in the book. The appendices contain nine Powerpoint presentations, useful in delivering the messages of the book.

Preface

Integrated project management, or *program management* as it is sometimes called, involves selecting, coordinating, and synchronizing projects in a company or agency, so that all the key factors for success are *optimized*. Program managers see both the big picture and the details of program and project work—all at the same time.

Integration involves analyzing project business value at the high level; mobilizing team performance and dynamics; monitoring projects to assure midstream adjustment and project recovery; resolving technical, resource, and interpersonal conflicts at every level; managing program interfaces and multitasking; identifying organizational constraints and *exploiting* them; keeping tabs on accountability; and reporting to avoid ethical and waste problems.

In an integrated project organization, program and project managers:

- See projects as capital investments made by the organization to achieve corporate business strategy and competitive advantage.

- Analyze a portfolio of candidate projects using net present value techniques in combination with risk assessment and other tools.

- "Read" team dynamics as they relate to team leadership, motivation, effectiveness, decision-making process, and conflict resolution.

- Formulate and evaluate alternative completion plans to optimize program quality, cost, and schedule. Select and apply appropriate project planning and tracking tools as well as project management leadership skills to recover the program.

- Develop an appropriate program "interface event management" plan to integrate and manage the projects effectively, and resolve any complexities that result from multitasking, within the networks or on the part of the project manager. Interface events are key milestones requiring cross functional coordination.

- Plan the development and implementation of suitable project management systems and methodology to support multiple projects. Identify best practices that lead to effective program management.

- Develop and manage an integrated program schedule. This includes the elements of the schedule, different types of schedules, schedule development, and the processes of schedule management.

- Work with the structures of schedules, based on the Integrated Master Plan (IMP), Integrated Master Schedule (IMS), supplier data integration, and the overall influences of the work breakdown structure (WBS).

- Establish requirements and a clear "make buy" decision; the reader will be able to identify those necessary contractor elements to include and integrate into the program master schedule.

- Work with networking basics, primary elements of the network, what a critical path is, the critical path method, and program networks.

- Work with integrated product and process teams (IPT), their outputs, and their relationships to each other, and recognize key product and process team tasks, their relationships in a program schedule, and be able to analyze the performance aspects of an IPT.

- Work to transition from IMP to IMS.

- Manage the integration of production recurring schedules with the nonrecurring program level schedules.

- Manage reporting of integrated schedule data to customers.

- Understand when and where to use Earned Value Management (EVM), and how this system is used to benefit the project management effort.

- Design and manage a resource assignment matrix (RAM).

- Serve as an effective cost account manager, and understand how project cost accounting supports the cost account manager.

- Provide a working level definition of a project/program baseline schedule to include the basic objectives of that schedule.

- Implement the planning and budgeting process within the resource loading activities of the schedule integration process.

- Produce a variance analysis report, and the process of arriving at the conclusions sited in the report.

- Define and integrate risk management, and elaborate on the process of risk analysis and risk management.

- Provide the definition for low risk, medium risk, and high risk, while being able to integrate the likelihood of the occurrence with the consequences of the occurrence onto the tailored risk matrix, and incorporate necessary mitigating elements.

Reviewing the current state of project management literature, it could be argued that the word "integration" is used in so many different contexts and applications that its practical usefulness is in question. Engineers integrate products and systems, managers integrate and coordinate their organizations, and planners integrate their plans. Yet despite its prolific use, the term still defines a critical aspect of successful organizations, projects, and teams—working together toward program and project objectives. The integration of product and system means that the components come together to produce product performance and customer satisfaction. They come together because people make them come together; integration just doesn't happen, it must be proactively encouraged by the participants in the program management process.

Integration as a Leadership Function

Organizations integrate their program and project work when their leaders encourage it. Systems do not integrate unless key people at the working and project levels actually *think* integration. Thinking integration is a way of looking at your work as interdependent, as a part of the whole. Information is shared in an integrated organization simply because the key people know that shared purpose and shared information serves the customer better, faster, and cheaper.

Leaders prepare their organizations for integration by loosening bureaucratic barriers and encouraging cross-functional training and work settings. Information systems encourage integration. For instance, an electronic time sheet system is tied into networked Microsoft Project software so that project managers can see actual costs in real time. Leaders insist on these supporting systems because they know the value of information sharing in building products that work.

Integration as a Wide Ranging Quality and Process Improvement Standard

Integration is addressed in a wide variety of quality standards for corporate management, and for program and project management, including the Project Management Institute PMBOK, the National Baldrige Quality Award, the PMI OPM 3 maturity model, balanced scorecard, and critical chain concepts. Along with increasing complexity in systems and projects, and the challenge of putting together the efforts of global outsourcing teams, the concept of integration becomes more and more important to achieve "cheaper, better, faster" project cycles.

For instance, the National Baldrige Quality Award criteria are used by many companies as benchmarks for best practice in integrating planning, operations, and project/process management. The Baldrige criteria address integration in terms of alignment and consistency of purpose and in the measurement of outcomes. For instance, the 2004 criteria state for health services organizations reads:

> This item examines your organization's selection, management, and use of data and information for performance measurement and analysis in support of organizational planning and performance improvement . . . This performance improvement includes efforts to improve health care results and outcomes (e.g., through the selection of statistically meaningful indicators, risk adjustment of data, and

linking outcomes to processes and provider decisions). The item serves as a central collection and analysis point in an integrated performance measurement and management system that relies on clinical, financial, and non-financial data and information. The aim of measurement and analysis is to guide your organization's process management toward the achievement of key organizational performance results and strategic objectives.

Alignment and integration are key concepts for successful implementation of your performance measurement system. They are viewed in terms of extent and effectiveness of use to meet your performance assessment needs. Alignment and integration include how measures are aligned throughout your organization, how they are integrated to yield organization-wide data/information, and how performance measurement requirements are deployed by your senior leaders to track departmental, work group, and process-level performance on key measures targeted for organization-wide significance and/or improvement. (2004 Baldrige Award Health Criteria, p. 40).

Translated to the project management environment, the Baldrige criteria stress the importance of selecting projects which implement business goals and plans, making sure that outcomes of multiproject portfolios and business processes such as project planning and control are tied together through alignment with the business direction.

The PMI PMBOK (PMI Body of Knowledge)

Addressed separately in Chap. 1, the PMBOK standard for project integration management is the global definition of project integration—the basis for the Project Management Professional (PMP) certification. This standard is the most comprehensive of the PMI standards, updated in 2004. It now includes project chartering, scope of work, project plan, project execution, monitoring and control, change control, and closeout. The implication here is that bringing together the efforts of a wide variety of project team members, stakeholders, and customers is a major challenge *from beginning to end*.

The Critical Chain Concept

Critical chain theory borrows heavily on integration concepts as it links scope and time management to risk management. The critical chain approach to project planning emphasizes developing a WBS and project network and focuses on identification of dependencies. Dependencies require coordination and integration. From systems theory, we recall that systems will go naturally into disorder, e.g., that the forces of system dynamics tend to push outward, away from the center. Integration, then, acts in contrast to the normal centrifugal forces in a project and its environment. Critical chain focuses on the use of buffers, or allotments of time that are "tapped" upfront by project managers and doled out as necessary to offset risk events and unanticipated problems. Because most networks are highly complex, a statistical analysis of all the inherent risks in starting tasks on time is usually impossible. Chains of tasks typically include a myriad of risks, many of which are the result of *disintegration*, the opposite of integration. Thus cost and schedule control tend to manage disintegration. For instance, as two components, one software and the other electrical, of a product are being designed, each effort tends to make design assumptions independent of the other, only to find in downstream integration and testing that different assumptions made product integration impossible. Thus the process of integration forces the electrical and software designers to share assumptions upfront, through concurrent work, constant cross-functional communication, information sharing, design reviews, and electronic integration tools.

PMI OPM 3 (Organizational Project Management 3)

PMI's OPM 3 maturity models, and in fact all such maturity models, actually measure the extent to which an organization is integrating its program and project work. OPM 3 integrates:

- Design and implementation of organizational strategic planning
- Identification of projects
- Determination of team and project chartering conditions
- Changes in priority and allocation of resources
- The process of managing the environment
- Management of the program and project portfolio

The overriding theme of OPM 3 is continuous improvement, the systematic and sustained improvement of business processes and products. This typically means linking information systems and teams to achieve standardization whenever possible.

Balanced Score Card

Measures are important because people tend to do what is measured. The balanced scorecard encourages the measurement of four main areas—financial, process, learning, and growth—framed overall in the customer's perspective. Project managers have traditionally focused on time more than cost simply because the customer typically focuses on time as the priority. Now financial measures are more important, due to Sarbanes-Oxley reporting and accounting requirements. Thus financial reporting at the project level now becomes important as a part of the earned value process, truly integrating cost and time.

eProcurement

The increasing use of electronic procurement systems has tended to tie businesses to businesses and customers in an unprecedented network of collaboration and cooperation in the acquisition of material, goods, and services. Product development teams now integrate contractors and vendors directly into the project through eProcurement systems that allow instant exchange of project and product information and documents.

What Is This Book About?

This book is about how to "nest" project management systems into a company organization and how to interrelate project management tools and techniques into the fabric of the company and its markets. The book will help to fill a major gap in the current literature on project management—the challenge of integration and implementation of the PMI standard. The book theme is that to be effective in a multiproject environment, the program or project manager will need to take a broad perspective, one that sees all aspects of the business and its customers and interrelates projects "seamlessly" into the business.

The book was first suggested by Dr. James Hiegel, curriculum manager for Keller Graduate School of Management, who emphasized the urgent need for a better book and text on project management integration. The concept stems from the growing popularity of project management tools and techniques and the stress that complex projects place on conventional business systems and teams. Here, integration is similar to the concept of enterprise project management, except that integration has an organizational and "soft" side, which is typically missed in the IT-oriented enterprise solution.

This book is not simply about systems; it is about people and how they work in a project environment. Integration allows project managers to grow into business managers because they see the business as a whole as they engage in integrating activity. The process will involve assuring that projects are not treated in isolated initiatives, insulated from the rest of the business. Rather individual projects, and indeed, portfolios of projects, will be seen as essentially the way the business "does business." Project management will be addressed as the central core process of the company to implement the business plan. Project success is enhanced by tying the projects to key business planning and system development, and to the training and "enculturation" of the workforce. Success is also enhanced when many projects can be managed all at once in a program management framework that reflects and controls "bottlenecks," as described in the theory of constraints and critical chain management.

The reason integrated project management is important is that we are increasingly aware that projects fail or underperform because of the lack of organizational and management support and dysfunctional separation of key financial, human resource, marketing, and IT systems from project management in the typical company. In fact, projects naturally *disintegrate*.

In the integrated model, the basic tools of project management, such as work breakdown, scheduling and schedule variance control, chartering, resource management and cost variance control, project team development, portfolio project selection, product development, quality control and assurance, project review and performance monitoring, and interface management, will be placed in a simple conceptual framework.

   The soft side of project management and the dynamics of organizational behavior are a major part of the book, advising project managers and support staff on effective ways to get things done. Leaning on insights about teams, but not necessarily endorsing teams for everything in the project process, the book will suggest a healthy skepticism about team effectiveness. The book addresses modern organizational behavior and leadership concepts to an integrated, "matrixed" company organization.

About the Author

Bruce T. Barkley has over 30 years of experience in project and program management, in both industry and government. He has taught at the University of Maryland and now teaches at DeVry University's Keller Graduate School of Management. Mr. Barkley is the author of *Project Risk Management*, and the coauthor of *Customer-Driven Project Management: Building Quality into Project Processes*.

Acknowledgments

The author would like to acknowledge the following sources for this book:

- The Universal Avionics Systems Corporation, Instrument Division, for valuable experience in supporting and managing integrated product development projects and processes, and writing program manuals and policy documents and conducting analyses in the program management office,

- The Alumax Aluminum Company (now Alcoa, Inc.), where the author was a project management and organizational development consultant, for valuable experience and case material in integrated strategic planning and SWOT analysis in a manufacturing work setting,

- Students and Faculty at DeVry University and Keller Graduate School of Management, Atlanta, where the author serves as senior faculty member and curriculum manager for project management, for valuable stories, cases, and exercises in integrated project and risk and cost management which serve as the basis for material in the book. Special thanks to a high performing MBA student at Keller–Maria Thompson–for her assistance in providing graphics to illustrate the capital rationing process through which ranked projects are funded based on their alignment with strategic objectives; and Curriculum Managers for Project Management at Keller Graduate School of Management for models and graphics to help explain integrated project management concepts,

- The Project Management Institute, Project Management Body of Knowledge (PMBOK), Project Integration Management Knowledge Area Guide, 2004

Project Integration

Introduction

This book presents a new view of program, project, and business management, an integrative *wrap-around*, of sorts, of the current state of the art. The book builds on the Project Management Institute (PMI) "Project Integration Management" standard in the Project Management Body of Knowledge (PMBOK), and then goes farther into the complex dynamics and interdependencies of modern project organization. Thus it will be useful to all current and prospective PMI members in testing for the Project Management Professional (PMP) certification and keeping current. Traditional project management tools and techniques are framed in a series of integration models or metaphors. The integration model is a *forward-looking* concept, beginning with the individual and *building out* to project outcomes, technology, team, organization, business systems, customer and market segment, the overall business regime, and, finally, the global economy. In this book, integration is defined at each level and builds toward a conceptual framework of *interconnection and purpose* that defines a successful project and program of projects.

Integration actually defines program management, that body of knowledge and practice dealing with multiproject portfolios, project selection methods, and long-term, complex programs with multiphases. Thus, the book is designed to support program managers as they seek out their roles in the upper reaches of the organization, working to implement business strategy through successful, integrated projects.

Chapter 1 introduces integration as a concept, presents the Project Management Institute Project Management Body of Knowledge (PMBOK, 2004 version) on integration (from the standard), and annotates the PMBOK discussion with the author's comments and applications.

Integration: Concepts and Models

What does integration *look like*? One way to answer this question quickly is to look at two ways to achieve cost control.

The simplest way to control cost is to match actual spending to the spending plan, pure and simple. An accounting office might do control that way, lacking any other information or perspective. This is a classic mistake in cost control that does not integrate with work performance or value.

The integrated cost control approach, on the other hand, involves looking at cost from the standpoint of work performed and quality/value achieved, not simply in terms of costs incurred. Integrated cost control is a *forward integration tool* that points toward completion of the work, keys on current progress, and matches costs to quality output. Forward cost control involves looking at the variance between the work performed in project execution against *what it should have cost to do that work*. It also looks at the value or quality of the deliverable at any given time to ensure that the customer is getting value for the dollar spent. In other words, a good indicator of whether you are forward integrating your cost control is whether invoices for work performed are paid.

What does integration *feel like*? In other words this overused term has a significant meaning in many fields, perhaps beyond its literal translation. Asking what integration feels like is not as superficial as it may sound. To explore when we have it is to explore how to get it. The following indicators come to mind:

1. When there is complete integration, a project deliverable reflects in its performance and value to the customer and stakeholders all the project requirements and components outlined for it in the project plan and work breakdown structure (WBS), along with horizontal and lateral coordination. Further, the design and performance of the product facilitates the customer's performance because it is integrated *into the customer's systems.*

2. When there is complete integration, all parties to a program and project—managers, team members, support people, suppliers, and customers—all are delighted with the project outcome and deliverables, and with their roles in its success.

3. When there is complete integration, all costs, schedule, quality, and risk factors, and changes along the way, are adequately reflected in the final outcome and due dates. The learning that occurs in a program or project is integrated into the product or service through *integrated* change controls.

4. When there is complete integration, the professional and technical project staffs, for instance, administrative staff, support people, software engineers, mechanical engineers, electrical engineers, and construction workers, who participated in defining specific components for a technical product deliverable, feel they have made a significant contribution and gained new working relationships with their colleagues.

5. When there is complete integration, there are no surprises and there has been an effective blending of cost, schedule, and quality considerations along the way in the project cycle; earned value has been maximized given project developments.

What significance does integration have for program and project managers in tomorrow's business settings?

Since the term integration is the key theme of this book, let's explore what integration means. The concept of integration has many dimensions, individual, technological, organizational, interpersonal, and informational, but the core concept of integration is grounded in *connection and alignment*. But why will integration be more important in tomorrow's business organization? What makes integration key to organization and product performance?

Integration means *completeness* and *closure*, bringing components of the "whole" together in an operating system. Components of a larger system, increasingly global in nature, are brought together to create performance; but what is the process of integration and how does it work generically? The answer lies in systems theory; a system is a series of parts working together with a common objective. Once the whole is defined, the analysis function breaks down the whole into its components for purposes of understanding, building, and managing the system. Integration then puts the "built components" of a system back together to create a performance model that is aligned, so that, all components work together as they were designed to.

Projects must be internally and externally integrated; internal integration means that project work packages, deliverables, and systems are connected; external integration means that the project interfaces with customer systems and produces value for the customer and the market/industry as a whole. Repeated internal and external project integration produces economic development in the larger community and societal framework.

The characteristics of integration that help to frame our understanding of program and project management and that underlie this book are as follows:

1. Systems don't integrate, people do. The individual and project team members, working with an external contingent of support people and stakeholders, is the beginning of integration. The way people who work in a project environment think about their roles, responsibilities, and tasks creates the conditions for integration. *Integration thinking* means that as people perform their functions, their behaviors reflect an awareness of impacts on other team members and on other product components, and most importantly on the customer's satisfaction with the outcome. *Integration support systems* connect key aspects of project performance, so that data are produced automatically on cost, schedule, and quality to allow informed decisions.

2. Forward integration means that communication and connection is focused *forward* on producing deliverables and creating customer satisfaction, not necessarily to bring a project back to its original plan. Plans are estimates; real work performance serves as the basis for corrective action. Forward integration is a downstream concept in which work is performed to provide value downstream toward the deliverable; sequence means that integration occurs at the right moment in the process. This is a horizontal function, cutting across traditional functions to create synergy and cooperation.

3. Top management builds the culture and mechanisms for successful connection and integration, involving extensive coordination by a centralized program

and project management function that works to avoid disconnected efforts throughout the enterprise.

4. Integration means integrity. There is a connection between integrity, e.g., producing what you promise and doing it in a professional and ethical way, and integration, making sure required connections occur at the right time. The outcome, product, or service has integrity because it is integrated.

5. Accountability requires integration; new requirements, including the Sarbanes-Oxley legislation, demand top management fiscal accountability, making financial and work performance integration imperative. The new requirement for internal accountability stresses internal control and checks and balances. Once seen as a low-level accounting and audit requirement, this new mandate now requires integration at every level of the organization, including programs and projects.

6. Integration begins at the business level. New forces require a new way of thinking about business itself, business strategy and operations, projects, and markets. These forces come about from developing changes in the landscape of business management, most notably at the global level; integration now occurs across geographical, economic, political, and system boundaries as never before.

7. The "regime" of business, the whole business enterprise system, is also changing as more and more middle and small businesses surface and disappear with the tides of business fortune. How does a business organization, designed as it is to grow and profit through serving customers, assure that it plays in the regime of business fairly and with integrity? Such a business plays by the rules not just to avoid regulatory and government interference, but because *the business equates success with integrity.*

Vertical and Horizontal Integration

There are two types of integration and they are both essential success factors, particularly in a multiproject program environment. They are vertical and horizontal integration.

Vertical integration looks *inside* and *up and down* into the business, program, project, and product/service components. This kind of integration targets the program, project, and product, and builds a product or service with integrity. It looks downstream in the project process to product performance and customer satisfaction.

Horizontal integration looks *outside and around* to the external, the environmental, and the *organizational assets that support the project*. It focuses on outside forces that create risk and opportunity, market forces that will shape the product or service.

Vertical integration is program integration; it proceeds down the project, going deep into the project processes and product configuration. It focuses on performance. Vertical integration is related to horizontal integration in the sense that a project that reflects outside factors and environmental scanning information is more apt to succeed in its performance because these factors can make or break a project.

Analysis, Selection, and Scheduling: Portfolio Integration

Vertical and horizontal integration factors are reflected in the analysis, selection, and scheduling of projects and portfolio integration. Programs or product lines are "chunks" of business development that will help define a portfolio of projects to improve business performance. Once these programs are identified, we can identify, say, five projects in each program as candidate projects to implement. In effect, you might be choosing three projects from a series of 15 projects for implementation.

We use a variety of program management tools in selecting the three projects that will be planned and scheduled in detail. These tools include

1. *Cash flow analysis.* This tool requires you to forecast the first 5+ years of cash flow for each project. Costs will come from a budget built up from a preliminary task list and schedule for the project, while revenues will come from your assessment of how the project deliverable or product will generate income or "value." Remember that a cash flow estimate can be identified for a project that does not produce a marketable product but adds value to the program portfolio. Simply allocate a dollar value each year to the benefits of the project to a user or customer in order to estimate the cash flow equivalent to the stream of project benefits.

2. *Net present value* (NPV). This tool requires you to take the cash flow analysis you have prepared and calculate the net present value of each so that you can compare all the projects regardless of how many years their cash flow is projected.

3. *Risk assessment and management.* This tool requires you to identify the high-level risks in each project and prepare a risk matrix, including task, task risk description, impact, probability, severity, and contingency plans.

4. *Weighted scoring model.* This tool allows you to score each project against the various strategic objectives of your company, to place weights on each strategic objective and multiply the scores by the weights to get a "weighted" score for each project.

Once you have performed this analysis for each project, you will be using the results to rank the projects in each program and to select three projects for detailed scheduling and budgeting using Microsoft Project. The selected projects may not be the ones most highly ranked in your rank ordered listing, but they will be the three projects that must be implemented first, to enable the remaining projects to be implemented to integrate the program and business strategic objectives.

eProcurement: Example of Horizontal Integration

Project managers must look and work across the organization with supporting departments that are not directly invested in the project but those who support it. This includes working with procurement and acquisition services that are sometimes at odds with short-term project goals. This means project managers must be attuned to these questions and issues at the interface with the project:

1. eProcurement and electronic data exchange with contractors and between businesses; new developments in Web-based supply management. Horizontal integration involves looking at the outside forces that will affect the project, working across an organization with supporting organizational assets. At the global level, this kind of integration involves looking at global supply chains, global economic and political factors, multinational corporate risks and opportunities, and the Internet. At the project level it involves looking at organizational assets that support the project such as eProcurement and Web-based acquisition strategies.

2. Supply chain management and the Web, building partnerships with suppliers across an industry to achieve cheaper, better, faster procurement, which, however, sometimes conflicts with short-term project goals.

3. Supplier quality management, e.g., ISO requirements for vendors, qualifying suppliers to business with many project managers in a multiproject environment.

4. New product information and sourcing systems, the digitized catalog, sometimes restricting project managers to choose from suppliers they may not want to work with.

PMBOK and Project Planning

The PMBOK standard on project integration management focuses on planning, execution, monitoring, and change control. This standard is the platform for all the other standards – providing the overall framework for subsequent concepts and tools. The PMBOK standard defines a *project management plan* as a plan to include *both* how the project will be *managed*, as well as how the *product or service itself will be produced*, for instance, technical characteristics, technical processes and stages, and product specifications as stated in the scope of work. PMBOK incorporates the scope of work in the plan, including technical and management/scheduling components.

Project management plan

The project integration management plan is a management document dealing with how resources are to be used, how project progress is to be monitored, how reporting will occur, and financial and funding issues relative to the project. The plan also includes the technical and product information necessary to produce the deliverable. This plan has the following elements:

1. Business plan and relevant strategic objectives
2. Project management process to be used (see program manual discussion in chapter 4)
3. Program and product line framework
4. Documentation requirements
5. Reporting and monitoring approach
6. Cost benefit analyses, cost control, and finance issues
7. Conflict resolution approach
8. Stage-gate review requirements
9. Business and program/project organization
10. Roles and responsibilities
11. Project schedule and key milestones
12. Change control procedures
13. Team contact directory
14. Customer performance and technical requirements document
15. Project deliverable definitions
16. Generic WBS and data dictionary
17. Technical stage-gate process and phases
18. Design review requirements
19. Industry standards
20. Testing and user approval procedures
21. Regulatory and international technical constraints
22. Configuration management requirements for transition to production

Strategic Planning

The Eastern case (Chap. 10) deals with global strategic planning, integration of risk into the business planning process, and the articulation of the company's approach to implementing its strategic objectives. The integration message of this case is that integration starts very early in the business planning and portfolio development process and that projects that are generated out of an integrated process at the top tend to have higher probabilities of project success. This is because one of the key reasons for project failure has been the lack of top management support; integration at the business plan level assures more visibility of the project at the top of the organization and more opportunity to develop reliable sponsors in upper management.

Ethics and Project Integration

There was a time when project accounting records, costs, and expenses of business projects were *beneath the eye level* of top business management. That time is past.

The integration of projects into a corporate portfolio has implications for corporate ethics and accountability. As the recent Enron case indicates, the source of Enron's problems in accountability and abuse of reporting accounting were grounded in part in the lack of an integrated project accounting system. Enron was a classic multiproject corporate environment. As such, top management had direct and continuous contact with the many natural gas project investments and projects in the company; in fact, they created many of these projects in their negotiations with their many potential customers, for instance, utilities, manufacturing plants, communities, and the like. Some top managers were paid bonuses based on profits *attributable to individual projects they generated.*

The new Sarbanes-Oxley legislation and regulation now requires that business officers sign-off on business and financial reporting and assure that internal controls are in place to track all business expenditures to make sure that they are legitimate. In project-oriented companies such as Enron, this means that now actual costs must be integrated into project planning and management. Project integration is associated with both program and project management.

Integration Model

The integration model that follows (Fig. 1.1) captures the essential factors requiring a new level of integration in program and project management.

People.   People integrate, not systems, so people are trained to coordinate and interact with program and project participants, forming a true interdisciplinary team.

Projects.   Projects become more cross-functional as project work is defined in terms of coordination and integration of work.

Technology.   Complex products are managed at the interface, placing more emphasis on product and service integration.

Financial, schedule, risk, and quality combined.   Through earned value and integrative tools, program and project progress is seen in terms of the combined impacts on financial, schedule, risk response, and quality issues.

Program management applications.   Integration defines the program manager's role; working between top management and project managers; program

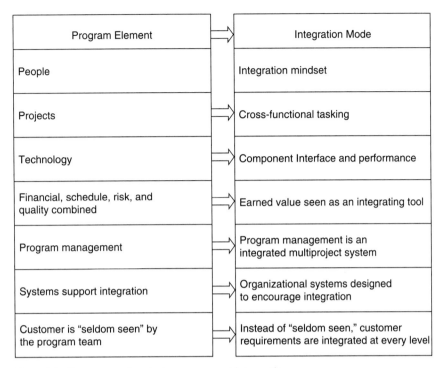

Program Element		Integration Mode
People	→	Integration mindset
Projects	→	Cross-functional tasking
Technology	→	Component Interface and performance
Financial, schedule, risk, and quality combined	→	Earned value seen as an integrating tool
Program management	→	Program management is an integrated multiproject system
Systems support integration	→	Organizational systems designed to encourage integration
Customer is "seldom seen" by the program team	→	Instead of "seldom seen," customer requirements are integrated at every level

Figure 1.1 Program and project management integration.

managers integrate projects with company plans and strategies, and work with enterprise-wide resource management systems.

Systems support integration.   Organizational and information technology systems are designed to interface with each other and to encourage integration.

Customer is "seen" by the program team.   All program and project activity is performed with the customer in full view, integrating the work with customer's expectations.

Project Integration Management: Organizational Issues

The model for successful project integration management starts with the organizational reform, with the key steps shown in Fig. 1.2.

Prepare the organization

As will be seen in the analysis of PMI PMBOK requirements for integration, the concept of organizational and technical coordination starts with a key business process focused on organizational integration. The process of putting things

Figure 1.2 Key steps for project integration management.

together and recognizing the interdependencies of the project process is the first priority. It starts with preparing a culture and supporting mechanism for working together for a shared outcome and deliverable, and designing systems to integrate rather than diffuse organizational performance. Preparing the organization starts with a corporate and enterprise policy on integration, backed up by top managers who *walk the talk* that brings people and system together, and treats the outcome as a shared vision.

Develop systems of integration

Systems of integration include business processes such as design reviews, project earned value analysis, configuration management, software compatibility, and interdisciplinary assignments. The more the organization provides mechanisms that in their very existence further integration, the more successful the integration process will be.

Develop integration skills

Integration skills start with a mindset that one's project tasks fit into a larger whole, and that the success of the project and the enterprise itself is dependent on the collective success and efficiency involved in producing the product or service.

Recognize integration success

What you recognize and measure is usually what you get, therefore the success of integration in planning and project management begins in what the company measures and rewards. Measurement of integration success can be accomplished using various indicators of integration:

1. Duration of integration tasks, looking for faster integration turnarounds

2. Conflict intensity during integration

3. Lessons learned

Integrate with the customer

The final integration is the alignment with customer expectations and systems, leading to a "perfect storm" of timing and performance with the customer's processes. This integration can be accomplished by keeping the customer involved and engaged throughout the project life cycle.

The Project Management Institute (PMI) standard for project integration has fundamentally changed from its early form—a narrow focus on project-only issues—to a broader treatment, published in 2005, of project integration from an organization-wide, global view. Project integration is now a project management knowledge area that includes the processes and activities needed to identify, define, combine, unify, and coordinate the various processes and project management activities within the project management groups, such as, initiating, planning, executing, monitoring, controlling, and closing. In the project management context, integration includes the characteristics of unification, consolidation, articulation, and integrative actions that are crucial to project completion, successfully meeting customer and other stakeholder requirements, and managing expectations. Integration, in the context of managing a project, is making choices about where to concentrate resources and effort on any given day, anticipating potential issues, dealing with these issues before they become critical, and coordinating work for the overall good of the project. The integration effort also involves making trade-offs among competing objectives and alternatives.

What this means in simple terms is that integration has become the essential pulling together of project and organizational systems and processes for a multiproject, portfolio approach to project management. Integration is essentially the major function of program management, running several projects simultaneously and using all the support systems of the organization.

Integration brings together all of the PMBOK processes, including cost management, time management, and risk management. These processes interact to provide opportunities for tradeoffs between schedule, cost, and performance of the deliverable. The deliverable should reflect the benefits of integration – the most cost-effective product possible, within resource and time constraints, that meets or exceeds customer expectations.

Most experienced project practitioners know that there is no single way to manage a project. They apply project management knowledge, skills, and processes in different orders and degrees of rigor to achieve the desired project performance. However, the perception that a particular process is not required, e.g. cost, does not mean that it should not be addressed. The project manager and project team must address every process, and the level of implementation for each process must be determined for each specific project.

Some integrative activities performed by the project management team include:

- Analyze and understand the scope. This includes the project and product requirements, criteria, assumptions, constraints, and other influences related to a project, and how each will be managed or addressed within the project.

- Document specific tradeoffs inherent in product requirements.

- Understand how to take the identified information and transform it into a project management plan using the planning process group described in the Project Management Body of Knowledge (PMBOK) guide.

- Prepare the work breakdown structure (WBS).

■ Take appropriate action to have the project performed in accordance with the project management plan, the planned set of integrated processes, and the planned scope.

■ Measure and monitor project status, processes, and products.

■ Analyze project risks.

PMBOK assumes separate "process groups," linked at various points, or "gates," in the project. The planning process group provides the executive process group with a documented project management plan early in the project and then facilitates updates to the project management plan if changes occur as the project progresses.

Integration is primarily concerned with effectively integrating the processes among the project management process groups that are required to accomplish project objectives within an organization's defined procedures. Figure 1.3 provides an overview of the major project management integrative processes. Figure 1.3 provides a process flow diagram of those processes and their inputs, outputs, and other related knowledge area processes. The integrative project management processes include the following steps:

a. Develop project charter.   Developing the project charter that formally authorizes a project or a project phase.

b. Develop preliminary project scope statement.   Developing the preliminary project scope statement that provides high-level scope narrative.

c. Develop project management plan.   Documenting the actions necessary to define, prepare, integrate, and coordinate all subsidiary plans into a project management plan.

d. Direct and manage project execution.   Executing the work defined in the project management plan to achieve the project's requirements defined in the project scope statement.

e. Monitor and control project work.   Monitoring and controlling the processes used to initiate, plan, execute, and close a project to meet performance objectives defined in the project management plan.

f. Integrated change control.   Reviewing all change requests, approving changes, and controlling changes to the deliverables and organizational process assets.

g. Close project.   Finalizing all activities across all the project management process groups to formally close the project or a project phase.

Develop Project Charter

The project charter is the document that formally authorizes a project. The project charter provides the project manager with the authority to apply organizational resources to project activities. A project manager is identified and assigned as early in the project as is feasible. The project manager should

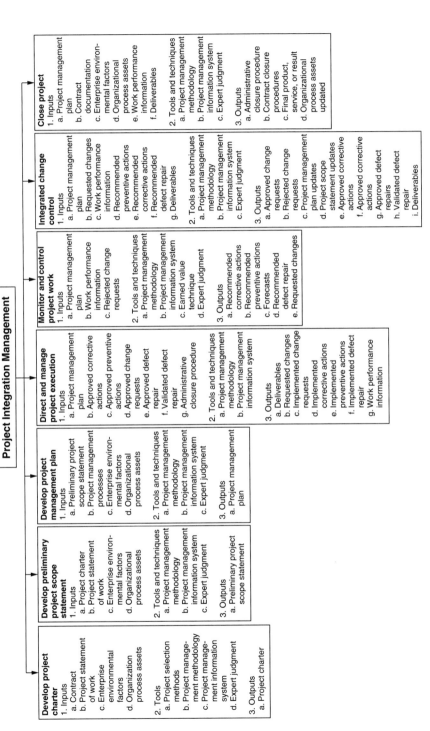

Figure 1.3 Project integration management overview.

always be assigned prior to the start of planning, and preferably while the project is being developed.

A project initiator or sponsor, external to the project organization, at a level that is appropriate to funding the project, issues a project charter. Projects are usually chartered and authorized by top management, a sponsor, a government agency, a partnering company, a program organization, or a portfolio organization, as a result of one or more of the following:

- A market demand (e.g., a car company authorizing the development of a product to provide more fuel-efficient cars in response to gasoline shortages)
- A business need (e.g., a training company authorizing a project to build a new substation to serve a new industrial park)
- A customer request (e.g., an electric utility authorizing a project to build a new substation to serve a new industrial park)
- A technological advance (e.g., an electronics firm authorizing a new project to develop a faster, cheaper, and smaller laptop after advances in computer memory and electronics technology)
- A legal requirement (e.g., a paint manufacturer authorizing a project to establish guidelines for handling toxic materials)
- A social need (e.g., a nongovernmental organization in a developing country authorizing a project to provide potable water systems, latrines, and sanitation education to communities suffering from high rates of cholera)

These factors that generate projects can also be called problems, opportunities, or business requirements. The central theme of all these stimuli is that management must make a decision about how to respond and what projects to authorize and charter. Project selection methods involve measuring value or attractiveness to the project owner or sponsor and may include other organizational decision criteria. Project selection also applies to choosing alternative ways of executing the project.

Charting a project links the project to the ongoing work of the organization. In some organizations, a project is not formally chartered and initiated until completion of a needs assessment, feasibility study, preliminary plan, or some other form of analysis that was separately initiated. Developing the project charter is primarily concerned with documenting the business needs, project justification, current understanding of the customer's requirements, and the new product, service, or result that is intended to satisfy those requirements. The project charter, either directly or by reference to other documents, should address the following information:

- Requirements that satisfy customer, sponsor, and other stakeholder needs, wants, and expectations
- Business needs, high-level project description, or product requirements that the project is undertaken to address

- Project purpose or justification
- Assigned project manager and authority level
- Summary of milestone schedule
- Stakeholder influences
- Functional organizations and their participation
- Organization, environmental, and external assumptions and constraints
- Business case justifying the project, including return on investment
- Summary budget

During subsequent phases of the multiphase projects, the "develop project charter" process validates the decisions made during the original chartering of the project. If required, it also authorizes the next project phase, and updates the charter.

The project charter commissions and challenges the project team, and the business itself, to work *with their eyes fully open to both the risks and opportunities of the project*. This means that the team is charged to plan, design, and monitor the program and/or project with an eye *outward* to customer expectations and requirements; cost, schedule, and quality trade-offs (using earned value tools); reaching out to supporting functions and systems (IT, functional departments such as accounting and purchasing/acquisition, technical test equipment, and tool managers); the costs of production and manufacturing of the project products and outputs; the need for strong configuration management to document and preserve the product; and other projects underway as part of the company's portfolio of projects. The team should look at the project as an investment in the company itself.

The charter will identify periodic stage-gate review points, the need for interfaces in those reviews, and will challenge the team to make the business case for the project at every stage-gate review.

Inputs

1. *Contract.*   A contract from the customer's acquiring organization is an input if the project is being done for an external customer.

2. *Project statement of work.*   The statement of work (SOW) is a narrative description of products or services to be supplied by the project. For internal purposes, the project initiator or sponsor provides the statement of work, based on business needs, product, or service requirements. For external purposes, the statement of work can be received from the customer as part of a bid document, for example, request for proposal, request for information, request for bid, or as part of a contract. The SOW indicates

- *Business need.*   An organization's business need can be based on needed training, market demand, technological advance, legal requirement, or governmental standard.

- *Product scope description.* Documents the product requirements and characteristics of the product or service that the project will undertake to create. The product requirements will generally have less detail during the initiation phase and more detail during later processes, as the product characteristics are progressively elaborated. These requirements should also document the relationship among the products or services being created and the business need or other stimulus that caused the need. While the form and substance of the product requirements document will vary, it should always be detailed enough to support later project planning.
- *A strategic plan.* All projects should support the organization's strategic goals. The strategic plan of the performing organization should be considered as a factor when making project selection decisions.

3. *Enterprise environmental factors.* When developing the project charter, any and all of the organization's enterprise environmental factors and systems that surround and influence the project's success must be considered. This includes items such as but not limited to

- Organizational or company culture and structure
- Governmental or industry standards (e.g., regulatory agency regulations, product standards, quality standards, and workmanship standards)
- Infrastructure (e.g., existing facilities and capital equipment)
- Existing human resources (e.g., skills, disciplines, and knowledge, such as design, development, legal, contracting, and purchasing)
- Personnel administration (e.g., hiring and firing guidelines, employee performance reviews, and training records)
- Company work authorization system
- Marketplace conditions
- Stakeholder risk tolerances
- Commercial databases (e.g., standardized cost-estimating data, industry risk study information, and risk databases)
- Project management information systems (e.g., an automated tool suite, such as a scheduling software tool, a configuration management system, an information collection and distribution system, or Web interfaces to other online automated systems)

4. *Organizational process assets.* When developing the project charter and subsequent project documentation, any and all of the assets that are used to influence the project's success can be drawn from organizational process assets. Any and all of the organizations involved in the project can have formal and informal policies, procedures, plans, and guidelines whose effects must be considered. Organizational process assets also represent the organization's learning and knowledge from previous projects; for example, completed schedules, risk data, and earned value data. Organizational process assets can be organized differently, depending on the type of industry, organization, and application area. For example, the organizational process assets could be grouped into two categories:

Organization's processes and procedures for conducting work:

- Organizational standard processes, such as standards, policies (e.g., safety, health, and project management policy), standard product and project life cycles, and quality policies and procedures (e.g., process audits, improvement targets, checklists, and standardized process definitions for use in the organization).
- Standardized guidelines, work instructions, proposal evaluation criteria, and performance measurement criteria.
- Templates (e.g., risk templates, WBS templates, and project schedule network diagram templates).
- Guidelines and criteria for tailoring the organization's set of standard processes to satisfy the specific needs of the project.
- Organizational communication requirements (e.g., specific communication technology available, allowed communication media, record retention, and security requirements).
- Project closure guidelines or requirements (e.g., final project audits, project evaluations, product validations, and acceptance criteria).
- Financial controls procedures (e.g., time reporting, required expenditure and disbursement reviews, accounting codes, and standard contract provisions).
- Issue and defect management procedures defining issue and defect controls, issue and defect identification and resolution, and action item tracking.
- Change control procedures, including the steps by which official company standards, policies, plans, and procedures or any project documents will be modified, and how any changes will be approved and validated.
- Risk control procedures, including risk categories, probability definition and impact, and probability and impact matrix.
- Procedures for approving and issuing work authorizations.

Organizational corporate knowledge base for storing and retrieving information:

- Process measurement database used to collect and make available measurement data on processes and products.
- Project files (e.g., scope, cost, schedule, and quality baselines, performance measurement baselines, project calendars, project schedule network diagrams, risk registers, planned response actions, and defined risk impact).
- Historical information and lessons learned knowledge base (e.g., project records and documents, all project closure information and documentation, information about both the results or previous project selection decisions and previous project performance information, and information from the risk management effort).
- Issue and defect management database containing issue and defect status, control information, issue and defect resolution, and action item results.

- Configuration management knowledge base containing the versions and baselines of all official company standards, policies, procedures, and any project documents.
- Financial database containing information such as labor hours, incurred costs, budgets, and any project cost overruns.

Tools and techniques

1. *Project selection methods.* Project selection methods are used to determine which project the organization will select. These methods generally fall into one of the two broad categories:

- Benefit measurement methods that are comparative approaches, scoring models, benefit contribution, or economic models
- Mathematical models that use linear, nonlinear, dynamic, integer, or multi-objective programming algorithms

2. *Project management methodology.* A project management methodology defines a set of project management process groups, their related processes, and the related control functions that are consolidated and combined into a functioning and unified whole. A project management methodology may or may not be an elaboration of a project management standard. A project management methodology can either be a formal mature process or an informal technique that aids a project management team in effectively developing a project charter.

3. *Project management information system.* The project management information system (PMIS) is a standardized set of automated tools available within the organization and integrated into a system. The PMIS is used by the project management team to support generation of a project charter, facilitate feedback as the document is refined, control changes to the project charter, and release the approved document.

4. *Expert judgment.* Expert judgment is often used to assess the inputs needed to develop the project charter. Such judgment and expertise is applied to any technical and management details during the process. Such expertise is provided by any group or individual with specialized knowledge or training, and is available from many sources, including

- Other units within the organization
- Consultants
- Stakeholders, including customers and sponsors
- Professional and technical associations
- Industry groups

Outputs

1. *Project charter.* (See the earlier introduction to the current section "Develop Project Charter.") One final point about the project team charter in terms of

integration. Teams that work together and communicate outward about the project with internal stakeholders, such as finance, purchasing, and engineering, tend to integrate their projects more effectively than teams that work in isolation. Therefore, the major determinant of successful integration is not technical but rather social and organizational. The way the team sees the priority of integration at all levels is to *see it explicitly in the charter itself*. Therefore, every charter should have a statement such as the following:

> The project team will integrate project activities at all levels, including with business planning and marketing, finance and budget, functional departments, and customers, to assure that the project outcomes reflect all the stakeholder interests to the extent possible. Project planning shall include a comprehensive project schedule which integrates cost, time, and quality factors to create an optimum outcome, cheaper, better, and faster.

The charter might address the following topics:

Project manager

Priority of project

Date

Owner/sponsor

Mission

Scope

Objectives

Assumptions

Constraints

Schedule and major milestones

Cost/budget/financial assumptions

Quality specifications

Major risks and contingencies

Project core team

Subject matter experts

Contractors

Develop Preliminary Project Scope Statement

The project scope statement is the definition of the project—what needs to be accomplished. The develop preliminary project scope statement process addresses and documents the characteristics and boundaries of the project and its associated products and services, as well as the methods of acceptance and scope control. A project scope statement includes

- Project and product objectives
- Product acceptance criteria
- Product or service requirements and characteristics
- Project boundaries
- Project requirements and deliverables
- Project constraints
- Project assumptions
- Initial project organization
- Initial defined risks
- Schedule milestones
- Initial WBS
- Order of magnitude cost estimate
- Project configuration management requirements
- Approval requirements

The preliminary project scope statement is developed from information provided by the initiator or sponsor. The project management team in the scope definition process further refines the preliminary project scope statement into the project scope statement. The project scope statement's content will vary, depending upon the application area and complexity of the project and can include some or all the components identified above. During subsequent phases of multiphase projects, the develop preliminary project scope statement process validates and refines, if required, the project scope defined for that phase.

Inputs

1. *Project charter*
2. *Project statement of work*
3. *Enterprise environmental factors*
4. *Organizational process assets*

Tools and techniques

1. *Project management methodology.*   The project management methodology defines a process that aids a project management team in developing and controlling changes to the preliminary project scope statement.

2. *Project management information system.*   The PMIS is used by the project management team to support generation of a preliminary project scope statement, facilitate feedback as the document is refined, control changes to the project scope statement, and release the approved document.

3. *Expert judgment.*   Expert judgment is applied to any technical and management details to be included in the preliminary scope statement.

Outputs

1. *Preliminary project scope statement*

Develop Project Management Plan

The develop project management plan process includes the actions necessary to define, integrate, and coordinate all subsidiary plans into a project management plan. The project management plan content will vary depending upon the application area and complexity of the project. This process results in a project management plan that is updated and revised through the integrated change control process. The project management plan defines how the project is executed, monitored, controlled, and closed. The project management plan documents the collection of outputs of the planning processes of the planning process group and includes

- The project management processes selected by the project management team
- The level of implementation of each selected process
- The descriptions of the tools and techniques to be used for accomplishing those processes
- How the selected processes will be used to manage the specific project, including the dependencies and interactions among those processes, and the essential inputs and outputs
- How work will be executed to accomplish the project objectives
- How changes will be monitored and controlled
- How configuration management will be performed
- How integrity of the performance measurement baselines will be maintained and used
- The need and techniques for communication among stakeholders
- The selected project life cycle and, for multiphase projects, the associated project phases
- Key management reviews for content, extent, and timing to facilitate addressing open issues and pending decisions

The project management plan can be composed of one or more subsidiary plans and other components. Each of the subsidiary plans and components is detailed to the extent required by the specific project. These subsidiary plans include, but are not limited to:

- Project scope management plan
- Schedule management plan
- Cost management plan
- Quality management plan

- Process improvement plan
- Staffing management plan
- Communication management plan
- Risk management plan
- Procurement management plan
- Milestone list
- Resource calendar
- Schedule baseline
- Cost baseline
- Quality baseline
- Risk register

Inputs

1. *Preliminary project scope statement*
2. *Project management processes*
3. *Enterprise environmental processes*
4. *Organizational process assets*

Tools and techniques

1. *Project management methodology*
2. *Project management information system*

- *Configuration management system.* The configuration management system is a subsystem of the overall PMIS. The system includes the process for submitting proposed changes, tracking systems for reviewing and approving proposed changes, defining approval levels for authorizing changes, and providing a method to validate approved changes. In most application areas, the configuration management system includes the change control system. The configuration management system is also a collection of formal documented procedures used to apply technical and administrative direction and surveillance to
  - Identify and document the functional and physical characteristics of a product or component.
  - Control any changes to such characteristics.
  - Record and report each change and its implementation status.
  - Support the audit of the products and components to verify conformance to requirements.
- *Change control system.* The change control system is a collection of formal documented procedures that define how project deliverables and documentation are controlled, changed, and approved. The change control system is a

subsystem of the configuration management system. For example, for information technology systems, a change control system can include the specifications (scripts, source code, data definition language, and the like) for each software component.

3. *Expert judgment.*   Expert judgment in the development of a project plan is typically obtained from outside experts on project planning in the consulting community.

Outputs

1. *Project management plan.*   In practice, the project management plan is a guide for the definition and control of the work. Therefore the plan must include control points, for instance, stage-gateway reviews, to ensure that management authorizes movement from one phase or stage to another. Reporting and monitoring strategies, including the use of earned value to integrate cost, schedule, and quality performance, should be made explicit.

The plan should also address accountability, particularly in view of the recent legislative and regulatory requirements of the Sarbanes-Oxley Act. This requirement is in compliance with internal control and accounting standards and is no longer optional for project managers. In fact, the price of disconnected and inconsistently applied efforts throughout a project and its interfaces, and lack of financial tracking systems that provide for audits, could be business-wide. Compliance with Sarbanes-Oxley therefore is not a choice but a requirement, and the plan should state standards for estimating costs, tracking the costs and relating costs to work performed, and the integrity of the closeout procedure and invoices to customers for work performed.

Direct and Manage Project Execution

The direct and manage project execution process requires the project manager and the project team to perform multiple actions to execute the project management plan to accomplish the work defined in the project scope statement. Some of these actions are

- Perform activities to accomplish project objectives.
- Expend effort and spend funds to accomplish the project objectives.
- Staff, train, and manage the project team members assigned to the project.
- Obtain quotations, bids, offers, or proposals as appropriate.
- Select sellers by choosing from among potential sellers.
- Obtain, manage, and use resources including materials, tools, equipment, and facilities.
- Implement the planning methods and standards.
- Create, control, verify, and validate project deliverables.

- Manage risks and implement risk response activities.

- Manage sellers and contractors.

- Adapt approved changes into the project's scope, plans, and environment.

- Establish and manage project communication channels, both external and internal to the project team.

- Collect project data and report cost, schedule, technical and quality progress, and status information to facilitate forecasting.

- Collect and document lessons learned, and implement approved process improvement activities.

The project manager, along with the project management team, directs the performance of the planning project activities, and manages various technical and organizational interfaces that exist within the project. The direct and manage project execution process is directly affected most by the project application area. Deliverables are produced as outputs from the processes performed to accomplish the project work planned and scheduled in the project management plan. Work performance information about the completion status of the deliverables, and what has been accomplished, is collected as part of project execution and is fed into the performance reporting process. Although the products, services, or results of the project are frequently in the form of tangible deliverables such as buildings, and roads, intangible deliverables, such as training, can also be provided.

Direct and manage project execution also requires implementation of:

- Approved corrective actions that will bring anticipated project performance into compliance with the project management plan

- Approved preventive actions to reduce the probability of potential negative consequences

- Approved defect repair requests to correct product defects found by the quality process

Inputs

1. *Project management plan.*

2. *Approved corrective actions.*   Approved corrective actions are documented, authorized directions required to bring expected future project performance in conformance with the project management plan.

3. *Approved preventive actions.*   Approved preventive actions are documented, authorized directions that reduce the probability of negative consequences associated with project risks.

4. *Approved change requests.*   Approved change requests are the documented, authorized changes to expand or contract project scope. The approved change requests can also modify policies, project management plans, procedures, costs

or budgets, or revise schedules. Approved change requests are scheduled for implementation by the project team.

5. *Approved defect repair.*   The approved defect repair is the documented, authorized request for product correction of a defect found during the quality inspection or the audit process.

6. *Validated defect repair.*   Notification that the reinspected repaired items have either been accepted or rejected.

7. *Administrative closure procedure.*   The administrative closure procedure documents all activities, interactions, and related roles and responsibilities needed in executing the administrative closure procedure for the project.

Tools and techniques

1. *Project management methodology*
2. *Project management information system*

Outputs

1. *Deliverables.*   A deliverable is any unique and verifiable product, result, or capability to perform a service that is identified in the project management planning documentation, and must be produced and provided to complete the project.

2. *Requested changes.*   Changes requested to expand or reduce project scope, to modify policies or procedures, to modify project cost or budget, or to revise the project schedule are often identified while project work is being performed. Requests for a change can be direct or indirect, externally or internally initiated, and can be optional or legally/contractually mandated.

3. *Implemented change requests.*   The approved change requests that have been implemented by the project management team during project execution.

4. *Implemented corrective actions.*   The approved corrective actions that have been implemented by the project management team to bring expected future project performance in conformance with the project management plan.

5. *Implemented preventive action.*   The approved preventive actions that have been implemented by the project management team to reduce the consequences of project risks.

6. *Implemented defect repair.*   During project execution, the project management team has implemented and approved product defect corrections.

7. *Work performance information.*   Information on the status of project activities being performed to accomplish the project work is routinely collected as part of the project management plan execution. This information includes, but is not limited to

- Schedule progress showing status information
- Deliverables that have been completed and those not completed

- Schedule activities that have started and those that have been finished
- Extent to which quality standards are being met
- Costs authorized and incurred
- Estimates to complete the schedule activities that have been started
- Percentage of completion of the inprogress schedule activities
- Documented lessons learned posted to the lessons learned knowledge base
- Resource utilization detail

Monitor and Control Project Work

The monitor and control project work process is performed to monitor project processes associated with initiating, planning, executing, and closing. Corrective or preventive actions are taken to control the project performance. Monitoring is an aspect of project management performed throughout the project. Monitoring includes collecting, measuring, and disseminating performance information, and assessing measurements and trends to effect process improvements. Continuous monitoring gives the project management team insight into the health of the project and identifies those areas that can require special attention. The monitor and control project work process is concerned with

- Comparing actual project performance against the project management plan
- Assessing performance to determine whether any corrective or preventive actions are indicated and then recommending those actions as necessary
- Analyzing, tracking, and monitoring project risks to make sure that the risks are identified, their status reported, and that appropriate risk response plans are being executed
- Maintaining an accurate and timely information base concerning the project's products and their associated documentation through project completion
- Providing information to support status reporting, progress measurement, and forecasting
- Monitoring implementation of approved changes as and when they occur

Inputs

1. *Project management plan*
2. *Work performance information*
3. *Rejected change requests.*   Rejected change requests include the change requests, their supporting documentation, and their change review status, showing a disposition of rejected change requests.

Tools and techniques

1. *Project management methodology*
2. *Project management information system*
3. *Earned value technique.*   The earned value technique measures perform-ance of the project as it moves from project initiation through project closure. The earned value management methodology also provides a means to forecast future performance based upon past performance.
4. *Expert judgment*

Outputs

1. *Recommended corrective actions.*   Corrective actions are documented rec-ommendations required to bring expected future project performance in con-formance with the project management plan.
2. *Recommended preventive actions*
3. *Forecasts.*   Forecasts include estimates or predictions of conditions and events in the project's future, based on information and knowledge available at the time of the forecast. Forecasts are updated and reissued based on work per-formance information that is provided as the project is executed. This infor-mation is about the project's past performance that could impact the project in the future; for example, estimate at completion.
4. *Recommended defect repair*
5. *Requested changes*

Integrated Change Control

The integrated change control process is performed from project inception through completion. Change control is necessary because projects seldom run exactly according to the project management plan. The project management plan, the project scope statement, and other deliverables must be maintained by carefully and continuously managing changes, either by rejecting changes or by approving changes so that those approved changes are incorporated into a revised baseline. The integrated change control process includes the follow-ing change management activities in differing levels of detail, based upon the completion of project execution:

- Identifying that a change needs to occur or has occurred.
- Influencing the factors that circumvent integrated change control so that only approved changes are implemented.
- Reviewing and approving requested changes.
- Managing the approved changes as and when they occur, by regulating the flow of requested changes.
- Maintaining the integrity of baselines by releasing only approved changes for incorporation into project products and services, and maintaining their related configuration and planning documentation.

- Reviewing and approving all recommended corrective and preventive actions.
- Controlling and updating the scope, cost, budget, schedule, and quality requirements based upon approved changes, by coordinating changes across the entire project. For example, a proposed schedule change will often affect cost, risk, quality, and staffing.
- Documenting the complete impact of a requested change.
- Validating defect repair.
- Controlling project quality to standards based on quality reports.

Proposed changes can require new or revised cost estimates, schedule activity sequences, schedule dates, resource requirements, and an analysis of risk response alternatives. These changes can require adjustments to the project management plan, project scope statement, or other project deliverables. The configuration management system with change control provides a standardized, effective, and efficient process to centrally manage changes within a project. Configuration management with change control includes identifying, documenting, and controlling changes to the baseline. The applied level of change control is dependent upon the application area, complexity of the specified project, contract requirements, and the context and environment in which the project is performed.

Project-wide application of the configuration management system, including change control processes, accomplishes three main objectives:

- Establishes an evolutionary method to consistently identify and request changes to established baselines, and to assess the value and effectiveness of those changes.
- Provides opportunities to continuously validate and improve the project by considering the impact of each change.
- Provides the mechanism for the project management team to consistently communicate all changes to the stakeholders.

In addition, some of the configuration management activities included in the integrated change control process are

- Providing the basis from which the configuration of products is defined and verified, products and documents are labeled, changes are managed, and accountability maintained.
- *Configuration status accounting.* Capturing, storing, and accessing configuration information needed to manage products and product information effectively.
- *Configuration verification and auditing.* Establishing that the performance and functional requirements defined in the configuration documentation have been met.

Every documented requested change must be either accepted or rejected by some authority within the project management team or an external organization representing the initiator, sponsor, or customer. Many times, the integrated change control process includes a change control board responsible for approving and rejecting the requested changes. The roles and responsibilities of these boards are clearly defined within the configuration control and change procedures, and are agreed to by the sponsor, customer, and other stakeholders. Many large organizations provide for a multitiered board structure, separating responsibilities among the boards. If the project is being provided under a contract, then some proposed changes would need to be approved by the customer.

Inputs

1. *Project management plan*
2. *Requested change*
3. *Work performance information*
4. *Recommended preventive actions*
5. *Recommended corrective actions*
6. *Recommended defect repair*
7. *Deliverables*

Tools and techniques

1. *Project management methodology*
2. *Project management information system*
3. *Expert judgment*

Outputs

1. *Approved change requests*
2. *Rejected change requests*
3. *Project management plan*
4. *Project scope statement*
5. *Approved corrective actions*
6. *Approved preventive actions*
7. *Approved defect repair*
8. *Validated defect epair*
9. *Deliverables*

Integrated change control requires, in practice, a clear understanding of the scope of work and what lies inside and outside the boundaries of the scope. Changes must be reviewed by top management and the customer in order to avoid new work generated by the team or by customer representatives. The project is seen as a contract, of sorts, and a change to the contract is considered "negotiable," but not given.

Cost control is driven by work done, not by budgets out of context from work performed. In other words, *cost control is seen as the process of aligning actual costs to the planned budget associated with the work performed.* This approach allows changes to be seen during a project *in terms of their impacts on remaining work*, and not on their original budget and work schedule.

Close Project

The close project process involves performing the project closure portion of the project management plan. In multiphase projects, the close project process closes out the portion of the project scope and associated activities applicable to a given phase. This process includes finalizing all activities completed across all project management process groups to formally close the project or a project phase, and transfer the completed or cancelled project as appropriate. The close project process also establishes the procedures to coordinate activities needed to verify and document the project deliverables, to coordinate and interact to formalize acceptance of those deliverables by the customer or sponsor, and to investigate and document the reasons for actions taken if a project is terminated before completion. Two procedures are developed to establish the interactions necessary to perform the closure activities across the entire project or for a project phase:

- *Administrative closure procedure.*   This procedure details all the activities, interactions, and related roles and responsibilities of the project team members and other stakeholders involved in executing the administrative closure procedure for the project. Performing the administrative closure process also includes integrated activities needed to collect project records, analyze project success or failure, gather lessons learned, and archive project information for future use by the organization.

- *Contract closure procedure.*   Includes all activities and interactions needed to settle and close any contract agreement established for the project, as well as define those related activities supporting the formal administrative closure of the project. This procedure involves both product verification (all work completed satisfactorily and correctly) and administrative closure (updating of contract records to reflect final results and archiving that information for future use). The contract terms and conditions can also prescribe specifications for contract closure that must be part of this procedure. Early termination of a contract is a special case of contract closure that could involve, for example, the inability to deliver the product, a budget overrun, or lack of required resources. This procedure is an input to the close contract process.

Inputs

1. *Project management plan*
2. *Contract documentation.*   Contract documentation is an input used to perform the contract closure process, and includes the contract itself, as well as

changes to the contract and other documentation (such as the technical approach, product description, or deliverable acceptance criteria and procedures).

3. *Enterprise environmental factors*
4. *Organizational process assets*
5. *Work performance information*
6. *Deliverables*

Tools and techniques

1. *Project management methodology*
2. *Project management information system*
3. *Expert judgment*

Outputs

1. *Administrative closure procedures.* This procedure contains all the activities and the related roles and responsibilities of the project team members involved in executing the administrative closure procedure. The procedures to transfer the project products or services to production and/or operations are developed and established. This procedure provides a step-by-step methodology for administrative closure that addresses

- Actions and activities to define the stakeholder approval requirements for changes and all levels of deliverables.
- Actions and activities that are necessary to confirm that the project has met all sponsor, customer, and other stakeholders' requirements, verify that all deliverables have been provided and accepted, and validate that completion and exit criteria have been met.
- Actions and activities necessary to satisfy completion or exit criteria for the project.

2. *Contract closure procedure.* This procedure is developed to provide a step-by-step methodology that addresses the terms and conditions of the contracts and any required completion or exit criteria for contract closure. It contains all activities and related responsibilities of the project team members, customers, and other stakeholders involved in the contract closure process. The actions performed formally close all contacts associated with the completed project.

3. *Final product, service, or result.* Formal acceptance and handover of the final product, service, or result that the project was authorized to produce. The acceptance includes receipt of a formal statement that the terms of the contract have been met.

4. *Organizational process assets (updates).* Closure will include the development of the index and location of project documentation using the configuration management system.

- *Formal acceptance documentation.* Formal confirmation has been received from the customer or sponsor that customer requirements and specifications for the project's product, service, or result have been met. This document formally indicates that the customer or sponsor has officially accepted the deliverables.

- *Project files.*   Documentation resulting from the project's activities, for example, project management plan, scope, cost, schedule and quality baselines, project calendar, risk registers, planned risk response actions, and risk impact.
- *Project closure documentation.*   Project closure documents consist of formal documentation indicating completion of the project and the transfer of the completed project deliverables to others, such as an operations group. If the project was terminated prior to completion, the formal documentation indicates why the project was terminated and formalizes the procedures for the transfer of the finished and unfinished deliverables of the cancelled project to others.
- *Historical information.*   Historical information and lessons learned from information are transferred to the lessons learned knowledge base for use by future projects.

In practice, closeout is often discounted by project managers and management in general as an *administrative* process, not worthy of much attention by *substantive* team members. Things have changed on that note. Now closeout is seen as the process of complying with Sarbanes-Oxley and the audit process to make sure that project work and expenditures are documented and traceable to customer requirements and project related expenditures.

Case Study of PMBOK Implementation: Integrated Transportation System

Using an integrated transportation system project case and the Microsoft Project schedule (Fig. 2.1), we will explore the application of the PMI PMBOK and other industry standards for integration. A Microsoft Project schedule for the case serves to illustrate how the work breakdown structure (WBS) is translated to project tasks, schedule, budget, and resource assignments.

This transportation program, entitled the Integrated Transportation System, involves the design and development of a product, a new transportation vehicle concept that will incorporate a controlled, line haul highway system for urban transportation. The case is scheduled into Microsoft Project and will be discussed, task level by task level to illustrate integration issues and opportunities in a typical such project. This product development project is organized in the stage-gateway framework, with entry from one stage to another controlled by an integration gateway review. This integration gateway review assesses progress, change, and impacts from each stage and provides the basis for a "go" or "no go" decision to proceed to the next stage.

The program is being developed in ITS, Inc., a research and development firm that designs transportation systems. Program stages are defined as separated projects to be *integrated forward* to the final program product. Forward integration is the process of looking forward to delivery rather than backwards to align with original baseline plans. Forward integration is based on earned value, that is, taking where we are in a project in both schedule and cost terms, and planning for remaining work. The scheduled tasks serve as the basis for this analysis in Figure 2.1.

Note that the gateway decision to proceed to the next stage is the summary output of each stage, thus highlighting the process of building in each stage to a *proceed* or *terminate* decision.

ID	% Complete	🔧	Task name	Duration	Start	Finish	Resource names
1	0%		**Integrated Transportation System**	**601 days?**	**Mon 6/25/07**	**Mon 10/12/09**	
2	0%		**Integration Gateway 1: Global interface**	**266 days**	**Mon 6/25/07**	**Mon 6/30/08**	John Shelter, CEO
3	0%	📋	International partnering and organizational integration	266 days	Mon 6/25/07	Mon 6/30/08	
4	0%		**Integration Gateway 2: Business planning**	**12 days**	**Tue 7/1/08**	**Wed 7/16/08**	John Shelter, CEO
5	0%		Develop strategic objectives	12 days	Tue 7/1/08	Wed 7/16/08	
6	0%		**Integration Gateway 3: Organizational development**	**9 days?**	**Thu 7/17/08**	**Tue 7/29/08**	John Shelter, CEO
7	0%		Prepare organization for integration	8 days	Thu 7/17/08	Mon 7/28/08	
8	0%		Prepare for internal control	1 day?	Tue 7/29/08	Tue 7/29/08	
9	0%		**Integration Gateway 4: Global team composition and development**	**11 days**	**Wed 7/30/08**	**Wed 8/13/08**	John Shelter, CEO
10	0%		Develop team and select program and project managers	11 days	Wed 7/30/08	Wed 8/13/08	
11	0%		**Integration Gateway 5: Support systems audit**	**4 days**	**Thu 8/14/08**	**Tue 8/19/08**	John Shelter, CEO
12	0%		Review all support organizational assets and systems for readiness	4 days	Thu 8/14/08	Tue 8/19/08	
13	0%		**Integration Gateway 6: Portfolio development and management**	**14 days**	**Wed 8/20/08**	**Mon 9/8/08**	
14	0%		Business strategy	6 days	Wed 8/20/08	Wed 8/27/08	John Shelter, CEO
15	0%		Portfolio development	4 days	Thu 8/28/08	Tue 9/2/08	John Shelter, CEO
16	0%		Project selection criteria	4 days	Wed 9/3/08	Mon 9/8/08	John Shelter, CEO

ID	% Complete	🔧	Task name	Duration	Start	Finish	Resource names
17	0%		**Integration Gateway 7: Market and customer interface**	**5 days**	**Tue 9/9/08**	**Mon 9/5/08**	
18	0%		Demand studies	5 days	Tue 9/9/08	Mon 9/15/08	John Shelter, CEO
19	0%		**Integration Gateway 8: Program integration management (PMBOK)**	**105 days**	**Tue 9/16/08**	**Mon 2/9/09**	
20	0%		Six sigma goals	4 days	Tue 9/16/08	Fri 9/19/08	Bob Smathers
21	0%		Business plan	2 days	Mon 9/22/08	Tue 9/23/08	
22	0%		**Develop project charter**	**39 days**	**Wed 9/24/08**	**Mon 11/17/08**	
23	0%	📋	Program plan	29 days	Wed 9/24/08	Mon 11/3/08	Bob Smathers
24	0%		Statement of work	2 days	Tue 11/4/08	Wed 11/5/08	
25	0%		Environmental scan	2 days	Thu 11/6/08	Fri 11/7/08	
26	0%		Organizational process assets	2 days	Mon 11/10/08	Tue 11/11/08	
27	0%	📋	Schedule baseline	2 days	Wed 11/12/08	Thu 11/13/08	Bob Smathers
28	0%		Project charter	2 days	Fri 11/14/08	Mon 11/17/08	
29	0%		**Develop preliminary project scope statement**	**4 days**	**Tue 11/18/08**	**Fri 11/21/08**	
30	0%		Draft scope statement	2 days	Tue 11/18/08	Wed 11/19/08	
31	0%		Integration review cycle	2 days	Thu 11/20/08	Fri 11/21/08	

ID	% Complete	🔧	Task name	Duration	Start	Finish	Resource names
32	0%		**Develop project management plan**	**38 days**	**Mon 11/24/08**	**Wed 1/14/09**	
33	0%		Project scope management plan	2 days	Mon 11/24/08	Tue 11/25/08	
34	0%		Generic work breakdown structure	2 days	Wed 11/26/08	Thu 11/27/08	
35	0%		Schedule management plan	2 days	Fri 11/28/08	Mon 12/1/08	
36	0%		Cost management plan	2 days	Tue 12/2/08	Wed 12/3/08	
37	0%		Quality management plan	2 days	Thu 12/4/08	Fri 12/5/08	
38	0%		Process improvement plan	2 days	Mon 12/8/08	Tue 12/9/08	
39	0%		Staffing management plan	2 days	Wed 12/10/08	Thu 12/11/08	
40	0%		Communication management plan	2 days	Fri 12/12/08	Mon 12/15/08	Bob Smathers
41	0%		Risk management plan	2 days	Tue 12/16/08	Wed 12/17/08	
42	0%		Procurement management plan	2 days	Thu 12/18/08	Fri 12/19/08	
43	0%		Milestone list	2 days	Mon 12/22/08	Tue 12/23/08	
44	0%		Resource calendar	2 days	Wed 12/24/08	Thu 12/25/08	
45	0%		Schedule baseline	2 days	Fri 12/26/08	Mon 12/29/08	
46	0%		Cost baseline	2 days	Tue 12/30/08	Wed 12/31/08	
47	0%		Quality baseline	2 days	Thu 1/1/09	Fri 1/2/09	

Figure 2.1   Integrated transportation system schedule in Microsoft Project.

ID	% Complete	🛈	Task name	Duration	Start	Finish	Resource names
48	0%		Risk register	2 days	Mon 1/5/09	Tue 1/6/09	
49	0%		Configuration management plan	2 days	Wed 1/7/09	Thu 1/8/09	
50	0%		Change control system concept	2 days	Fri 1/9/09	Mon 1/12/09	
51	0%		Contract management plan	2 days	Tue 1/13/09	Wed 1/14/09	
52	0%		**Direct and manage project execution**	**4 days**	**Thu 1/15/09**	**Tue 1/20/09**	
53	0%		Authorize and supervise work	2 days	Thu 1/15/09	Fri 1/16/09	
54	0%		Assign work	2 days	Mon 1/19/09	Tue 1/20/09	
55	0%		**Monitor and control project work**	**10 days**	**Wed 1/21/09**	**Tue 2/3/09**	
56	0%		**Assess earned value**	**6 days**	**Wed 1/21/09**	**Wed 1/28/09**	
57	0%		Cost variance	2 days	Wed 1/21/09	Thu 1/22/09	
58	0%		Schedule variance	2 days	Fri 1/23/09	Mon 1/26/09	
59	0%		Implement corretive actions	2 days	Tue 1/27/09	Wed 1/28/09	
60	0%		**Integrated change control**	**4 days**	**Thu 1/29/09**	**Tue 2/3/09**	
61	0%		Review and approve change requests	2 days	Thu 1/29/09	Fri 1/30/09	
62	0%		Prepare change impact statements	2 days	Mon 2/2/09	Tue 2/3/09	
63	0%		**Plan for project closeout**	**6 days**	**Mon 2/2/09**	**Mon 2/9/09**	

ID	% Complete	🛈	Task name	Duration	Start	Finish	Resource names
64	0%		Administrative	2 days	Mon 2/2/09	Tue 2/3/09	
65	0%		Contract	2 days	Wed 2/4/09	Thu 2/5/09	
66	0%		Financial	2 days	Fri 2/6/09	Mon 2/9/09	
67	0%		**Integration Gateway 9: Systems safety and reliability engineering (requirements definition**	**80 days**	**Tue 2/10/09**	**Mon 6/1/09**	
68	0%	🖼	System architecture	3 wks	Tue 2/10/09	Mon 3/2/09	Bill Carter[25%]
69	0%		Test requirements	6 wks	Tue 3/3/09	Mon 4/13/09	Bill Carter[25%]
70	0%		System design review (SDR)	0 days	Mon 4/13/09	Mon 4/13/09	John Smoltz[25%]
71	0%	📑	System requirements specification (SRS)	7 wks	Tue 3/3/09	Mon 4/20/09	Ryan Brookings[25%]
72	0%		Test architecture	4 wks	Tue 4/14/09	Mon 5/11/09	Ryan Brookings[25%]
73	0%	🖼	Functional hazard assessment to determine level C/B	15 days	Tue 5/12/09	Mon 6/1/09	Ryan Brown
74	0%	📑	**Integration Gateway 10: Chassis, mechanical and electronics design and development**	**95 days**	**Mon 6/1/09**	**Mon 10/12/09**	
75	0%		**Power assembly**	**1 day**	**Tue 6/2/09**	**Tue 6/2/09**	
76	0%	📑	I/O drawing	1 day	Tue 6/2/09	Tue 6/2/09	Bill Dow
77	0%	📑	Performance spec	1 day	Tue 6/2/09	Tue 6/2/09	Bill Dow
78	0%	📑	Test requirements	1 day	Tue 6/2/09	Tue 6/2/09	Ben Gay

ID	% Complete	🛈	Task name	Duration	Start	Finish	Resource names
79	0%		Full drawings	1 day	Tue 6/2/09	Tue 6/2/09	Bob Harris
80	0%		**Chassis concept**	**91 days**	**Mon 6/1/09**	**Tue 10/6/09**	
81	0%	🖼	Layout	40 days	Tue 6/2/09	Mon 7/27/09	Bart Starr
82	0%		Layout drawing	2 days	Tue 6/2/09	Wed 6/3/09	Dennis Bloom
83	0%		**Chassis design**	**91 days**	**Mon 6/1/09**	**Tue 10/6/09**	
84	0%	🖼	Assy design	29 days	Tue 6/2/09	Fri 7/10/09	Bud Manaker
85	0%	🖼	Approval	10 days	Tue 6/2/09	Mon 6/15/09	Bart Werrel
86	0%	🖼	Interpret guidelines and conditions in approval	0 days	Mon 6/1/09	Mon 6/1/09	Ben Schwartz
87	0%		Release	1 day	Tue 6/2/09	Tue 6/2/09	Brant Strong
88	0%	🖼	Procurement	15 days	Tue 6/2/09	Mon 6/22/09	Purchasing Dept
89	0%	🖼	Procurement check	18.2 wks	Tue 6/2/09	Tue 10/6/09	Purchasing Dept
90	0%		**Computer package**	**67 days**	**Mon 6/1/09**	**Wed 9/2/09**	
91	0%	🖼	Systems design	0 days	Mon 6/1/09	Mon 6/1/09	Ben Sheets
92	0%	🖼	Hardware	0 days	Mon 6/1/09	Mon 6/1/09	Ben Sheets
93	0%	🖼	Software	16 days	Tue 6/2/09	Tue 6/23/09	Lakeisha Werner
94	0%	🖼	Embedded integration	5 days	Tue 6/2/09	Mon 6/8/09	Sheila Bentley

Figure 2.1   (*Continued*)

ID	% Complete	ℹ	Task name	Duration	Start	Finish	Resource names
95	0%		Special safety and security issues	1 day	Tue 6/2/09	Tue 6/2/09	Sheila Bentley
96	0%		Dedection systems	2 days	Tue 6/2/09	Wed 6/3/09	Sheila Bentley
97	0%		Interface with diagnotic systems	3 days	Tue 6/2/09	Thu 6/4/09	Sheila Bentley
98	0%		Software code	2 days	Tue 6/2/09	Wed 6/3/09	Sheila Bentley
99	0%		Software integration	3 days	Tue 6/2/09	Thu 6/4/09	Sheila Bentley
100	0%	▥	Mechanical housings	13.4 wks	Tue 6/2/09	Wed 9/2/09	Sheila Bentley
101	0%	▥	In engine sensors	0 days	Mon 6/1/09	Mon 6/1/09	Sheila Bentley
102	0%	▥	Brake systems	20 days	Tue 6/2/09	Mon 6/29/09	Sheila Bentley
103	0%	▥	Automatic systems	6.8 wks	Tue 6/2/09	Fri 7/17/09	Sheila Bentley
104	**0%**		**Exhaust and emission control**	**20 days**	**Tue 6/2/09**	**Mon 6/29/09**	
105	0%		Standards	20 days	Tue 6/2/09	Mon 6/29/09	Ben Dowd
106	0%	▥	International issues	3 wks	*Tue 6/2/09*	Mon 6/22/09	Ben Dowd
107	0%	▥	Hardware	3 days	Tue 6/2/09	Thu 6/4/09	Ben Dowd
108	0%	▥	Computer controls	17 days	Tue 6/2/09	Wed 6/24/09	Ben Dowd
109	0%		Self reguation system	3 days	Tue 6/2/09	Thu 6/4/09	Ben Dowd

ID	% Complete	ℹ	Task name	Duration	Start	Finish	Resource names
110	**0%**		**Supply chain contracts**	**8 days**	**Mon 6/1/09**	**Thu 6/11/09**	
111	0%	▥	Systems	3 days	Tue 6/2/09	Thu 6/4/09	Butch Rends
112	0%		Vertical integration	2 days	Tue 6/2/09	Wed 6/3/09	Butch Rends
113	0%		International consortia	0 days	Mon 6/1/09	Mon 6/1/09	Butch Rends
114	0%		Supply interfaces	8 days	Tue 6/2/09	Thu 6/11/09	Butch Rends
115	**0%**		**Configuration management**	**5 days**	**Tue 6/2/09**	**Mon 6/8/09**	
116	0%	▥	Software tailoring	5 days	Tue 6/2/09	Mon 6/8/09	Bart Sharr
117	0%	▥	Data entry	1 day	Tue 6/2/09	Tue 6/2/09	Bart Sharr
118	0%		Change management	1 day	Tue 6/2/09	Tue 6/2/09	Bart Sharr
119	**0%**		**Tooling**	**5 days**	**Tue 6/2/09**	**Mon 6/8/09**	
120	0%		Premanufacturing inspection	1 wk	Tue 6/2/09	Mon 6/8/09	Bret How
121	0%	▥	Safety system	1 wk	Tue 6/2/09	Mon 6/8/09	Bret How
122	0%		Drawing	1 wk	Tue 6/2/09	Mon 6/8/09	Bret How
123	0%	▥	Alignment	1 wk	Tue 6/2/09	Mon 6/8/09	Bret How
124	**0%**		**Electrical components**	**4 days**	**Tue 6/2/09**	**Fri 6/5/09**	

ID	% Complete	ℹ	Task name	Duration	Start	Finish	Resource names
125	0%		Component designs	4 days	Tue 6/2/09	Fri 6/5/09	Sheve Brent
126	**0%**		**Chassis assembly**	**65 days**	**Mon 6/1/09**	**Mon 8/31/09**	
127	0%	▥	Panels	*65 days*	Tue 6/2/09	Mon 8/31/09	Scott Brust
128	0%		Insulation	5 days	Tue 6/2/09	Mon 6/8/09	Scott Brust
129	0%	▥	Welding	24 days	Tue 6/2/09	Fri 7/3/09	Scott Brust
130	0%		Trunk	2 days	Tue 6/2/09	Thu 6/4/09	Scott Brust
131	0%	▥	Hood	11.4 wks	Tue 6/2/09	Wed 8/19/09	Scott Brust
132	0%	▥	Doors	6 wks	Tue 6/2/09	Mon 7/13/09	Scott Brust
133	0%	▥	Windows	*5.6 wks*	Tue 6/2/09	Thu 7/9/09	Scott Brust
134	**0%**		**Computer systems**	**24 days**	**Mon 6/1/09**	**Fri 7/3/09**	
135	0%		Sensors	5 days	Tue 6/2/09	Mon 6/8/09	Scott Brust
136	0%		Network	3 days	Tue 6/2/09	Thu 6/4/09	Scott Brust
137	0%		Wiring	0 days	Mon 6/1/09	Mon 6/1/09	Scott Brust
138	0%		Embedded software	2 days	Tue 6/2/09	Wed 6/3/09	Scott Brust
139	0%	▥	Safety and security	0 days	Mon 6/1/09	Mon 6/1/09	Scott Brust
140	0%		Fail proof systems	3 wks	Tue 6/2/09	Mon 6/22/09	Scott Brust

Figure 2.1   (*Continued*)

ID	% Complete	❶	Task name	Duration	Start	Finish	Resource names
141	0%	▦	Lighting systems	4 wks	Tue 6/2/09	Mon 6/29/09	Scott Brust
142	0%	▦	Engine injection	4.8 wks	Tue 6/2/09	Fri 7/3/09	Scott Brust
143	0%		**Electric assembly builds**	**5 days**	**Tue 6/2/09**	**Mon 6/8/09**	
144	0%	▦	Prototype	5 days	Tue 6/2/09	Mon 6/8/09	Scott Brust
145	0%	▦	Systems design	1 day	Tue 6/2/09	Tue 6/2/09	Scott Brust
146	0%		Wiring	1 day	Tue 6/2/09	Tue 6/2/09	Scott Brust
147	0%		**Prototype assembly**	**10 days**	**Tue 6/2/09**	**Mon 6/15/09**	
148	0%		Molding	10 days	Tue 6/2/09	Mon 6/15/09	*Scott Brust*
149	0%	▦	Mold development	1 day	Tue 6/2/09	Tue 6/2/09	*Scott Brust*
150	0%		Shaping	2 days	Tue 6/2/09	Wed 6/3/09	*Scott Brust*
151	0%		**Customer requirements**	**54 days**	**Mon 6/1/09**	**Fri 8/14/09**	
152	0%		Comfort	0 days	Mon 6/1/09	Mon 6/1/09	Larry Constatine
153	0%	▦	Safety	10.8 wks	Tue 6/2/09	Fri 8/14/09	Larry Constatine
154	0%		Security	14 days	Tue 6/2/09	Fri 6/19/09	Larry Constatine
155	0%		Seating	2 wks	Tue 6/2/09	Mon 6/15/09	Larry Constatine

ID	% Complete	❶	Task name	Duration	Start	Finish	Resource names
156	0%		Visibility	1 day	Tue 6/2/09	Tue 6/2/09	Larry Constatine
157	0%		Controls	2 days	Tue 6/2/09	Wed 6/3/09	Larry Constatine
158	0%	▦	Dashboard	3 days	Tue 6/2/09	Thu 6/4/09	Larry Constatine
159	0%		Trunk	10 days	Tue 6/2/09	Thu 6/25/09	Larry Constatine
160	0%	▦	Hood	5 days	Tue 6/2/09	Mon 6/8/09	Larry Constatine
161	0%	▦	Tires	3 days	Tue 6/2/09	Mon 6/8/09	Larry Constatine
162	0%		Capacity	5 days	Tue 6/2/09	Mon 6/8/09	Larry Constatine
163	0%		**Six sigma supplier management**	**86.81 days**	**Tue 6/2/09**	**Wed 9/30/09**	
164	0%		Key processes	11.5 days	Tue 6/2/09	Wed 6/17/09	Larry Constatine
165	0%	▦	Process performance indicators	8 wks	Tue 6/2/09	Wed 9/30/09	Larry Constatine
166	0%		Process improvement strategy	3 wks	Tue 6/2/09	Mon 6/22/09	Larry Constatine
167	0%		Measures	3 days	Tue 6/2/09	Thu 6/4/09	Larry Constatine
168	0%		Data collection	3 days	Tue 6/2/09	Thu 6/4/09	Larry Constatine
169	0%		Data analysis	2 days	Tue 6/2/09	Wed 6/3/09	Larry Constatine
170	0%		Process improvement teams	15 days	Tue 6/2/09	Mon 6/22/09	Larry Constatine
171	0%		Review of competition	3 days	Tue 6/2/09	Thu 6/4/09	Larry Constatine

ID	% Complete	❶	Task name	Duration	Start	Finish	Resource names
172	0%		Benchmarking	10 days	Tue 6/2/09	Mon 6/15/09	Larry Constatine
173	0%		Internal reviews	15 days	Tue 6/2/09	Mon 6/22/09	Larry Constatine
174	0%		Supplier quality	5 days	Tue 6/2/09	Mon 6/8/09	Larry Constatine
175	0%		Documentation	5 days	Tue 6/2/09	Mon 6/8/09	Larry Constatine
176	0%		**Performance requirements**	**95 days**	**Mon 6/1/09**	**Mon 10/12/09**	
177	0%	▦	Requirements analysis	15 days	Tue 6/2/09	Mon 6/22/09	Larry Constatine
178	0%	▦	Data analysis	19 wks	Mon 6/1/09	Mon 10/12/09	Larry Constatine
179	0%		Simulation studies	14 days	Tue 6/2/09	Fri 6/19/09	Larry Constatine
180	0%		**Interface integration**	**70 days**	**Tue 6/2/09**	**Mon 9/7/09**	
181	0%		Electrical	16.5 days	Tue 6/2/09	Wed 6/24/09	Bill Short
182	0%	▦	Mechanical	5 wks	Tue 6/2/09	Mon 7/6/09	Bill Short
183	0%		Software	4 wks	Tue 6/2/09	Mon 6/29/09	Bill Short
184	0%	▦	Powertrain	*14 wks*	Tue 6/2/09	Mon 9/7/09	Bill Short
185	0%	▦	Wheels	0.6 wks	Tue 6/2/09	Thu 6/4/09	Bill Short
186	0%		**Outsource controls**	**5 days**	**Tue 6/2/09**	**Mon 6/8/09**	
187	0%	▦	Contracts	0.1 wks	Tue 6/2/09	Tue 6/2/09	Bill Fitch

Figure 2.1   (*Continued*)

ID	% Complete	❶	Task name	Duration	Start	Finish	Resource names
188	0%		Supplier negotiations	2.5 days	Tue 6/2/09	Thu 6/4/09	Bill Fitch
189	0%	▦	Collaboration and partnering	1 wk	Tue 6/2/09	Mon 6/8/09	Bill Fitch
190	0%		Outshoring	3 days	Tue 6/2/09	Thu 6/4/09	Bill Fitch
191	0%		**Integration Gateway 11: Software design and development**	**10 days**	**Mon 4/20/09**	**Mon 5/4/09**	
192	0%		**Iteration 1**	**10 days**	**Tue 4/21/09**	**Mon 5/4/09**	
193	0%		Inception	1 wk	Tue 4/21/09	Mon 4/27/09	John Miller
194	0%		Elaboration	2 wks	Tue 4/21/09	Mon 5/4/09	John Miller
195	0%		**Radio and communication**	**10 days**	**Tue 4/21/09**	**Mon 5/4/09**	
196	0%		Learn environment	2 wks	Tue 4/21/09	Mon 5/4/09	Bill Done
197	0%		Write to requirements	1 wk	Tue 4/21/09	Mon 4/27/09	Bill Done
198	0%		Draw line	1 wk	Tue 4/21/09	Mon 4/27/09	Bill Done
199	0%		Draw character	4 days	Tue 4/21/09	Fri 4/24/09	Bill Done
200	0%		Research radios	1 wk	Tue 4/21/09	Mon 4/27/09	Bill Done
201	0%		**Transition**	**5 days**	**Tue 4/21/09**	**Mon 4/27/09**	
202	0%		Architecture document	1 wk	Tue 4/21/09	Mon 4/27/09	Charlie Howe
203	0%		**Iteration 2 - S/W application**	**10 days**	**Mon 4/20/09**	**Mon 5/4/09**	

ID	% Complete	❶	Task name	Duration	Start	Finish	Resource names
204	0%		Inception (planning)	10 days	Tue 4/21/09	Mon 5/4/09	Chuck York
205	0%		**Elaboration (analysis & design)**	**5 days**	**Mon 4/20/09**	**Mon 4/27/09**	
206	0%		Write use cases	1 wk	Tue 4/21/09	Mon 4/27/09	Bill Verdon
207	0%		Class and sequence diagrams	1 wk	Tue 4/21/09	Mon 4/27/09	Bill Verdon
208	0%		Preliminary software requirements	0.8 wks	Tue 4/21/09	Fri 4/24/09	Bill Verdon
209	0%		Software requirements review	0.2 wks	Tue 4/21/09	Tue 4/21/09	Bill Verdon
210	0%		High-level requirements complete	0 wks	Mon 4/20/09	Mon 4/20/09	Bill Verdon
211	0%		Refine class diagrams	1 wk	Tue 4/21/09	Mon 4/27/09	Bill Verdon
212	0%		Collaboration diagrams	1 wk	Tue 4/21/09	Mon 4/27/09	Bill Verdon
213	0%		**Integration testing**	**5 days**	**Tue 4/21/09**	**Mon 4/27/09**	
214	0%		Test protocol	1 wk	Tue 4/21/09	Mon 4/27/09	Bill Verdon
215	0%		Test the test	1 wk	Tue 4/21/09	Mon 4/27/09	Bill Verdon
216	0%		Conduct test	1 wk	Tue 4/21/09	Mon 4/27/09	Bill Verdon
217	0%		**Iteration 3 - Hardware Integration**	**10 days**	**Tue 4/21/09**	**Mon 5/4/09**	
218	0%		Inception (planning)	80 hrs	Tue 4/21/09	Mon 5/4/09	Bill Bartol
219	0%		**Application development**	**10 days**	**Tue 4/21/09**	**Mon 5/4/09**	

ID	% Complete	❶	Task name	Duration	Start	Finish	Resource names
220	0%		Hardware setup	0.8 wks	Tue 4/21/09	Fri 4/24/09	Jim Schwartz
221	0%		Learning curve	2 wks	Tue 4/21/09	Mon 5/4/09	Jim Schwartz
222	0%		Design for software support layer	1 wk	Tue 4/21/09	Mon 4/27/09	Jim Schwartz
223	0%		Message manager	1 wk	Tue 4/21/09	Thu 4/30/09	Jim Schwartz
224	0%		Radio control	1 wk	Tue 4/21/09	Mon 4/27/09	Jim Schwartz
225	0%		**Hardware support**	**9 days**	**Tue 4/21/09**	**Fri 5/1/09**	
226	0%		Design for hardware support	1.8 wks	Tue 4/21/09	Fri 5/1/09	Bill Woren
227	0%		**Integration Gateway 12: Test equipment and testing**	**50 days**	**Tue 4/21/09**	**Mon 6/29/09**	
228	0%		**Integration test equipment**	**50 days**	**Tue 4/21/09**	**Mon 6/29/09**	
229	0%	▦	Requirements definition	2 wks	Tue 4/21/09	Mon 5/4/09	LOU Betx
230	0%		Detailed design	10 wks	Tue 4/21/09	Mon 6/29/09	LOU Betx
231	0%		Procurement	7.5 wks	Tue 4/21/09	Thu 6/11/09	LOU Betx
232	0%		Assemble	4 wks	Tue 4/21/09	Mon 6/8/09	LOU Betx
233	0%		Test	0.5 wks	Tue 4/21/09	Thu 4/23/09	LOU Betx
234	0%		Documentation release	1 wk	Tue 4/21/09	Mon 4/27/09	LOU Betx
235	0%		**Integration Gateway 13: Integration of software/hardware**	**20 days**	**Mon 4/20/09**	**Mon 5/18/09**	

Figure 2.1 *(Continued)*

ID	% Complete	☺	Task name	Duration	Start	Finish	Resource names
236	0%		**Subassembly Availability - Prototype 2X**	**0 days**	**Mon 4/20/09**	**Mon 4/20/09**	**Lour Bentt**
237	0%		Part 1 available	0 days	Mon 4/20/09	Mon 4/20/09	Lour Bentt
238	0%		Part 2 available	0 days	Mon 4/20/09	Mon 4/20/09	Lour Bentt
239	0%		Kit available	0 days	Mon 4/20/09	Mon 4/20/09	Lour Bentt
240	0%	▦	Chassis available	0 days	Mon 4/20/09	Mon 4/20/09	Lour Bentt
241	0%		**Prototype full integration**	**20 days**	**Tue 4/21/09**	**Mon 5/18/09**	
242	0%		Build	*20 days*	Tue 4/21/09	Mon 5/18/09	David Bart

Figure 2.1   (*Continued*)

Integration Gateway 1: Global Interface

The first step in integration is a business planning function (often called environmental scanning), looking outward to integrate with global partners and customers. *The first line of integration is global.* According to Thomas Friedman in the *World is Flat*, the "playing field" for resources, partnerships, and systems is now global—beyond traditional political and economic jurisdictions. Thus, ITS must first position itself to be successful in this program area by building interfaces with key customer groups, supplying partners, and perhaps, with governmental agencies globally because of the "public" nature of transportation and the need to take advantage of worldwide supply and design sources.

Customer groups would include a set of public transportation companies and agencies, which would represent stakeholders in a new transportation system product. Integration, in this case, would involve understanding the strategic and business plans of these agencies and "building in" requirements and conditions as the new product is developed.

International partnering and organizational integration

This integration step involves setting up an internal business staff to provide liaison with global partners and customers. Completion of this step "rolls up" in the project schedule to "Global Interface." Organizational integration means actually studying and understanding the system dynamics of candidate transportation agencies and systems in order to fully integrate product prototypes with customer expectations.

The concept of stage-gateway project management assures that integration is achieved during each stage or phase of the project. Integration implies that there has been coordination and collaboration across functions and among participants *at the scale of the particular stage.* For instance, in the global interface stage, the gateway integration issue is, "Has the business positioned itself globally to exploit supplier, customer, and stakeholder values worldwide?" Thus, here integration is seen on a global scale and targets the forces and factors that will create risk and opportunity for the business and its developing portfolio of projects.

Integration Gateway 2: Business Planning

Business planning is an integrative function and gateway because it involves the integration and combination of business objectives and strategies with candidate projects, resulting in a company strategy and aligned program and project portfolio. Here the business integrates its core competency and global partnerships with its internal business objectives and plans. Candidate projects are designed to carry out business investment goals. The integration of business interest and direction, with projects such as this ITS case study, is the second line of interface in fully integrating the project. Integration of business planning involves the use of the weighted scoring model and other integrative tools to score projects against business objectives.

In the case of ITS, one of its strategic objectives is to develop and test the feasibility of a variety of new transportation systems that would provide future customers and passengers with new levels of efficiency and effectiveness. The ITS project would score highly against this objective, simply because it is directly connected to that business objective. ITS is "aligned" and thus integrated with the business itself, its capacity, its competencies, and its intended future.

Develop strategic objectives

The development of strategic objectives is a "roll up" task to business planning. Strategic objectives are developed after an audit of the business capacity and competencies, and the interests of stakeholders and management in directing business growth. Strategic objectives are developed as part of a brainstorming process, and then confirmed by top management and the board of directors. Objectives are then weighted, based on their relative importance, providing a basis for later assessment of candidate programs of projects against weighted objectives.

The integration of business strategy and programs is the second line of integration, following global interface. Integration assures that all the business owner and management expectations are embodied in documented strategic objectives, and that the global opportunities, both for markets and suppliers, are integrated into business decisions.

Integration Gateway 3: Organizational Development

If the organization cannot handle the challenges and risks associated with a given business purpose and direction, this stage assures that work does not proceed until it can. The stage addresses the core competency of the company or agency to design, develop, and produce in a given program area, in this case, the transportation system development. In effect, this is an audit of company capacity, and this stage involves taking stock of company capacity in terms of people, support system infrastructure, information technology, facilities, business processes, and, perhaps most importantly, energy and commitment.

This stage is, in effect, an assessment of the company's *integrative capacity*, its proven competence in pulling together its people, systems, and processes to overcome risks and create opportunities in a given program area. If the gateway review uncovers weaknesses in this capacity, e.g., a proven tendency to deliver project deliverables late and overbudget, then the business undertakes improvement projects to increase its capacity to produce on time and within budget, before entering the next stage.

Integration Gateway 4: Global Team Composition and Development

This stage involves setting up partnerships and team relationships in all areas necessary to achieve the global objectives of the business and to support candidate programs and projects. The composition of the team must be aligned with business direction. Teams are composed of team members who possess the competencies and interests globally, across functions, suppliers, and customers that support the broad business plan. Teams are set up at each gateway level of the program, beginning with worldwide partnerships down to program and project teams. The stage is important because integration at every level requires commitments and trusting relationships between key company stakeholders.

The concept of integration is often not associated with people in a work setting as much as it is with systems and equipment. In a social or political setting, integration has meant many things to many people, such as, racial and religious integration and economic integration. But the concept has rarely been applied to organizational dynamics. Other concepts, e.g., team harmony and team alignment, refer to teams where team members contribute according to their capacities and support each other.

However, team integration as used in this book is more than a simple team concept. It is not the question of whether the team members get along. It is, rather, grounded in the need for the team to be integrated across the organization and across the global marketplace in which it is working. Team members reach out to various support systems and stakeholders of the organization and to the customer base, and *bring value* to the team. There is true integration when team members create team value because they are connected to key forces and factors outside the team. For instance, an engineer on the ITS team is in direct contact with governmental regulations that govern the dimensions and performance characteristics of the ITS. Thus, his or her engineering contribution is informed by the external constraints and conditions, which the project product must meet.

Virtual team tools are utilized to integrate people across geographical boundaries. Thus integration is not spatial; it is informational. The integration of ideas is facilitated by online working relationships and teleconferencing, and customers and suppliers are integrated into team deliberations through online tools. This is true integration of the team into the global fabric of the business and its constituency.

Develop a team, select key program and project managers

The selection of the program and project managers in an integrated project organization is keyed to training and cross-functional experience. Managers who have played many functional roles in a project management process will likely coordinate and collaborate more effectively than managers who have not. Thus rotating talent across functions builds project management competency in integrating and delivering project outcomes.

Integration Gateway 5: Support Systems Audit

This stage involves assurance that the organization or agency can support a complex program of projects; this is the "positioning" of the infrastructure of the organization, much like an engineering study of the readiness of a bridge for heavy traffic. Termed organizational process assets by the Project Management Institute in the PMBOK, the targets here are key business processes, e.g., functional and technical support, procurement, contracting, human resources, accounting and financial cost capture and reporting, configuration management, information technology, and a project management office (PMO), that can *make or break* a program of projects. In these organizations, integration of the project, both during the planning and implementation stages, is facilitated by responsive and integrated support systems and services. These are the so-called tools of program management. No project can be successful in isolation from its parent business, and no project can be successful without a strong support system in the key *asset* areas. Integration is made possible by integrating systems.

This basic system audit task provides for reviews of the company's support systems and capacity to support program management in the following areas. Each system helps to integrate a particular business system support with project team needs:

- *Functional, technical support.*   The presence of a matrix of functional capability, such as, engineering, facilities, and technical processes that support project management

- *eProcurement and contracting.*   The capacity to develop a supplier community and work with suppliers and contractors in a seamless, eProcurement (electronic procurement system) environment

- *Human resources.*   The support of an HR department that looks after the welfare of employees and the morale and well-being of the workforce

- *Accounting and financial reporting.*   A project-oriented accounting and reporting system that captures costs at the project code level and is able to report real-time actual costs within 24 hours to project managers

- *Configuration management.*   A staff and software that preserves and documents the project deliverables and their components, with disciplined numbering and filing systems, to serve transition to manufacturing and production

- *Information technology.*   A company intranet system for facilitating the visibility of program and project information, e.g., schedules, plans, budgets, status reports, project review agendas, and a Web-based customer reporting system that allows project managers to share project information with stakeholders and customers

- *Project management office.*   A staff function to program managers and project managers that provides analytic and administrative support to projects through generic WBS, tools, and techniques for scheduling, and monitoring guidelines to assure consistent management across all company projects

Integration Gateway 6: Portfolio Development and Management

The process of producing and managing a portfolio of projects is an integrative function from beginning to end. Portfolio development involves aligning new projects so that the entire organization is positioned to implement top-level strategic and business plans. The integration of projects with business direction is a key high-level activity that begins the portfolio process. Integration, in this case, means that projects are made part of the fabric of the business; projects are seen as instruments of the business plan, focused on business growth and expansion. The way integration is accomplished at this level involves the following steps:

- Review of business strategic objectives
- Weighting business objectives relative to each other
- Scoring each candidate project against each strategic objective
- Integrating weights of the objectives and project scores

The weighted scoring model is a tool to assure that projects are seen in terms of how projects "rack up" against the business strategies, weighted to reflect their relative importance to the business. The tool is flexible, so weighted objectives can be changed as the business changes, and scoring can be enhanced by modification of project plans.

The development of a portfolio and scoring of candidate projects is largely a subjective system performed through a group meeting of key business management and experts. Integration in this case occurs in the thinking process of the participants as well, reflecting the views and insights of thoughtful participants.

The gateway decision here is whether projects fit the organization's direction and purpose and serve as capital assets to grow the business. Projects enter the portfolio pipeline and are budgeted and funded by a *capital rationing* technique. Capital rationing integrates the company's allocation of available program resources with its strategic objectives through a weighted scoring model. Through the budgeting process, funds are allocated to strategic objectives according to their relative importance (triggered by their relative weights), then project costs and scores against objectives are used to fund projects until funds run out.

Integration Gateway 7:
Market and Customer Interface

The integration of projects with the company's market and customer base is accomplished *through an organizational process*, not a technical one. The organization is vertically integrated to tie marketing and sales to project planning and management. This is accomplished by linking the marketing and sales departments in a matrix relationship with program and project management. Marketing and sales representatives are tied virtually to project team status and review meetings, and project design and development can be interrupted by marketing and sales inputs *at any time* through the change control process.

Integrated project management opens the change control process to its own marketing and sales people through this linkage. This is not easily done in many companies because of the traditional separation of project, marketing, and sales departments. This separation is functional because marketing and sales are outward bound activities, while projects are inward bound activities. Cultural differences stem from different workforce and incentive systems. Sales is *incentivized* by actual bottom line sales transactions, while projects are typically unbound by customer acceptance transactions, with the exception of user acceptance tasks.

This institutional integration of marketing, sales, and project dynamics is a key ingredient to flexible project management, focused on better, cheaper, and faster. While traditional project deliverables are constrained by generic processes and requirements, under this system customized changes in real time from marketing and sales are *injected* seamlessly into project processes at any stage gateway. Sales transactions on the customer's site can be made on the spot as salespeople and project people are in real-time communication on project outcomes and design specifications. New marketing research information can *be blended into project designs as they are surfaced and interpreted.*

Integration Gateway 8: Project
Integration Management

This stage gateway is the key management action—the *change intervention* that empowers the company to carry out project integration. The stage actions facilitate consistency with PMI's Project Body of Knowledge section on project integration management. Here the organization *shows* the face of coordination, integration, and teamwork through its processes. Good program planning is reflected in employees who are disciplined to do what is necessary to integrate, even when such activity may seem "bureaucratic" and overly administrative in nature. In other words, engineers may be uncomfortable with preparing a project charter when the ingredients of such a charter are already in their heads, until they see that the charter is necessary to *mobilize* the whole team.

An integrated environment also involves setting up the work of the organization at every level to allow monitoring for earned value. The concept of integration begins at the task level. Interface factors such as key earned value milestones and cost factors in a project should be built into individual task structure in the project planning process. If the task is structured correctly, project integration is practical and routine; if not, project integration becomes difficult because there is no objective set of indicators for project performance against time and cost.

The major stages of PMI's project integration management are as follows:

- *Develop project charter.*   A full and detailed discussion of the charter of the project team.

- *Develop preliminary scope statement.*   A statement of the work of the project and how the staged, gateway system would work, including criteria for passage from one stage to another.

- *Develop project management plan.*   An overall project plan including plans for scope, generic WBS, schedule, cost, quality, staffing, risk, procurement and contracting, resources, configuration management, and change control.

- *Direct and manage project execution.*   This would be a statement of the administrative and managerial actions that will be triggered to authorize work, to assign work, and to generate teamwork in the project team.

- *Monitor and control project work.*   This includes the approach to monitoring progress and remaining work, through the use of earned value (cost and schedule variance) tools.

- *Plan for project closeout.*   This stage would include procedures to terminate the project, including financial, contract, and resource disposition.

Integration Gateway 9: Systems Safety and Reliability

This is the technical design stage, the process of linking the requirements document with the design of the system and product prototype. System safety and reliability sets the design boundaries for making sure the ITS system is safe, that it performs to minimum "mean time between failure" standards, and that it is reliable, e.g., that it performs to minimum "mean time between maintenance standards."

Integration at the systems level changes the context of integration to the system and product being produced by the project. But again, technical integration does not occur without organizational integration. A quality electronic product requires that mechanical, software, and electronic engineers consult with each other in defining, designing, and building system components that must perform in the system being produced.

Outputs of this stage also include system architecture, test requirements, system design review criteria for gateway reviews, system requirements specifications, test architecture, and functional hazard assessment requirements. The gateway "go" or "no go" decision is based on a direct tracing of design to functional requirements.

Integration Gateway 10: Chassis, Mechanical, and Electronics Design and Development

This stage covers the design and development of the prototype product following designs produced in the previous stage.

Here, the hardware prototype components are produced with the support of the manufacturing engineering staff. Integration of manufacturing factors and design factors are assured by involving manufacturing engineers in producing prototypes for testing and user approval. Components include power assembly, chassis, computer package, exhaust and emission control, supply chain contract partnerships, electrical components, and necessary drawings and graphics. Components are tested against six sigma quality standards set in the design.

Integration Gateway 11: Software Design and Development

Software design is seen as a high-risk activity because of the high probability of failure in integration; thus, this activity has its own gateway. This stage involves inception and elaboration phases of software design and development, a separate stage to assure control over the design and development of software design.

Integration Gateway 12: Test Equipment and Testing

Test equipment is a separate stage because of the key role of testing equipment in integration. Test equipment must be aligned with testing requirements to allow for the next stage, integration of software and hardware.

Integration Gateway 13: Integration of Software and Hardware

Full integration of software and hardware is accomplished in this stage. In a product development project, this is where software, electrical, and mechanical engineers work together to integrate their components into a fully functioning prototype for testing and acceptance.

This stage is not primarily a technical one, but rather a teaming activity, where success is determined by past work between functional specialists. Integration is a coming together of trained specialists who have been working together while producing their components.

Case Application: Integration Issues in Portfolio and Project Planning Life Cycles

The purpose of this case is to illustrate, using a real project, how integration is achieved at each stage of a portfolio and project life cycle. The process described below includes many of the traditional project planning and control steps, simplified and "demystified," for practical use. This discussion is followed by a more in-depth treatment of integration, including technology and technical integration issues that typically characterize technical projects.

Integrating a project involves 13 basic steps:

1. Business and strategic planning
2. Portfolio development and project selection
3. Definition, work breakdown structure, and scope
4. Task list, with estimated durations, linkages and interfaces, and resources
5. Network diagram
6. Time-based network diagram
7. Baseline Gantt chart (schedule interfaces)
8. Resource integration
9. Project initiation
10. Project work assignment and performance
11. Team integration
12. Project monitoring
13. Project closeout

The Case: QuickTech Building Systems

The case is a project involving QuickTech, a development company in the commercial real estate and building industry. The case involves the selection, planning, and implementation of a complex building project involving a high-level technical component of building support systems. QuickTech employs a new automated system of building architecture and planning that accelerates the completion of commercial buildings for specialized technical tenants who require tailored facility support and security.

Business and strategic planning

QuickTech uses a classic portfolio development process, first identifying broad business plans and then developing a strategic plan using SWOT (strengths, weaknesses, opportunities, and threats) analysis. The company's SWOT analysis has identified key SWOT issues in all four areas, concentrating on contingencies and integration challenges.

Integration issues

We can define the process of integration as "the process of bringing the parts of a system together to produce a deliverable" through a proactive management approach that encourages people to worry about whether "the left hand knows what the right hand is doing." Integration is made necessary because to design and build a project deliverable, that deliverable must be broken down into its "configuration" parts and produced from the bottom up. The "rolling up" of a deliverable is called integration because it requires both vertical and horizontal activity to bring pieces together from work package all the way up to the final project outcome.

We can further describe the integration process as coordinating:

1. The work of the project with the plans and ongoing operations of the performing organization, and
2. Product and project scope.

Integration at the highest level, business and strategic planning, involves the coordination of company and business planning with project selection and financial planning. This means that the beginning of project integration is making sure that the project itself is aligned with the company's strategy and plan for growth, whether written or is simply a shared vision of company leadership.

Analysis of weaknesses in the strategic planning process, for instance, would be performed in the light of the company's past performance and market analysis. Integration of business plans with marketing plans means that a project is selected with a full view of how the project will serve the company in its growth objectives. From a personal standpoint, this means that the company leadership coordinates and communicates with program and project managers, and has access to information that facilitates project integration management.

The Portfolio: Integration Issues and Procedures in Development

The business portfolio is coordinated with key company processes and workforce capacity. Resources are reviewed against the demands of the company's project portfolio.

Integration issues

The early integration of the portfolio with other company processes means that the financial and resource implications of the portfolio are reviewed by company leadership across the board. Each top manager of the company has veto authority over proposed projects and a portfolio council is organized to resolve differences and move the portfolio on through development.

This building project would first appear in the business plan as a marketing or "ideation" concept or program objective to enter into a commercial building project, consistent with the company's growth plans. Integration of portfolio issues with other company processes requires a planning information system with the following characteristics:

1. Provides a database on current workforce commitments

2. Provides for a business impact statement for each new project proposed for the portfolio

The database can be handled through a networked Microsoft Project "resource pool," a database of all current projects and committed resources against a calendar.

Integrated portfolio business impact statement

The business impact statement is a tool to assure integration of the new portfolio with key business processes and plans. The impact statement is completed and shared widely at the top of the company, in order to flesh out issues before further project commitments are made. This is the first and highest level integration tool tailored to weed out projects that would have adverse impacts on other company commitments or plans.

Impact statement format.   The format is given in Table 3.1, completed with the building case now under consideration:

The value of this statement is that each functional department completes its portion of the statement after review of the project proposal. This achieves the integration of the key perspectives in the company—many of which may be odds—at its highest level. Thus integration activity may be completed by electronic forms, which are made part of the company business planning process.

TABLE 3.1 Integrated Portfolio Business Impact Statement

Proposed portfolio project	Impact on current project schedules	Impact of current workforce	Impact on current financial condition	Impact on current risk posture of company	Impact of current market and customer base	Impact on current company technology and processes	Impact on company culture
Commercial "technical" building support project.	On proposed schedule, project would commit over 500 hours of building design engineer staff.	Current proposed project team will require hiring three draftsmen with technical and building support background.	Upfront financing of proposed project will require finding a venture capital source to earmark support of this highly risky project. However, company does not now have project level accounting and cost capture system to record costs.	Current portfolio balance in high risk; this project will add to the current imbalance of highly risky projects with no committed customer contract.	Company relies on technical clients which need this kind of building and support system, thus project is aligned with strategic objective of growing in this industry sector.	Current company tooling is already there; capacity to perform with little new investment makes this an attractive project.	Current company culture has moved away from research and applied new systems to manufacturing. This project could face problems because the culture of the company no longer supports high-risk, creative projects. This may require finding a venture capitalist to fund the project and share major risks.

Definition: Work Breakdown Structure

Generic WBS

Before the process begins, the company defines a generic work breakdown structure (WBS). The generic WBS defines the company's prescribed technical and project process cycle for a given family or programs of projects. This is the standard for every project life cycle designed to deliver product and services and includes a set of generic tasks, linkages, and definitions, which represents the company's learning system based on past performance.

First level: the deliverable

The first step in defining the work necessary to produce the deliverable is to complete a WBS from the top (the deliverable) down to the third or fourth level of tasks. We will do this in outline form. The top of the WBS is the first level of this organization chart of the work, called a WBS. It represents the final product or service outcome of the project, performing to specification and accepted by the sponsor, client, and/or user. In our case it is the building itself. The building at the top of the WBS implies a finished product accepted by the user or customer.

Second level: summary tasks

The second level across the organization chart of the deliverable includes the five or six basic "chunks" of high-level work that serve as the basic components of the project, the summary tasks that are integrated at the end of the project to complete the job. For our building project, these chunks of work might include the architectural drawing, building supplies, ventilation systems, water, and electrical systems. (For a software project, these chunks might include hardware platform, software, interfaces, training program, and financing. For a health management system, they might include the clinic population, health information system, medical personnel, space, and equipment.)

Third level: subtasks

The third level includes a breakdown of the summary tasks outlined above, into two or more subtasks, which would be necessary to complete, to produce the second level summary task. For our building project, under the summary task "architectural drawing," this might include three tasks, get an architect, prepare preliminary blueprint, and check against standard blueprint template.

Fourth level: work package

The fourth level is another level of detail at the real tasking level—the work package. These are the individual tasks assigned to team members. For instance, breaking down the summary task to "get an architect" to the fourth level, we identify nine work packages—build list of candidate architects, develop criteria for selection, screen candidates, interview candidates, conduct reference checks, compile candidate information, distribute candidate information, convene meeting, and conduct process of selection.

It is this last level that is used to create the task list, the actual work assignments that will be necessary to identify and schedule before the work can begin. These are the "schedulable" tasks.

The resultant WBS outline (can be shown as an organization chart) looks as follows:

The building

Architectural drawings
    Get an architect
    Prepare preliminary blueprint
    Check standard blueprint template
        Building supplies
        Ventilation system
        Water system
        Electrical system

Of course, in this case we have filled out only one summary task to the fourth level; all levels are filled out in a real project. The concept is that all project tasks at the lowest level of the WBS "roll up" to produce the deliverable.

Integration issues

The WBS is the first integration challenge after the alignment of the project with the business strategy is assured. The tool for integrating a project WBS is a generic WBS. The generic WBS is a standard business process, which defines the company's core project and product development process and project codes. All WBSs are checked against the generic WBS to assure alignment and workforce competency.

This is the way it works. First, the generic WBS is developed by a cross company team representing all key functions and support systems. A project management office is typically in charge of the effort, but the main thrust is to develop a "standardized" WBS and a task list on each product deliverable the company produces. Key coordination steps across the company are built into the generic WBS, thus ensuring all perspectives are reflected.

An example of a generic WBS and how it works to integrate is as follows:

Technical building design and support systems

Architectural drawings
  Get an architect
    Build list of candidate architects
    Check with building system department for past architect performance records
    Develop criteria for selection
    Get customer input on criteria
    Screen candidates
    Interview candidates, conduct reference checks
    Compile candidate information
    Distribute candidate information
    Convene meeting
    Conduct process of selection
  Prepare preliminary blueprint
  Check standard blueprint template

Plan Tasks for Earned Value

In order to be able to interpret progress reports on tasks in terms of %complete (as a precursor to earned value, schedule and cost variance analysis), tasks are structured so that key milestones align with %complete determinations. For instance, if *conduct process of selection* is a 2-week activity, one-week deliverable could be *meet and discuss*, and the other could be *vote and decide*. Each costs the same in project labor costs. Thus 50% complete would coincide with meet and discuss, 100% complete would indicate that a decision has been made. This is an integrated approach to task structuring that enables meaningful earned value assessment later; without it, progress reports cannot be related to real deliverables.

Task list

The task list includes the fourth level of the building project referenced above. This step defines the "work" for several purposes:

- To serve as the basic definition of the work of each task, consistent with the definition of work in MS Project (work = duration × resource)

- To serve as the basis for the network diagram, each task will be an arrow in the network diagram

- To serve as the basis for identifying risks, the first opportunity to identify high-risk tasks

Tasks are listed and durations for each are estimated as follows by the task manager who will be accountable for that task, along with dependencies (predecessors) and assigned resources.

ID	Task	Duration (total estimated elapsed time) (weeks)	Predecessor (linkage or dependencies)	Resources
A	Build candidate list	6	0	HR Specialist Plans Department
B	Define criteria for selection	3	0	Project Manager and Architectural Drawing Task Manager
C	Screen candidates	50	A	Architectural Drawing Task Manager
D	Interview candidates	30	A, B	Project Manager
E	Reference checks	25	B	HR Specialist
F	Compile information	35	C	HR Specialist
G	Distribute information	3	F	HR Specialist
H	Conduct selection process	3	E, G	Project Manager

Network Diagram

Having identified the basic tasks of this summary task, you now build a network diagram of this summary task, which is later integrated with other summary tasks diagrams to create the whole project network, as follows.

Start with a network template. Always start your network diagramming with a template or model of the typical network, and adjust it to the project you are planning. A typical template looks like this, with three paths and parallel activities, ending in one task.

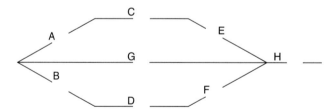

Then tailor your model to your project as follows.

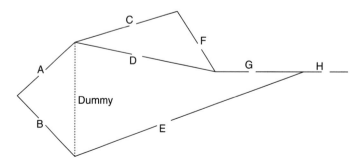

(The Dummy arrow connecting A and B is not a task but a link. This arrow shows that A and B are interdependent with D. D is dependent on both A and B, not just A.)

Project paths: A, C, F, G, H = 6 + 50 + 35 + 3 + 3 = 97 weeks (critical path)

A, D, G, H = 6 + 30 + 3 + 3 = 42 weeks

B, E, H = 3 + 25 + 3 = 31 weeks

Time-based network diagram

Here you simply place the network diagram on a time-based graph. Draw the length of the arrows representing each task to equate with their actual durations as aligned with the bottom calendar of 97 days. Note that this figure shows float, or slack, the dotted lines that represent the flexibility in what time slot you determine to do the noncritical path tasks. Note also that the critical path, A, C, F, G, and H, a continuous arrow with no breaks, represents the critical path.

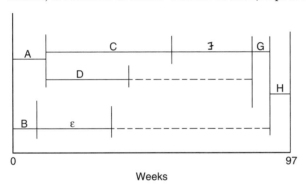

Analysis of Early and Late Starts

In order to determine what slack you have in the project plan to move tasks that are not on the critical path, do an analysis of early and late starts and early and late finishes, and slack, as follows.

ID	Task	Duration (total estimated elapsed time) (weeks)	Early start (week)	Late start	Early finish	Late finish	Slack
A	Build candidate list	6	0	0	6	6	0
B	Define criteria for selection	3	0	66	3	69	66
C	Screen candidates	50	6	6	56	56	0
D	Interview candidates	30	6	66	36	96	60
E	Reference checks	25	3	69	28	94	66
F	Compile information	35	56	56	91	91	0
G	Distribute information	3	91	91	94	94	0
H	Conduct selection process	3	94	94	97	97	0

Project paths: A, C, F, G, H = 6 + 50 + 35 + 3 + 3 = 97 weeks (critical path)

A, D, G, H = 6 + 30 + 3 + 3 = 42 weeks

B, E, H = 3 + 25 + 3 = 31 weeks

Gantt Chart

The final Gantt chart (Microsoft Project) takes the task list information entries and builds a bar chart representing the whole project graphically, based on linkages and durations.

ID	ⓘ	Task name	Duration	Start	Finish	1st Half Qtr 1	Qtr 2	2nd Half Qtr 3	Qtr 4	1st Half Qtr 1	Qtr 2	2nd Half Qtr 3	Qtr 4	1st Half Qtr 1	Qtr 2	2nd Half Qtr 3	Qtr 4	1st Half Qtr 1	Qtr 2	2nd Ha Qtr 3
1		A Build candidate list	6 wks	Mon 7/28/03	Fri 9/5/03															
2		B Define criteria for selection	3 wks	Mon 7/28/03	Fri 8/15/03															
3		C Screen candidates	50 wks	Mon 9/8/03	Fri 8/20/04															
4		D Interview candidates	30 wks	Mon 9/8/03	Fri 4/2/04															
5		E Reference checks	25 wks	Mon 8/18/03	Fri 2/6/04															
6		F Compile information	35 wks	Mon 8/23/04	Fri 4/22/05															
7		G Distribtute information	3 wks	Mon 4/25/05	Fri 5/13/05															
8		H Conduct selection process	3 wks	Mon 5/16/05	Fri 6/3/05															
9																			
10																			
11																			
12																			
13																			
14																			
15																			
16																			
17																			
18																			
19																			
20																			
21																			
22																			
23																			
24			1 day	Mon 7/28/03	Mon 7/28/03															

Resource Integration

Resource integration involves interfacing project planning with workforce and manpower planning. A successful resource integration system characterizes the workforce and makes it possible to know

1. What resources are required to accomplish selected projects

2. What resources are available in-house, when and where

3. What resource outsourcing or contracting is needed, when and where

The integration of project planning with resource planning assures that the company does not take on more than it can handle and can avoid the kind of resource constraints or bottlenecks characterized in the critical chain concept.

Scale and Integration

This is just a reminder that integration occurs at different scales, or has different perspectives. This makes decision making difficult in a complex company facing many trade-offs in its management of multiprojects.

Integration occurs at five levels—global, industry, company, program, and project.

Global. The global scale of integration, which works in the regime of global markets, supply chains, and new product development. Thomas Friedman's book, *The World is Flat: A Brief History of the Twenty First Century*, reminds us that we are passing through the business based, global economy and moving into a new era of individual-based information sharing and open source partnering that has no limits. Project management will be different in this new flat world, and project integration will be increasingly instantaneous and virtual.

Industry. Integrating with industry standards and the state of the art in the markets served.

Company. Company or organizational integration is the successful combination of program and project work with the assortment of supporting organizational "assets," as PMI calls them, the systems that support integration.

Program. Since a program is an integrated set of related projects and/or phases, integration of project work within a program is accomplished by a program manager to assure that the system outcome is consistent with customer requirements.

Project. Project integration is the internal coordination and integration practice of the project team, working with each other in a seamless and open system.

Integrated Monitoring

The concept of an integrated monitoring system illustrates integrated project management. Integrated planning encourages the joint assessment of impacts of various project scenarios on cost, schedule, quality, customer satisfaction, corporate competency, and growth. But regardless of how well project plans are put together and integrated, it is in monitoring that integration produces its most effective results. This is because the "system" as described in the project plan, rarely plays out in actual performance.

Monitoring project performance requires trade-offs, and trade-offs are an application of integration. For instance, trading off cost and time requires the project manager to see *time and cost as a whole—and both in the context of risk.* Rather than simply looking at the "burn rate" of the project and making decisions on cost based on rate of expenditure, an integrated approach requires looking at *both cost and schedule.* As cost variance from an original plan is positive, that is, as the project is able to produce to its milestones at lower than expected costs, the schedule implications of positive cost variance must be viewed at the same time. Thus integration of cost, risk, and time is achieved. Thus, as cost variance becomes more positive, it is quite possible that reductions in cost are at the expense of time.

Integration gets more complicated when three or more variables are being viewed and traded off. For instance, as time and cost variances are more positive, it is possible that potential impacts on product quality are being sacrificed. Substantial variances in cost and time either suggest that the baseline estimates are incorrect or that achievement of a quality deliverable is affected. Cost and time efficiencies could suggest skipping important quality processes, such as testing, and overages suggest that quality standards are coming at unexpectedly high costs and schedule.

Real integration during the project cycle is even more complicated when internal variables are added to the integration mix, such as company profit margins or resource efficiencies. Thus, at the same time when the project manager is keeping tabs on cost, time, and quality, the dynamics of the project may be having unexpected impacts on the business itself. Here we see that picture of the project perhaps doing well but using valuable resources that are needed elsewhere to achieve the company's overall strategic plan. This means that integration now occurs not only at the deliverable, process, and project team level, but also importantly at the business level. Trade-offs at the company level may result in reversing decisions made for fully integrated rational reasons at the project level. For instance, a project doing well in terms of budget and time and likely to satisfy a customer may be negatively impacted or even terminated for "bigger picture" issues, such as marketing, company finances, or acquisition and merger. Thus one expects that top management will integrate at a different level than the program or project manager; a company that generates respect for upper management is more likely to be able to resolve this built-in tension than one that ignores the potential of it happening.

"Reading" the Project as an Integrated Whole

Gareth Morgan made the concept of "reading" an organization popular in *Images of Organization*. His breakthrough analysis of organizations using metaphors provides a useful backdrop for viewing the challenges of program and project integration management. The higher the level of visibility in the organization, the more important it is to be able to *read* the project and the parent organization. Reading in this sense means seeing the full dynamics of many projects and decisions in perspective, judging the collective results and impacts of the "tyranny of small decisions." Good project managers make decisions on the basis of integrating the factors and variables *they see in the larger context, requiring them to think terms of integration.*

Integration mixes art and science, intuition and data. Managers must make decisions with incomplete information; thus integration is both analytical and interpersonal. Analysis provides data on real impacts, but sometimes a full picture of the complete dynamics of a project cannot be provided with data and information. Thus integration usually requires communication with key people who can read the impacts at their accountability level, e.g., how project decisions will affect project finances.

Integration of Cost, Schedule, Risk, and Quality

Project integration in practice in a real work setting often means *juggling* several factors and forces during the project planning and control process. Contrary to academic and professional association rubric that segments project management as if it were pieces of a pie, "real" project planning and management does not occur in distinct phases nor in convenient buckets called planning, risk management, scheduling, scope, cost estimation, and the like. In fact, these functions and activities occur all at once as a project takes shape and is implemented.

Integration then becomes first a mindset, an approach that requires a project manager to monitor several factors at once. This discussion places this "multitasking" environment of integration into perspective. Let us try to integrate risk, schedule, cost, and quality in a typical project setting.

First, planning *is* risk management. Every project plan approaches work structure and tasks in terms of overcoming uncertainty and barriers to project completion. So risk is inherent in a project simply because projects are usually new and different from past work and because there is a level of uncertainty and risk involved in every aspect of the project. The impact of failure because a risk is not "managed" well is felt in project outcomes such as cost, schedule, and quality. Bad risk management is bad cost and schedule control.

Integration involves making sure that all aspects of a project are attended to during the whole project life cycle.

- Work and task planning is structured so that earned value (schedule and cost variance) can be assessed at milestones, built into the task definition and schedule. In other words, the way you build cost and schedule control into planning is to define the work in segments which correspond with %complete determinations.

- Work and task planning is reviewed in terms of potential failures, such as risks, and high-risk tasks are presented in a risk matrix that includes a contingency plan *build right into the project schedule.*

- Quality is integrated into project planning by not only shaping scope and work around customer requirements but also by structuring work around quality. This means that earned value determinations, e.g., %complete reports, assume that when a team member reports a piece of work completed that this means *completed according to user or customer requirements.*

- Projects are seen as decision systems, not just task planning and control. This means that the project manager anticipates decisions that have to be made and the expected value of these decisions downstream. This assures that the schedule is flexible and includes alternative decision paths and scenarios when appropriate. Project plans become more than a single, linear look at the process; they start to reflect alternative directions as key decisions are made.

Project integration is first a personal and professional issue, not a process or technical issue. Project managers must be able to see the "big picture" as they proceed through the project process; they lead and direct the team to keep their eyes on all the major factors that need to be integrated to ensure success. They know the key players who can reflect different perspectives on the project, accountants, technical specialists and engineers, human resource people, contract and purchasing people, and top management. They are "plugged into" customers and users during the process to assure integration of customer learning and change into the project.

The indicator of good project integration is that there are no surprises in the project that have not been addressed in planning and project design. Thus, if project integration is unsuccessful, we see that unanticipated costs appear, schedule delays occur that were not planned, quality problems are seen too late to resolve without costly change, and "outside forces" intervene in project decisions.

Steps in the Integration Process

There are four steps in integration. These steps are part of the normal project life cycle, not separate from them.

1. *Project alignment.*   Projects are aligned and integrated with company strategy and financial goals. Projects that are not aligned with where the company or agency is going are destined to fail. Integration with the "home" competency and culture is key to success. Tools used to assure such integration include a weighted scoring model, portfolio process, and top management interface.
2. *Interface management.*   All stakeholders in the project are involved in project planning through effective interface management.

    Projects are continually interfaced with the following perspectives and functions:

    - Accounting
    - Purchasing
    - Engineering
    - Human resources
    - Marketing
    - IT
    - Manufacturing or production
    - Customer

3. *Project trade-off management.*   Cost, schedule, risk, and quality are built into project work and task definition so that trade-offs can be made between them.
   Work is defined in terms that can be monitored; if the monitoring system is attuned to the way work is planned, then progress reporting can be successful.
4. *Earned value control.*   Project progress is assessed through indicators of schedule, cost, and quality variance. In addition to the traditional focus on schedule and cost variance, a new concept called quality variance, is introduced. Quality variance is distinct assessment of the gap between customer expectations and product or service delivery.

Integration Skills of the Program and Project Manager

We explore here the progression from project manager to program manager in an organization, and the new skills and competencies required to make the transition from leading a single project to integrating a longer-range, multiproject program. While there are many gray areas in the transition from project to program, it is clear that new competencies and skills are called up as the focus shifts to long-term program and the broader scope needed to monitor many projects at once.

Single Project Management

The management of single projects requires several analytical and leadership skills in addition to proficiency in project management software. Project managers must be capable of working with a customer to develop the scope of work for the project and to prepare a WBS that captures the deliverable in an organizational chart or outline. The project manager must be familiar with the technical field and changes in technology. The manager must be able to put a team together, assigning team members to activity and task areas in the WBS, and lead the team through the project life cycle. The manager must have the capacity to use project management software to prepare Gantt charts, assign resources, estimate costs, produce reports, and make presentations on the project.

There is an active debate in the field on the extent to which the project manager must be familiar with the technology of the project and technical aspects of design, development, testing, and product delivery. Some say the manager need only have a cursory sense of the deliverable and the technology involved, relying on team members and subject matter experts for technical assistance. Others say the manager must know enough "not to be snowed" by the customer, team members, or suppliers and subcontractors. They indicate that the manager will have to interpret technical progress reports of team members and be able to communicate with technical counterparts in the customer organization. In any case, it is clear that the project manager must have a good grasp of the deliverable and be comfortable in the field, if not an expert. If the field is changing rapidly, it is especially important for the project manager to grasp the implications of change for the current project.

Single project managers must be wholly focused on the day-to-day dynamics of the project because the project environment is always changing and shifting unexpectedly. The horizon is short in project management. This requires that the project manager manage through the 80-hour rule, that is, the focus in each weekly review is the current status of projects, indicated in earned value analysis, and anticipating the next 80 hours of work. This way the team is reminded of the next two weeks' work, challenges that can be anticipated, and key milestones in that 80-hour period. The single project manager is typically wrapped up in the project at hand.

Project managers must have several key skills: the ability to lead a team and resolve team problems; the ability to communicate and report effectively to a wide variety of customers and stakeholders on technical and project issues; the ability to manage a number of technical assignments all at once; the capacity to deploy project management tools, such as Gantt charts and schedules; a full understanding of the project life cycle; and proficiency in project management software. In addition, the project manager must have judgment skills to make trade-offs between cost, schedule, and quality during the progress of the project and to make difficult decisions quickly to keep a project moving.

Finally, project managers are expected to be advocates of their projects and to make effective arguments for resources and priorities, based on their project needs and their project critical path. They are not necessarily expected to see the big picture or to make decisions on sharing resources with other project managers. They are expected to be narrowly focused on making their project goals, objectives, and deliverables regardless of what else is happening in the company. If they start compromising their focus in the context of the needs of other projects, they do a disservice to their customers and to their project team.

Program (or Multiproject) Management

Program management is a different kettle of fish altogether. Program management is the process of managing and integrating a portfolio of projects, some of which are going on at the same time and some linked in a sequence of product enhancements over a longer time period. In either case, the program manager's span of control is wider and broader than the project manager's responsibility. Program managers can be responsible for a long line of products and product enhancements in one program area over time, say over a 10-year period, transitioning from one project to another based on customer and market feedback. Program managers can also be responsible for many projects and project managers across programs or product areas, thus complicating the management process. Program managers often have responsibility for broad corporate product lines and markets across wide technical boundaries.

Program managers typically hire and supervise other project managers. They are responsible for developing the company's project manager workforce, building and advancing project managers into higher levels of responsibility. They coach project managers. Program managers serve as the interface between projects and broader company strategies and business plans; thus they are called on to communicate broad purpose to individual project managers and to report individual project results to corporate executives in high-level program reviews.

The complex, multiproject environment that program managers face requires different skills in managing information. The program manager cannot get lost in the details of one project or one project schedule or report, but must have an enterprise-wide perspective. Information on many projects must be managed so that the program manager can see the big picture and make the necessary trade-offs between projects, if necessary to resolve resource and priority problems. Program managers must be able to step away from project details, see the broader implications, and make decisions on the basis of corporate-wide considerations and impacts.

Program managers mix in the milieu of vice presidents and CEOs of both their corporations and those of the customer. They tend to integrate at high–levels, where decisions impact broad business performance, business-to-business relationships, workforce planning and management, regulatory issues, financial performance, stockholders, partnerships, and major supplier and contract issues. These factors often bring program managers into play with issues, which their single project managers may not fully understand, especially if they get in the way of achieving narrow project goals. This is the essence of program management; balancing between individual projects with broader performance issues and implications across projects.

There are many working definitions of a program manager. In Europe, the program manager is seen differently. The focus of most UK program managers is likely to be change and change management. This view says that the program manager has the broad perspective to be able to manage several projects aimed at changing the company in fundamental ways, across a wide variety of company activities and divisions.

BuildIt: A Sample Integrated Program Structure

Let's look at a small, 100-employee, construction firm, BuildIt, Inc., that builds high-density housing around transportation hubs and transit stations. The business has built several complexes in the Atlanta area aimed at middle-income families—specializing on small, compact cluster housing.

Organization

The firm does business through projects, with project managers leading teams of architects, engineers, electricians, carpenters, concrete specialists, and other home-building specialists. The organization is a matrix, with functional managers for architecture, engineering, electrical, concrete, and drywall departments, who assign employees to various project teams.

Strategic Statement

BuildIt's overall strategy is to capture the market in the Atlanta area for high density home building and development around transportation hubs, particularly Metropolitan Atlanta Rapid Transit Authority (MARTA) stations. The strategy is to work with the area wide planners and MARTA to get early information on where stations will be built and improved, and to use that information to acquire land and build developments adjacent to stations.

1- to 5-year strategic objectives

Objective 1:   To build home developments around current MARTA stations

Objective 2:   To research plans and programs for future MARTA sites

Objective 3:   To build home developments around the intersections of major interstate highways

Program of Projects

The program of projects for BuildIt is a broad description of a series of short-term projects and other support activities necessary to carry out the strategic intent of the company to increase its market share in transit related community development. The program includes three different but related program areas: program areas 1, 2, and 3

1. *Program Area 1*:   Near-term community development

Program Goal: To build home developments around current MARTA stations. This program of projects includes all the program planning activity that will produce a set of short term projects to design, plan, and build home developments around current MARTA stations.

Marketing program: The marketing program of projects includes all program and project activity focused on identifying opportunities and markets for current MARTA oriented housing development. The marketing program involves gaining a better understanding of not only what potential lies in building high-density homes around stations, but also about the capacity of BuildIt to implement such a program. Marketing will dimension the needs but also the challenges of designing and building complexes in terms of the company's strengths, weaknesses, opportunities, and threats. Included in this program of projects are the following:

- Project 1: Perform market research on potential construction planning and engineering studies for Sandy Springs Station.
- Project 2: Perform market research on potential construction proposal for major downtown development around Underground, including major land redevelopment.
- Project 3: Perform feasibility study on options for high-density homes and development around the Atlanta airport station.

- Project 4: Contract out a survey and produce a comprehensive report to describe resident needs and services around MARTA stations.
- Project 5: Develop a model home design and build near the MARTA station in order to market housing development concepts.
- Project 6: Design an Internet marketing program and campaign to identify needs for high-density residences near MARTA stations.

Program Area 2
Program Area 3

Project plans.   Projects from the above programs are selected through net present value (NPV), analysis of alignment with strategy (weighted scoring model) and risk assessment using the program evaluation and review technique (PERT) analysis in Microsoft Project.

In sum, the integration challenge for the BuildIt company program manager is to coordinate the staging, execution, and delivery of a series of related projects. This requires continual interface with a multitude of stakeholders with potentially conflicting interests, keeping the focus on business profitability and customer satisfaction.

PCAS

A key program management tool is the PCAS. Project Cost Accounting Systems (PCAS) integrate work packages, cost accounts, and project schedules into a unified project control package. They permit cost and scheduling overruns to be identified and causes to be quickly pinpointed among numerous work packages or cost accounts. Two elements common to most of these systems are the use of work packages and cost accounts, as basic data collection units, and the concept of earned value to measure project performance.

4

A Program Management Manual for Integrated Project Management

Writing integration into a program or project management manual requires the writer to see a broader, big picture of the process. Below is a sample manual emphasizing integration and coordination.

Program Management Principles

It is company policy that all programs and projects will be planned and managed in a way consistent with project integration standards. The process will be managed by a program manager who is responsible for integrating and producing products that satisfy customer requirements. Customer requirements are documented in a system requirements specification (SRS). Products are produced through a product development process, which meets customer requirements. It is company policy that in collaboration with department managers, program managers will follow this guide in planning, scheduling, and tracking programs through the product development cycle.

The following principles underlie the program management process.

Meet customer requirements

We are a customer-driven company, striving to meet or exceed customer requirements. The customer's technical requirements are embodied in an SRS prepared by the project team. The customer's schedule and resource requirements are embodied in a baseline program schedule prepared by the program manager and approved by the director of product development. In addition, the program manager maintains close contact with the customer to assure integration at every level required.

Follow integrated, generic WBS—product development process

The program management process will ensure that products are managed through the integrated product development process, tailored to particular product requirements. Program managers use the generic work breakdown structure (WBS) in that policy as the basis for scheduling a program, with exceptions for special programs.

Standard work breakdown structure

The standard WBS for schedules is specified as follows:

- *Program.*   This is the display product line incorporating a basic set of features and functionality.
- *Project Phase.*   This is the particular set of features and functionality for a program, based on particular customer need.
- *Stages.*   These are the steps in the product development process: requirements, detailed design, prototype development, design validation, verification, and manufacturing transition.
- *Functions.*   This is the task level within a stage, e.g., mechanical/optical, electrical, and software design within detailed design.
- *Tasks.*   This is the operating component level where work is achieved through individual or small team activity.

Teamwork

Program managers and functional managers establish integrated teams to carry out the work with the objective of building an environment of high-performance teamwork and collaboration. To the extent possible, staff will be assigned tasks that are consistent with their backgrounds and expressed professional interests. Job descriptions will be written to encourage interface and integration of each individual's work. Program teams will be composed of professionals who are suited to the work they are expected to perform. Team staff members will be oriented and trained as necessary to enable them to perform assigned tasks.

Define and communicate the scope of work and assignments clearly

Product requirements and job assignments will be defined and communicated to the program team clearly through the program schedule and individual assignments. This is to empower staff to understand how their work contributes to the overall customer requirement and to prepare for work assignments with appropriate training and development.

Collaboration across the organization

Collaboration between the program managers, department managers, and the program team is an essential ingredient to the success of program management.

The company encourages continuous, professional communication and information exchange among program team members and department and system managers in a concurrent engineering framework. The objective is to create both individual team member and joint team accountability for particular tasks and a broad support system to ensure individual success.

Work will be quality and schedule driven

Maximum emphasis will be placed on preparing tight program schedules that incorporate all the work necessary to meet requirements on time. Program schedules will be planned and "scrubbed" in a collaborative process which ensures that all necessary work is included and all task durations, interdependencies, and resources are tightly planned and estimated. Schedule baselines will be established and work initiated only after schedules have been tightened through this process.

Ensure timely procurement
of product components

Program managers pay special attention in early program scheduling to ensure the availability of required product components and test equipment. Hardware specifications, parts, test equipment, and supply items will be included in initial program schedules, and appropriate lead times established. Procurement actions will be generated in a timely way to avoid schedule delays attributable to lack of components.

Change will be managed

The company will administer the engineering change notice and configuration management processes to ensure that requirements and product component changes are managed and controlled. A systematic change management process ensures that specifications can be met within schedule and resource constraints.

Program progress will be tracked
and periodically reviewed

Program managers will track program progress, prepare weekly reports, and prepare for weekly program reviews conducted by the director of product development. Department managers and selected team members will participate in tracking and program reviews as and when appropriate.

Integrated Program Management: Roles
and Responsibilities

The organizational framework for integrated program management is a collaborative, team-based organization requiring cooperation between program managers and functional department managers. In that framework, the program manager's responsibility is delivery of the product within quality, schedule, and resource requirements. Department management is responsible for supervising staff and maintaining the technical capacity of their departments to support program management.

Program Management Office

The program management department includes all program managers and the program administrator/planner. The program management office (PMO) is responsible for assuring consistency in the application of this program management guide throughout the product development process. The PMO tracks performance of the overall program management process.

Within the department, program managers will consult regularly with each other on scheduling and resource plans and potential conflicts, and assure consistent approaches to scheduling details, WBS, budgeting, and sharing schedule information. On the initiation of new programs, program managers will consult with each other on potential resource impacts and issues.

Program manager role

The program manager is ultimately responsible for meeting customer requirements and delivering the program within schedule. The program manager provides leadership to the program team, assures that the program meets product specifications, delivers the product on time and within resource constraints, and in general controls the "what and when" of the project. The program manager produces time-phased schedules for each program, tracks progress and anticipates future impact, and assures linkages with related programs and projects.

The program manager requires that design reviews at every phase are conducted and documented to assure integration, and all actions resolved.

The program manager has the primary responsibility for creating a program plan for each program and a program schedule composed of tasks and milestones. The program plan is created with support from the customer, program team members, and department managers. Once the program is underway, the program manager is required to keep the program schedule current, track progress, and incorporate changes as required. The program manager utilizes project management software to produce and update schedules and resource reports, and is expected to be proficient in the use of such software for control and presentation purposes.

The program has the primary responsibility to create and maintain a detailed program schedule that meets all program objectives. The schedule must be consistent with the generic WBS, and include:

- Summary tasks and task structure along with key milestones that correspond to all major program objectives contained in the program plan

- All product development activities and tasks required to execute a given program, including systems design, detailed design, certification, test equipment, reliability, safety, design reviews, manufacturing, procurement, test assets, and the like

- Tasks detailed to the lowest practical level (Activities and tasks should generally be built four levels down)

- Resources assigned to activities and tasks and leveled to reflect a realistic workload

Departmental Manager Roles in the Matrix

Department managers for systems engineering, mechanical/optical design, electrical design, software design, and certification are responsible for building and maintaining the resource and technical capacity of their departments to support the product development process. Here are some key functions of department managers in the program management process:

- Assign programs to staff and support assignments.
- Ensure technical processes and systems are in place to accomplish programs.
- Prepare and maintain department schedules for each program, identifying department level assignments.
- Attend program review meetings and provide advice and support to program managers.

Each program team member is responsible for understanding his or her individual tasks and for general support to overall team performance. Team members are accountable for staying technically proficient and performing their assigned tasks in a timely way, consistent with the schedule. Team members are responsible for communicating with their program managers and functional managers on issues or problems encountered in their team tasks. Team members collaborate with each other and with the program manager, promptly attend program team meetings, and report to their program managers and department managers on schedule and technical issues, respectively.

Role of the Program Administrator/Planner

The role of the program planner in the PMO is to promote consistent best practice in ID program management. The administrator/planner provides administrative support to program managers and departments with scheduling, resource planning, and reporting service, and prepares analysis of resource impacts to identify and resolve conflicts. In addition, the program administrator/planner prepares program management guidelines, provides training, and develops program evaluation metrics, and maintains individual program schedules for the director of product development and/or program managers.

Program planning, scheduling, and resource management

The product development process is primarily schedule driven. Effective and disciplined scheduling and tracking of work and resources is directly related to customer satisfaction since customer expectations always include timely delivery as a key priority.

The scheduling process begins with a program plan that describes the overall program in general terms. It is a reference source for all documents that impact on the program. The program plan includes:

- Program overview
- Program strategy
- Customer identification
- Program objectives
- Measures of program success
- Program scope and requirements (summary)
- Program management, including team roles, schedule, resource plan, and milestones, program review, and risk management
- Program development and review process
- Reference documents

Once a program plan is approved, good scheduling is at the heart of the program management process. Program schedules, created in Microsoft Project, linked to a central resource pool file and posted on the network, constitute the basis for program development, tracking, and review. A good scheduling process provides adequate time to ensure that the work breakdown is comprehensive and responds to the customer requirement and product functionality, that scheduled task durations and predecessors are as accurate as possible, that key linkages are made, and that people and resources, once assigned, understand interdependencies and are available and committed to the program when they are needed.

Before a schedule is drawn up, the work itself must be clearly defined in a WBS. Thus scheduling provides for an SRS (in the requirements stage), which defines the *what and why* of the program or product, e.g., a description of the product and its functionality. The scheduling process helps to flesh out requirements as individual features are programmed into various iterations of the schedule, leading to the baseline.

Once the work scope is understood and signed off by the customer, scheduling defines *when and how* the work is going to be done, key interdependencies, *when* the deliverable will be produced, and *who* will do the work. The scheduling process assigns staff to scheduled work and commits staff to do the work within the time constraints in the schedule. Scheduling is a resource planning tool, providing a high degree of discipline to the assignment of staff since each task is specifically described and time-constrained. Thus scheduling requires that those who actually are going to do the work—*those who are being scheduled*—also be part of the process. Since scheduling "signs up" and mobilizes staff to fit new work into their schedules, which typically includes other program work, it requires that there be a clear picture of staff availability—the current resource picture. New program schedules are phased-in based on the timelines and resource impacts of current work.

The integrity of a schedule is only as good as the description of the work, the processes in place to do the work, a good picture of interdependencies and resource availability, and the commitment of the people who are slated to do the work. This process becomes more complicated when there are several programs or projects operating at the same time and where staff time is always limited by previous commitments driven by earlier or concurrent projects, and by anticipated and unplanned work. In the end, it is the quality of the planning and communication process and the capacity, commitment, and motivation of the individuals actually doing the work that drives a successful schedule.

Project management software makes it easier to accomplish the scheduling process by capturing important planning and scheduling data and making it available to a wide cross section of people, and facilitating presentations and progress tracking. The following process assumes access and proficiency in Microsoft Project as the support software as a network-based planning and communication tool.

Scheduling tailors the product development process to real time and available resources, and flags conflicts and new resource needs. Scheduling provides time-phase and links tasks and milestones, assigns resources to complete the work, and supports the monitoring of performance, resource allocations, budget, and earned value.

An example of an integrated baselined program schedule (Gantt chart) is as follows. Note the inserted column for %complete, added through the insert toolbar, then column. Note that predecessor for ID 88 is 87FF+1, entered through the task information dialogue box, predecessors, and type of linkage. 87FF+1 indicates that the task has a finish-to-finish relationship with ID 87, plus one day.

ID	% Com	ⓘ	Task name	Duration	Start	Finish	Predecessor	1st Half	
								Mar	Apr
82	0%		453210-950 Chassis detailed design	20 days	Tue 4/24/01	Mon 5/21/01	81		
83	**0%**		**RCU optics assemblies**	**93 days**	**Mon 1/15/01**	**Wed 5/23/01**			
84	0%	▦	RCU optics preliminary layout	40 days	Mon 1/15/01	Fri 3/9/01			
85	**0%**		**453110-950XXX bezel assy**	**16 days**	**Tue 3/13/01**	**Tue 4/3/01**			
86	0%		453110-950 Bezel assy design	10 days	Tue 3/13/01	Mon 3/26/01	70		
87	0%	✎	Send bezel assy to tucson / RDE	0 days	Mon 3/26/01	Mon 3/26/01	86		
88	0%		Receive approval from tucson / R	0 days	Mon 4/2/01	Mon 4/2/01	87FF+1		
89	0%		453110-950 Bezel assy release	1 day	Tue 4/3/01	Tue 4/3/01	88		
90	**0%**		**RCU LCD assembly**	**30 days**	**Wed 4/4/01**	**Tue 5/15/01**			
91	0%		453122-950 RCU front filter	3 days	Wed 4/4/01	Fri 4/6/01	85		
92	0%		453115-950 tray design - prelimin	5 days	Mon 4/9/01	Fri 4/13/01	91		
93	0%		453180-950 DIB outline	5 days	Mon 4/16/01	Fri 4/20/01	92		
94	0%		453127-950 bezel flex outline	5 days	Mon 4/16/01	Fri 4/20/01	92		
95	0%		453120-950 assembly drawing	3 days	Mon 4/23/01	Wed 4/25/01	94,93		
96	0%		453129-950 LCD altered item draw	1 day	Thu 4/26/01	Thu 4/26/01	95		
97	0%		453121-950 LCD mount adhesive	3 days	Fri 4/27/01	Tue 5/1/01	96		
98	0%		453128-950 diffuser design	3 days	Wed 5/2/01	Fri 5/4/01	97		
99	0%		453115-950 tray final design	2 days	Mon 5/14/01	Tue 5/15/01	**123**		
100	**0%**		**RCU backlight assembly**	**13 days**	**Mon 5/7/01**	**Wed 5/23/01**			
101	0%		453142-950 lamp design	5 days	Mon 5/7/01	Fri 5/11/01	98		
102	0%		453132-950 front element design	3 days	Mon 5/14/01	Wed 5/16/01	101		
103	0%		453136-950 lamp housing	5 days	Thu 5/17/01	Wed 5/23/01	102		
104	**0%**		**RCU assembly drawings**	**50 days**	**Tue 4/24/01**	**Tue 7/3/01**			
105	0%		453290-950 rear panel assembly draw	2 days	Tue 4/24/01	Wed 4/25/01	78		
106	0%		453270-950 I/O #1 assembly drawing	1 day	Tue 7/3/01	Tue 7/3/01	128		
107	0%		453250-950 LVPS assembly drawing	1 day	Tue 5/29/01	Tue 5/29/01	132		

The resource usage view of that same schedule is as follows. The program manager and the project team can see from this view what resources are assigned to the project and the level of assignment in terms of hours, against a calendar.

ID	ⓘ	Resource name	Initials	Details	2/11	2/18	2/25	3/4	March 3/11	3/18	3/25	April 4/1
11		Bruce Barkley	SA	Work	40h	40h	40h	40h	32h	40h	8h	32h
		RCU Optics Preliminary Lay	SA	Work	40h	40h	40h	40h				
		453110-950 Bezel Assy Des	SA	Work					32h	40h	8h	
		Send Bezel Assy to Tucson	SA	Work							0h	
		Receive Approval from Tucs	SA	Work								0h
		453110-950 Bezel Assy Rel	SA	Work								8h
		453122-950 RCU Front Filte	SA	Work								24h
		453115-950 Tray Design - P	SA	Work								
		453180-950 DIB Outline	SA	Work								
		453127-950 Bezel Flex Outl	SA	Work								
		453120-950 Assembly Draw	SA	Work								
		453129-950 LCD Altered Ite	SA	Work								
		453121-950 LCD Mount Adh	SA	Work								
		453128-950 Diffuser Design	SA	Work								
		453142-950 Lamp Design	SA	Work								
		453132-950 Front Element D	SA	Work								
		453136-950 Lamp Housing	SA	Work								
12		Joe Stern	BS	Work	40h	40h	40h	40h	32h	40h	40h	40h
		453210-950 Chassis Prelimi	BS	Work	40h	40h	40h	40h				
		453270-950 I/O #1 CCA Ou	BS	Work					16h	4h		
		453250-950 LVPS CCA Out	BS	Work					16h	4h		
		453230-950 CPU CCA Outli	BS	Work						16h	4h	
		453280-950 I/O #2 CCA Ou	BS	Work						16h	4h	
		453225-950 Ballast Drawing	BS	Work							32h	8h
		453211-950 Rear Card Guid	BS	Work								16h
		453291-950 Rear Panel Des	BS	Work								16h
		453210-950 Chassis Details	BS	Work								
13	◈		DH	Work								

The Tracking Gantt view of the schedule after a schedule has been updated. Note that the tracking view includes a %complete column with actual completion percentages.

ID	ⓘ	Task name	Duration	Start	Finish	Predecessor	% Complete
1		**Stage 1 systems design and requirements defintio**	**195 days**	**Fri 3/3/00**	**Fri 12/1/00**		**33%**
2		**Program management**	**136 days**	**Fri 3/3/00**	**Mon 9/11/00**		**95%**
3	✓	Detailed program schedule	6 days	Fri 3/3/00	Fri 3/10/00		100%
4	✓	Manpower planning	6 days	Fri 3/3/00	Fri 3/10/00		100%
5	✓	Schedule management review	4 days	Tue 6/13/00	Fri 6/16/00		100%
6	✓	Program plan (internal)	2 days	Mon 6/19/00	Tue 6/20/00		100%
7	▦	Schedule baseline established	1 day	Mon 9/11/00	Mon 9/11/00	6,5	0%
8		**System engineering**	**56 days**	**Mon 8/28/00**	**Tue 11/14/00**		**60%**
24		**Reliability engineering**	**10 days**	**Mon 9/11/00**	**Fri 9/22/00**		**0%**
27		**Safety engineering**	**50 days**	**Mon 9/25/00**	**Fri 12/1/00**		**0%**
32		**Stage 2 detailed design**	**302 days**	**Fri 11/19/99**	**Tue 1/16/01**		**44%**
33		**Electronics design & development**	**71 days**	**Mon 6/19/00**	**Tue 9/26/00**		**72%**
34		**Attitude/revert panel redesign**	**16 days**	**Tue 9/5/00**	**Tue 9/26/00**		**52%**
35	✓	Mechanical specification	2 days	Mon 9/11/00	Tue 9/12/00		100%
36	✓	Procure	2 wks	Wed 9/13/00	Tue 9/26/00	35	100%
37		**Validate**	**11 days**	**Tue 9/5/00**	**Tue 9/19/00**		**0%**
38	▦🖉	Tester design and fabricate	2 wks	Tue 9/5/00	Mon 9/18/00		0%
39		Evaluate panel	1 day	Tue 9/19/00	Tue 9/19/00	38	0%
40		**RDR-1E/F**	**63 days**	**Mon 6/19/00**	**Thu 9/14/00**		**87%**
41	✓	Electrical design changes	1 wk	Mon 6/19/00	Fri 6/23/00		100%
42	✓	Incorporate lightning/EMI Mods	5 days	Mon 6/26/00	Fri 6/30/00	41	100%
43	✓	Procure PWB	3 wks	Wed 7/5/00	Tue 7/25/00	42	100%
44	✓	Build CCA	2 days	Wed 8/23/00	Thu 8/24/00		100%
45	▦🖉	Verification and test	1 day	Mon 9/11/00	Mon 9/11/00	44	0%
46	🖉	Integrate four CCAs in chassis	3 days	Tue 9/12/00	Thu 9/14/00	45	0%
47		**Software requirements documentation**	**235 days**	**Tue 2/1/00**	**Tue 12/26/00**		**27%**

The following is the Tracking Gantt with bar chart, which shows actual progress (black bar) within the planned duration (blue bar).

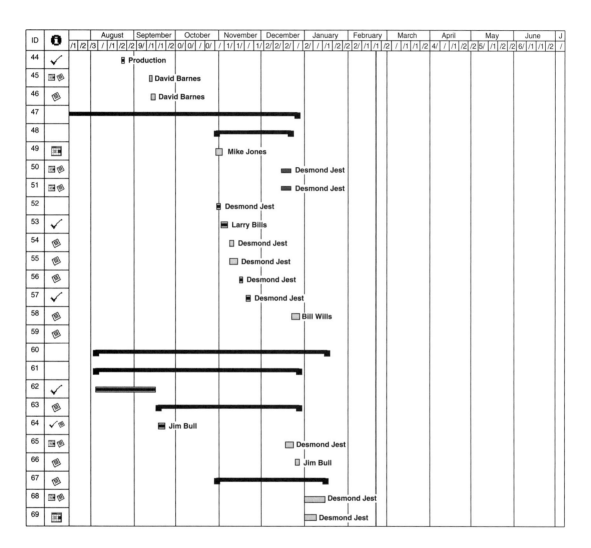

Five-Step Scheduling Process

The program manager generates the scheduling process; the department manager serves as a resource on product functionality and department resources and assures that the technical procedures are in place to complete the work. This process works effectively only with a constant dialogue between program managers, department managers, system engineers, and the team.

The scheduling process for product development involves five steps, culminating in the product deliverable. The general sequence of work is first to define the work from customer requirements; structure the work into an outline or WBS; define an overall, top-level task structure and work flow; then identify tasks, durations, and interdependencies, and then develop department-staffing plans to accomplish the work, estimate the costs, and kick off, monitor, and close out the program.

The following is a table outlining the five functions, a description of the function, and the roles of the program manager, department manager, director of product development, and project team.

The integrated scheduling process

Scheduling function	Description of function	Program manager role	Department manager role	Director of product development role	Project team role
1. Develop top-level work breakdown in Microsoft Project	Develop top-level program structure consistent with product development process	Lead role: working with systems engineer and department management	Participates in developing top-level structure	Reviews, comments, approves	Helps program manager develop structure, as requested
2. Flesh out schedule, establishing task and subtasks, durations, interdependencies, and constraints	Prepare preliminary schedule	Lead role with inputs from department staff: works to find ways to accelerate work in concurrent tasks when feasible and address risks	Helps define how scheduled work can take advantage of prior work, supports concurrency in work schedules	Reviews, comments, approves	Helps department manager find efficient ways to work in parallel
3. Assign resources to schedule, estimating hourly requirements for each task	Establish resource needs to support schedule; assign work from scheduled tasks to staff; confirm resource availability	Works with departments to identify program team and meet other resource requirements	Lead role, department managers are responsible for staffing program with competent, adequately trained personnel and providing adequate resources	Reviews, comments	Participates with department manager and program manager in fitting assignments into current and projected workload

(Continued)

Scheduling function	Description of function	Program manager role	Department manager role	Director of product development role	Project team role
4. Establish schedule baseline, confirming program "kick-off"	Save schedule as "baseline" in Microsoft Project software, placing file in central directory on network	Takes lead to kick-off program, handing out hardcopy of baseline schedule at meeting, along with resource usage table which defines resource commitments	Participates in kick-off meeting, supports resource usage plan	Approves baseline before it is saved as such	Reviews, comments
5. Monitor performance against baseline, report on performance, variances, and cost to complete, manage change	Enter actual data on %complete and/or cost data from time-sheet project codes; revises start and finish dates as appropriate	Gets %complete and other performance information from project team members; report weekly to director of product development	Reviews actual and planned, BCWP, and makes recommendations	Reviews actual and planned	Recommends corrective action in case of schedule slippage

Schedule control

Product specification changes that impact schedules are approved by the program manager and departments involved. The program manager initiates two kinds of changes, schedule updates based on tracking information, such as %complete, and more fundamental changes from customer inputs, design change notices, and other more substantial changes in the scope of work. Affected department managers and the appropriate program manager must agree to all schedule changes. After the baseline schedule is saved, the director of product development must approve any slips or changes in scheduled milestones on the critical path.

Baselining the schedule

After a preliminary schedule is prepared and analyzed, cross-program resource conflicts resolved, and successful delivery of the product within the schedule determined to be feasible by the program manager, the schedule is baselined. Establishing the baseline schedule is a significant action in the ID program management process, signifying the official kickoff of the work and indicating a strong commitment to the schedule and resource plan. The baseline is the point of departure for monitoring and tracking process. When a project is baselined, the project schedule is complete. Here are some rules of thumb for baselining:

1. The purpose is to get to a baseline schedule that captures all the work to be done. This includes key documentation and procurement tasks. The baseline schedule does not change unless the basic scope changes. Once agreement is reached, the program manager confirms the baseline by saving it and making it available on the network *as the baseline*. There is no uncertainty where the baseline is and how to access it.

2. The baseline schedule is the agreed-upon, scrubbed schedule for the program, linked to the resource pool. The baseline shows all interdependencies, linkages, and resource requirements, includes all tasks necessary to get the work done, and shows impacts on parallel programs and resources. All procurements and test equipment are covered in the schedule.

3. The baseline schedule is resource-leveled—the schedule can be implemented with current, available resources. Assigned staff members are aware of the commitments and have "signed-on" to complete their tasks to meet the schedule milestones.

4. Getting to the schedule baseline involves collaboration between the program manager and all departments and staff involved in planning and implementing the schedule. A baseline meeting is held to arrive at final agreement on schedule and resources committed before the baseline is saved to the network. The program manager facilitates the meeting, and all department managers attend and come prepared to commit their resources to the final, agreed upon baseline schedule.

5. The final review of the schedule at the baseline meeting involves reviewing all stages and tasks, linkages, and resources assigned line by line.

6. The baseline schedule is monitored weekly, with actual %complete data and changes in start and finish dates entered weekly and reported at program review.

Baseline procedures

The program manager uses Microsoft's Planning Wizard (or Tools, Tracking, Save Baseline) to set a baseline schedule. When a baseline is created, a backup copy of the project file is created as a permanent archive of the original schedule for later reference and comparison to actuals.

Sometimes it is necessary to create a baseline schedule before the complete schedule and task structure is determined, simply to serve as a basis for capturing actual progress. This is because some work, which is clearly on the critical path, such as mechanical design or long lead-time procurement, must begin immediately to meet key milestones, sometimes before all the details of a schedule are worked out. To accommodate this, when the final schedule is completed, the baseline can be updated by saving an "interim plan." The interim plan saves particular start and finish date changes that are made after a baseline has been saved. Interim changes can be made for the entire project or for selected tasks.

Managing schedules on the network

The basic objectives of network management of program schedules are to (1) enable the program management department to control schedule updates and schedule versions, and (2) provide department managers and staff with an easy way to review and provide input to schedules and schedule assumptions. Here are the steps involved:

1. All schedules will be housed on the server in individual program manager folders.

2. The central resource pool file will be named "Integrated Resources, project file name" and will be housed in the schedule folder. Archive versions of schedules will be housed in a separate folder.

3. The program management department will control access to schedule files. The director of product development and the program management department (program managers and program administrator/planner) will have "write" access to the schedules. Department managers, systems engineers, and team staff and other users will have "read" access to program schedules.

4. The program management department is responsible for maintaining and updating program schedules on the network. Once the director of product development, the program manager, and department managers agree on a proposed schedule and/or update, the schedule will be linked to the resource file and resource conflicts will be identified and resolved. The program manager will then save the schedule as a baseline schedule. Once baselined, the schedule will be placed in a project manager-administrator directory. The baseline schedule will be the only version of that schedule housed on the network (except for archives) and will serve as the source of "planned versus actual" tracking information.

Integrated Resource Planning and Control

Scheduling is essentially the process of planning for use of personnel and equipment resources. Good program management requires that there be a process to plan for the acquisition of future resources, to allocate current and projected resources to schedules, and to make shifts in resource management as required. The process provides for a central resource pool to identify impacts of project schedules and assure the efficient utilization of the workforce. The resource pool information on the network is shared with management staff and all team members to allow each team member to evaluate the scheduled work assigned and to provide guidance on task definition, durations, start and finish dates, and interdependencies.

While work actually done on a project is tracked automatically by project when %complete data is entered, the program management and finance departments collect actual work done from time sheets to gain a more accurate assessment of actual work. Actual work is tracked from time sheets, which collect hours of work against the project account-numbering scheme. The program manager is responsible for establishing the account numbers for charges to the project and for ensuring that time sheets are kept for all work on the project. The project administrator/planner is responsible for working with finance department to collect data each week and enter it into appropriate schedules.

Integrated Tracking and Program Review

The director of product development will hold weekly program review meetings to discuss broad program issues, detailed technical, resource, and schedule problems, project team performance, and risk mitigation. Program managers are responsible for preparing presentations for these reviews and identifying key agenda items. Department managers and team members attend program review meetings as appropriate.

The program manager tracks the progress of the program on an ongoing basis and updates the schedule on a weekly basis. The program plan is to be updated as changes in plans warrant. Program managers hold periodic reviews with the program team in preparation for reporting and to support task assignments and feedback, either as a single meeting with all functions represented, or as a series of meetings with major functional areas represented at each meeting. Program managers report progress for their portions of the weekly report, due to the director of product development each week.

Schedule Update Procedures

Using Microsoft Project, program managers can track and update actual performance information once a project is underway, including % complete for each task; change in task start date; change in task finish date; task duration; task cost; and total work.

1. *Percent complete on a task.*   At the very minimum, the program manager updates %complete for each task on which work has been done during the past week. These data are gathered from the appropriate project team members based on their assessment of the percentage of work actually done, compared to the baseline work definition. Program managers are responsible for briefing team members on the importance of accurate assessments of %complete and how their estimates are used to update project performance. When %complete is entered, Project changes the actual start date to match the scheduled start date and calculates the actual duration and remaining duration.

2. Add a new task to a baseline or interim plan.

3. Enter actual duration of a task.

4. Enter actual start and finish dates for a task.

5. Enter actual work (e.g., hours) completed on each task (from time sheets.)

6. Reschedule uncompleted work.

Analyzing Variance

The program manager uses tracking data to determine how the actual progress of the scheduled work compares to the original baseline schedule, but more importantly to determine impacts of actual work done on the overall schedule and on critical milestones.

Variances that are tracked include:

1. *Tasks that are starting or finishing late.*   Along with updating the task start and finish dates through the tools/tracking command, the program manager identifies impacts of the change on linked tasks.

2. *Tasks that require more or less work than scheduled.*   Changed durations and/or additional resources can be assigned to tasks that are running late; Project will shift durations and start and finish dates automatically when resource units are changed.

3. *Tasks that are progressing more slowly than planned.*   Tasks on the critical path which are progressing more slowly than planned must be addressed, either through redefining the task to stay within the schedule or adding resources. Tasks off the critical path provide the program manager with some slack time, or "safety buffer" before they go onto the critical path because of delays.

4. *Resources that aren't working hours as scheduled.*   If there are major variances in actual work versus planned work, this can have implications for several projects. Based on actual work hours, program managers reassign resources and link to the resource pool to identify broad impacts and conflicts. Project's resource leveling capability can be used to address resource conflicts as well.

5. *Earned value.*   Earned value is an indicator of cost and schedule variance. It is important to track both whether the actual work is on schedule and whether the actual resources expended on the work is consistent with what it should have cost to get the work done based on the baseline budget. In other words, earned value tracks whether the work accomplished actually cost what it should have cost, given the original budget. Reports on earned value show schedule variance and cost variance.

6. *Corrective action.*   The real issue in variance analysis and earned value is what corrective action the program manager takes to put a program, which is showing substantial schedule variance back on schedule. Program managers are responsible for alerting the team to these variances, reporting them in program review, and coming up with corrective actions. Some corrective actions include:

   a. Making sure there is no scope creep, that is, the work the team is doing that is not on the system requirements specification *b.* Changing task dependencies and linkages

  c. Assigning overtime work

  d. Hiring or assigning additional resources

  e. Decreasing amount of work necessary to do a task

  f. Reassigning resources

  g. Delaying selected tasks

  h. Changing working hours

In support of tracking and program review, the program administrator/planner:

- Serves as a resource for Microsoft Project procedures and training

- At the request of a program manager, tracks progress against the schedule and anticipates future schedule problems

- Flags current and new issues for the week from current schedules

- Distributes assignments in the central resource pool to project team staff and gathers feedback

- Identifies conflicts and facilitates resolution

Program Closeout and Lessons Learned

Each program manager meets with the program team at the end of a program to go over the project, identify uncompleted documentation or other tasks, and identify lessons learned. Lessons learned are captured and reported back to the director of product development and the PMO for follow up.

Earned Value and Other Integrating Functions and Forces

Programs will use earned value to integrate cost, schedule, and quality.

Earned value

Earned value is an integrating concept because it allows review of project progress based on: (1) separate analyses of schedule and cost variance, and (2) a combined analysis of both schedule and cost, based on *work performed.* The reviewer is able to *see the project* from two different perspectives and then from a single earned value standpoint. Earned value is the value that a project has earned, based on work performed; in effect, earned value is the dollar value of work progress, the amount that a customer would pay for the work.

1. *Identifying earned value.*   Earned value is identified by project team members' estimates of work performed, either in terms of %complete or hours worked.

2. *Understanding earned value management systems*

Tools.   Earned value can be documented and calculated by Microsoft Project; tools include %complete reporting formats, calculated schedule and cost variance, and capacity to enter actual costs from accounting records to assure that cost variance is based on real project costs during the Gateway period.

Process.   The process is triggered by project and Gateway reviews. Data on schedule and cost variance are reported and review meetings focus on interpretation of root causes and corrective actions.

Planning.   Work is planned in increments that allow earned value assessment. Tasks are broken down into task milestones that correspond with %complete determinations.

Execution.   Execution is accomplished by program and project managers who must "walk the talk" on earned value by scheduling and holding project and gateway reviews to assess earned value.

Control.   Control of schedule and cost is accomplished by interpretation of earned value and taking corrective action. A key concept in control is *forward corrective* action—the process of looking at where you are in the project (not where you plan to be) and determining remaining work. Control does not point backward to the original plan; it directs attention and action forward to completion and customer satisfaction.

Reporting.   Reporting is conducted through electronic reporting of %complete on key tasks at the lowest level of the WBS where actual costs can be collected. Team members must determine %complete based on the structure of the planned work and must report progress accurately, even when progress is disappointing. This requires the establishment of a collaborative and open project team.

Management data.   Management data are collected and documented in a Microsoft Project or a tailored project management information system, and posted in a company intranet and Web-based customer reporting system.

Scope.   The scope is embodied in the project plan and serves as the basis for controlling work. Scope "creep" is avoided by the establishment of a WBS and baseline schedule bounded by work in the scope.

Content.   The quality of the content of management data is assured by documentation and verification of earned value information through frequent audits.

Frequency.   The timing of major Gateway reviews determine major review frequencies; bi-weekly project reviews are made within the gateway period to assess progress, based on the 80-hour rule (project manager reviews at the earned value level and can plan to look ahead about 80 hours in most projects).

Quality.   The quality of the process is determined by the extent of trust and reliability in the reporting system. If a team member determines that a task is 100% complete, it must mean that the customer would accept the deliverable of this task in a user approval transaction.

Earned value criteria

These are standards that are used in the earned value process.

1. *Performance management.*   Performance management is an approach to managing projects that relies on actual performance of a project against project goals and objectives, and against actual costs incurred.

2. *Task definition.*   Tasks must be defined in a WBS dictionary (see below) and structured in the schedule to align milestones with %complete determinations. *WBS.*   The WBS is a structured outline of work, defined by the company to control project management. A generic WBS describes each task in a key project business process, e.g., new product development process, as a company exercise. The generic WBS controls all project work; if a project takes on a task that is not covered in the generic WBS, the WBS is modified to accommodate the new task.

3. *WBS dictionary.*   The data dictionary is a detailed definition of each task to control the work and provide a basis for each team member to see what is expected in each project task assignment.

4. *WBS indexing.*   Indexing is a project coding system that allows cost capture and reporting earned value data.

5. *Organization.*   The organization of the project team is an important factor in the success of an earned value system. The team member roles are delineated in terms of tasks in the WBS of the project.

6. *Control account.*   Accounts are structured around project tasks and project codes so that each team member can record actual work in terms of hours on each project task. Time sheets are integrated into project management software so that actual costs are calculated in real time and reported in earned value reports.

Control account manager

Control account manager roles and responsibilities.   The control account manger is the accountable manager in charge of tasks and cost accounts at a given level of the project WBS.

Team relationships.   Team members must have collaborative relationships that facilitate honest and accurate representation of work progress.

Work authorization.   Under an earned value system, each task is authorized by a project manager or team task manager.

Establish schedule baseline.   An official schedule is established during the project planning process after all project work is captured in a linked, cost, and resource assigned project.

What.   The "what" question is the issue of what work is to be performed; a documented project schedule and WBS determines the what of the project.

When. The "when" is determined by a calendar-based Gantt chart that places tasks in a calendar, based on durations, start and finish dates, and linkages between tasks.

How. The "how" of the system is determined by the WBS and data dictionary; the definition of the task includes a discussion of how the work is to be accomplished, e.g., tools, equipment, methodology, techniques, and the like.

Why. The "why" of the process is determined by the scope of work and customer requirements; each task is being conducted because it is part of the process of creating value in the project deliverable design to satisfy a customer.

Schedule objectives. Schedule objectives in terms of deliverable due dates are set by the baseline schedule and by customer requirements. If there is a gap between the customer's schedule requirement and the baseline schedule, a final schedule objective must be negotiated.

Top down. The top down WBS is organized top down, beginning with the deliverable at the top and breaking down tasks to the fourth level.

Vertical integration. Vertical integration is the process of aligning the scope of work down into the WBS and project schedule.

Horizontal integration. Horizontal integration is the process of aligning work across the project at a given level of the WBS. Integration of parallel work is important to ensure that work going on under different components is coordinated, during the process of design and development.

Critical path and critical chain. Critical chain is based on integrating time and resources in scheduling work. Critical path reflects task durations only without focusing on resource bottlenecks in noncritical tasks; critical chain establishes a line of control in the project schedule that controls key resources that drive the project outcome.

Budgeting, planning, and resource loading

Budgeting process. Budgeting is a company process that allocates financing to key business plans and priorities.

Cost schedule integration. Cost schedule integration is accomplished through earned value determinations; cost and schedule are monitored separately, but both are used in determining corrective action.

Undistributed budget. This is a reserve account that can be used as a buffer fund to fund unanticipated tasks and delays created by key resource bottlenecks.

Control Account. The control account is the finance accounting system that provides the project coding for cost capture and reporting purposes.

Work package. The work package is the third level of breakdown in a WBS, below task and subtask, and provides for work by a team in a 2- to 3-week period. Below the work package is the level of effort that typically defines an individual's task.

Planning package.   The planning package is the collection of project plan, scope of work, schedule and budget, along with appropriate customer requirement documents.

Rolling wave.   The rolling wave is the contour of the bar chart that provides for a gradual movement down the project WBS for linked tasks, ending up with the deliverable at the bottom farthest out to the right.

EVM measurement techniques.   Measurement of EVM is accomplished by %complete determinations and actual costs captured in a project coding system.

Variance analysis.   Variance analysis focuses on cost variance, or difference between budgeted cost of work performed and actual cost of work performed; and schedule variance is the difference between budgeted cost of work performed and budgeted cost of work scheduled.

Calculating variances.   Calculations are automatic in MS Project.

Reporting of variances.   Variances are typically reported by the project manager or project management office.

Schedule risk management

Risk is an integrating function because it combines so many factors that determine project success, including time, cost, quality, decision options, commercial value, contingency, risk-based scheduling, and planning process.

Define risk process.   The risk process involves the identification, assessment, qualitative and quantitative analysis, and response to risk in projects.

Familiarity with risk tools.   Risk tools include the risk matrix (embodies task, risk, impact, probability, severity, and contingency actions), risk-based scheduling, decision analysis, and probability analysis.

Risk-based scheduling.   In MS Project, for any given project or task, risk-based scheduling takes the project manager's three estimated task duration scenarios based on risk analysis—expected, optimistic, and pessimistic—gives weights to them and then calculates a new task duration based on the estimates and weights.

Schedule risk analysis.   Reviews risk events with schedule impacts in terms of root causes and contingencies.

Definition of low, medium, high risk.   Subjective ranking based on low, not requiring any contingency; medium, requiring a contingency but not the insertion of the contingency into the project schedule; and high, anticipated major impact requiring the integration of contingency actions into the project schedule.

Mitigation techniques.   These are actions to prevent or offset anticipated risk events. Mitigation, or control tasks, require the development of alternative actions.

Integrated schedule fundamentals

Fundamentals of preparing an integrated program schedule.   An integrated program schedule includes all factors in baseline schedules, including risk, contingency, linkages, concurrency, resource availability, cost, quality, and technical performance.

Schedule development.   Schedules are developed in an iterative process involving the structuring of the WBS, the use of MS Project or equivalent for the listing of the task outline to the third or fourth level, the assignment of resources, the estimation of resource costs and entering costs, the linking of tasks, estimation of task durations, and the determination of the start date.

Processes of schedule management.   Schedule management involves reviewing the schedule every two weeks in a project review session, adjusting as necessary with actual data, and a major review at the stage Gateway point.

Supplier data integration.   Supplier information is documented in a supplier database program, and related to components in a configuration management system that documents the supplier of every outsourced component and how it was designed and built, or produced.

Influences of the WBS.   The generic WBS is an enormous aid in controlling project plans and schedules and in clarifying what each task means. Project managers learn to rely on a generic WBS, if it is properly maintained, as the source of all issues on task clarity and outputs.

Data incorporation

Drivers of supplier schedules.   Supplier schedules are integrated into the scheduling process by making sure all supplier tasks are identified and all suppliers maintain their own task schedules in the context of linkages to the project. Suppliers must have scheduling and project control capacity comparable to the buyer.

Supplier management.   Suppliers are managed in a partnership relationship and informed on the owner's quality, time, and cost standards for a given project and for all work.

Critical chain management.   Critical chain management focuses control not only on critical path tasks, but also on all the resources that drive project outcomes as determined by sensitivity analysis.

Schedule networks

Networking basics.   Arrow diagrams (e.g., network diagrams from MS Project) are produced for each project to graphically depict interdependencies.

The critical path method identifies the linkage of tasks, any delay in which will drive the project due date out from its current date.

Program networks.   Program networks depict how multiple projects are scheduled out over time in order to facilitate resource planning.

Product and process teams

What product and process teams do.   Teams work cooperatively to produce components of the final project deliverable, then integrate those components into a final product or service.

Product and process team relationships with each other.   Program and project managers build teams that are capable of moving through the difficult periods of group development, such as forming, storming, and norming, to high levels of performing.

Recognition of key product and process team tasks.   Team and individual tasks are made clear by the project plans, including scope of work, WBS, project schedule, and resource plan.

IPT.   Integrated product teams are teams in which the members are dedicated solely to their project tasks and work in concurrent engineering processes to produce fast cycle products to market.

Programmatic transitions

Transition from the integrated master plan to the integrated master schedule. The integrated master plan is the final baseline plan, including program objectives, scope, work methodology, and budget. The master schedule is prepared and becomes the baseline schedule.

Customer reporting

Requirements.   For any project, customer requirements are captured in a customer requirement document, then translated to a scope of work. All work is then traced periodically back, both to scope and customer requirements.

Processes.   Customers receive monthly or biweekly reports on project progress, variances, and exceptions.

Integrated product teams

Integrated product teams (IPTs) are the organizational arrangement, resulting from integrated product development (IPD) implementation. IPT membership is made up of multifunctional stakeholders, working together with a product-oriented focus. This team is empowered to make critical life cycle decisions for the weapon system. Because the product and system development activities change and evolve over its life, team membership and leadership will likewise evolve. While marketing personnel, acquisition planners, project managers, and design engineers may be the most prominent members early in the life cycle, provisioners and item managers gain a bigger voice during engineering and manufacturing development. Equipment specialists and mechanics may be the lead members during the operations and maintenance phase, with the design engineers returning once again, if a major modification is needed.

Why are they important in integration?

IPTs are what make integrated product development (IPD) work. They are created for the express purpose of delivering a product or managing a process for their customer(s). Implementation of IPD represents a transition from a functional stovepipe focus to a customer product focus. Teamwork within the framework of IPD drives the functional and product disciplines into a mutually reinforcing relationship that helps remove barriers to the IPT success.

When are they used?

IPTs are applied at various levels ranging from the overall structure of an organization to informal groups functioning across existing units. The purpose of an IPT is to bring together all the functions that have a stake in the performance of a product/process and concurrently make integrated decisions affecting that product or process. The teams can be created, formed, and their talents applied at all levels of the organization ranging from the overall structure of the organization to ad hoc teams that address specific problems.

What are the key characteristics?

- A team is established to produce a specific product or service.
- Multidisciplinary—all team members/functions working together toward common goal.
- Members have mutual, as well as individual accountability.
- Integrated, concurrent decision making.
- Empowered to make decisions within specific product or service goal.

Rebuilding New Orleans: A Case in Integrated Program and Project Management

As we have stressed earlier, the concept of integrated project management can be applied to a wide variety of policy, program, and project management decision levels, from top level policy/political strategic and portfolio decisions to low level, individual, and technical tasks to integrate project components. Integration becomes more and more important as the complexity of the program and projects increases, simply because there are more points of contact, more risks associated with lack of coordination, and more stakeholders and customers to satisfy. When integration is applied to a public program of projects, e.g., a community development initiative, the key role of integration is clear.

In view of the general interest in the effort to recover from the hurricane Katrina's impacts in the Gulf Coast, especially in the New Orleans community, we will address the issue of integration in a proposal for coordinated action there, involving all the many stakeholders, customers, and participants in the process.

Let's say that Development Associates, Inc., DAI, a new town development corporation, has planned many community complexes throughout the world. DAI has been selected by the newly created New Orleans Community Development District, to serve as a prime integrator in rebuilding New Orleans. Your company New Vision, Inc, has been selected by DAI to serve as their prime, to design, develop, and erect a redesigned New Orleans, a recovery community in the New Orleans proper area that would resurrect the city to its preKatrina hurricane status, or better. This is to develop an integrated community on a 42,900 acre site made available by the city through the new development district created under special state legislation to manage the process.

The Concept: Leased Land under Public Ownership

The concept of the new community is based on private leasing of community land which will be condemned by eminent domain because of hurricane destruction. In other words, the community will be owned by a public corporation enabled by state legislation, but populated by residents who lease land for private residences. The concept borrows from many communities on the coastline, such as Maryland's eastern shore. Individual residential plots will be purchased by the district at market value, the owners becoming shareholders in the new development district. Those residents will participate in the design and building of new residences, and then lease them back from the district.

This arrangement allows the public district to control the land in the event of a natural disaster such as another Katrina. This kind of control would allow evacuation to occur in a much more orderly fashion because the choice would not be left to individual residences.

The Integration Challenge

Projects and product outcomes are integrated most effectively when the framework for integration is established, e.g., where integration has occurred first at the "top," at the program and policy-making levels. The challenge in returning New Orleans to a viable and safe community involves a complex arrangement of partnerships and interlocking contracts starting at the top, all integrated by a special purpose district established by the state legislation.

Integration must occur at five basic levels:

- Public-private community policy and program integration
- Contractor-community integration
- Subcontractor business-to-business integration
- Multiproject integration
- Project integration

Public-private community policy and program integration

The level of cooperation and integration at the public-private community is a political process. But its essence is *choice*, choice of funding source, choice of priority housing and community development programs, and choice of design and plan. The special district must make the difficult decisions on how to develop a portfolio of projects, how to rank them, and how to finance them in order to bring the private sector back to the New Orleans area. The integration process involves a horizontal sweep across current political jurisdictions and business and community leaders to establish a consensus on direction and purpose for the development.

A design team is established to create ideas and proposals for consideration by the special district leaders. Plans are framed in terms of project plan, schedule, and cost, and all projects are analyzed using cash flow projections, discounted by net present value factors, a weighted scoring model that ranks projects according to the relative importance of several community objectives, and a risk assessment that identifies project risks, impacts, probabilities, severity, and contingency actions.

The development of an integrated portfolio involves ranking projects using the tools described above and then generating a public-hearing process to raise community awareness of proposals and projects. Contractors are chosen through competitive bidding on segments of the community plan and are bonded to avoid misuse of funding or fraud and waste.

Funding for the proposal would come from an integrated financial package providing for 80% federal funding from the Department of Housing and Development, and the Department of Transportation, and 20% state funding from a special state tax assessment. Private funding from charitable organizations and service agencies such as Red Cross will be welcomed.

Control of finances and strict accountability will be maintained by the special inspector general function managed at the state level by the Governor's office.

Contractor community integration

The contractors then enter the community of prospective residents and facilitate public hearings in neighborhoods to share designs and ideas and to solicit feedback from prospective residents. Integration of resident ideas and design team ideas occurs through the development of an iterative series of plans, which eventually become well-developed programs of projects.

Planning and construction begins using baseline schedules and contractor-subcontractor arrangements that serve to coordinate the construction process.

Subcontractor and business-to-business integration

Business leaders are brought into the process in the same way as private residences. The special district purchases businesses and then proposes designs and plans for approval by prospective business owners who will lease the land to reopen their businesses.

Multiproject integration

Multiproject integration will occur through the use of Microsoft Project software, consolidating individual project schedules, and integrating contractor activity to maximize the use of local labor and materials. A prime contractor will serve as liaison between the leadership of the special purpose district and the individual contractors planning and building local single and multiresident housing and business facilities.

Project integration

Project integration will be managed using the PMBOK standards, providing for integrated plans and programs, and using earned value as the indicator of progress. Quality is maintained through building a commitment to the overall purposes of the program. Progress reports in terms of %complete and milestone achievement will be conditioned on honest and straightforward assessment of work status.

Motivation

Motivation of the workforce will not be difficult since many of those who will work for the district will be the residents themselves. The strategy would be to employ local residents in the planning and development process, so that they can build their local values and visions into the work itself.

Contract Goals

Basically, the contract goal throughout the process is getting the best value possible for a reasonable cost. Your company, New Vision, understands that new systems exist today that reduce construction costs while improving construction quality. Additionally, this project will produce the same kind of technological jump, and infuse "smart systems" into the community that will greatly improve not only the housing program itself, but also the environment. The contractor will participate in an incentive award fee process that rewards the successful implementation of this goal. It must be measurable and verifiable.

Secondly, New Visions has reviewed the complexities of this project and determined that with a moderate risk project, the proposed two-year development process is most favorable for a project of this size within the region. However, early completion is desired. Therefore New Visions has established the following incentive award fee for the contractor, in the event of an early completion.

Award fee	Complete in months from contract award
$2,000,000	15
$1,000,000	18
$500,000	21
$0	24

Contract Objectives

Under its contract from the special district, New Visions will provide:

- 1000 new private residences, designed and built in the old French architecture style of old New Orleans
- 1000 new private residences designed and built in a new Afro-American style design to be determined by the residents

- 500 new businesses, each to be designed by individual business owners and blended into the neighborhood fabric
- A comprehensive electronic, Web-based community Internet system
- A new public rental vehicle system for the community, providing for publicly owned hybrid vehicles to be available to all citizens on demand for local trips, funded by the special district and private contributions

Technical Requirements for Community Internet System

Technical requirements for the community Internet system will be set by a special committee of residents who will be commissioned to work with the company to set standards for cable or satellite hookups and internal electrical system requirements.

Security Systems

The community will be developed with a complete network of video and audio surveillance systems built into the infrastructure, and monitored through a central security office, housed within each complex. All necessary steps will be taken to ensure rapid response to all issues and security breaches. The security systems will necessarily include the capability to provide medical attention, and immediate communication capability of the security team.

Structure

The structure of the individual buildings in the community will be constructed to take full advantage of the digital information, electrical, water, and communications capabilities within the complex. It is anticipated that the structure will be a smart structure with built-in sensors to communicate on a variety of levels regarding failures, damage, risk, fire, and air issues.

Fire Suppression Systems

The fire suppression systems within the community complex will provide instant communication if a fire breaks out. Notification will include electrically lighted egress markers, and fire suppression facilities capable of retarding fire and holding an outbreak within a limited location for 1 hour.

Transportation

With the community site location already close to several transportation facilities and arteries, the transportation system will be developed to accommodate pedestrian and fuel efficient, publicly owned vehicles for intracommunity transit. Parking facilities will be developed with access ramps to the Interstate

Highway system. Autonomous operating robotic tram connections will be provided to each community, with a new railroad station facility to tie to current Amtrak services.

Management Approach

The management of the development process will be an integration challenge since all activity will be in a "fish bowl" environment that will be of direct interest not only locally, but also nationally and internationally. The special district will employ a career executive director to coordinate the process, who will report to the special district board of directors (local, state, and federal officials). A partnership arrangement will be negotiated so that all contractors report to the special district executive director.

Project Reporting Requirements

The company, New Vision, is a privately owned and operated enterprise. However, the land use for this project is under the control of the New Orleans Special Community Development District, which holds ownership of the property to be developed. Therefore, all rights and privileges are held by the district administration. You as the contractor will be required to obtain all permits and easements through the district. Reporting requirements on project performance will include cost reporting at the third level of the work breakdown structure (WBS). Performance-reporting requirements include schedule, cost, and technical reporting on a weekly basis, with reports being provided to the district.

Stage Gate Process and Payment Milestones

All projects will be managed using the stage gate process. Projects will enter each phase after a Gate review and explicit authorization from the district management to proceed to the next phase. Gate reviews will consider an integrated set of measures of progress, including earned value, customer satisfaction, and cost effectiveness.

Payment milestones have been established for every quarter, starting 90 days after contract award and geared to Stage Gate reviews. Payment milestones shall be tied to measurable and verifiable work accomplishment. The exit criteria for each phase will be provided to your company during the first performance review. Accomplishments must be substantial and mark a point of project progress, consistent with Sarbanes-Oxley; accountability records and documentation of actual costs will be maintained by an independent audit arm of the U.S. Army Audit Agency.

Affordability Requirements

The determination of affordability of new property for residents has to do with the quality and sophistication of the financing arrangements for the lease of publicly owned land. New leasing arrangements will be designed to allow low income residents to lease their land and residences at low interest loan provided by Freddie Mac. Therefore, the contractor will ensure a best value development that provides a sound internal rate of return and earliest break-even point for the district operation as possible. Income streams to be considered will be for a 25-year period.

The New Vision Program

The New Vision program will include a proposal package with the following elements:

- An executive overview.
- Program master schedule—develop a program schedule that outlines the contracted development.
- Schedule will be developed in MS Project and delivered in hardcopy form.
- The schedule will include the WBS element number, task description, percent complete, start, finish, actual start, actual finish, and predecessor.
- A schedule of Gateway reviews to provide status and earned value information to the district management.
- Schedule detail that clearly provides a concise viewable plan of the project elements required for building and that provides visibility and a network to at least level 4 of the WBS.
- The schedule is required to address minimally each of the elements outlined in the requirements section of this document.

Schedule structure

- The schedule is required to be a product-and-outcome–based schedule of events and activities based on the WBS.
- The schedule will provide sufficient summary tasks as to provide an intelligent and organized flow of the development.

Questions for New Visions in Setting up Its Integrated Project Management Approach

Sound scheduling processes

New Vision will conduct scheduling using a five-step, integrated schedule process as elaborated in Chap 4, WBS, scheduling, resource assignment, program "kick-off" and baselining, and monitoring. Within New Visions, the program manager generates the scheduling process; the department manager serves as a resource on product functionality and department resources and assures that the technical procedures are in place to complete the work. High-Quality scheduling products.

Project integration requires that scheduling becomes a high-level, visible activity taken seriously from the project team upward to the district, stakeholder level. This means that schedules are seen as commitments of people and organizations to perform work as scheduled and within budgets, specified for each task. *Schedules are baselined and managed as the basic ingredient of integration.* In practice, this means that the company manages the critical chain resources and activities that drive the project outcomes, not just the critical path. Schedule information is summarized and packaged in Powerpoint presentations for Gateway reviews and Microsoft Project schedules are used as backup to individual issues of work progress as necessary.

Accurate Performance Assessment

Accurate performance assessment is the cornerstone of an integrated project management system. This means that reports on tasks partially or wholly complete from task managers are accurate estimates from those doing the work. A culture of honesty and integrity in the organization and the district itself creates the standard for accurate reporting, with a premium on "bad news going up."

Actual costs are captured by a time sheet and purchase requisition process that is project based, with project codes linked to a generic WBS-coding system. Thus, actual cost variance is continually calculated based on costs incurred.

Reliable Prediction of Future Performance

The focus of integrated project management for New Visions is that monitoring will be based on a forward oriented approach to remaining work and *not a backward mapping to original plans*. In other words, variances are based on work performed and the focus of corrective action is on the remaining work, using Microsoft Project's capacity to provide remaining work information.

Timely Management Action

Corrective action is generated by risk assessment information and contingency plans prepared in the baselining process. In other words, mitigation actions for most anticipated risks in the project are already available to project managers because those corrective actions have been planned early in the project.

Scheduling terms

There are four basic elements that make up a schedule.

Task. Identification of work that requires the expenditure of resources

Time. Duration required for the expenditure of resources against a piece of work

Resources. A commodity of labor, equipment, or dollars expended to accomplish a task

Constraints.   Relationships between two or more tasks that govern which one is required to support the other's activity

Schedule Categories

Three types of integrated schedules will be used:

1. Gantt type of schedules

    a. *Activity.*   Activity schedules derive from the WBS of the project "decomposed" to at least the fourth level. Tasks are outlined activities in a "roll up" hierarchy to a summary task and each activity is defined in a generic WBS data dictionary that defines the activity and its inputs and outputs.
    b. *Lead time.*   Lead-time scheduling is based on estimating lead times and establishing milestones that anticipate the "triggering" of actions downstream. For instance, if the lead time for beginning activity A is 5 weeks because of necessary supporting material purchase, the linkage of activity A to purchasing as a predecessor establishes the lead time for activity A.
    c. *Milestone.*   A milestone is an intermediate or final point in the schedule where significant deliverables are due or when a phase or stage is to be completed. Milestones are planned for each activity to allow earned value determinations, e.g., 50% complete is aligned with half the work of the activity and a specific deliverable is associated with 50% complete in the baseline schedule. This allows earned value to be based on work progress that is specifically aligned with outputs.
    d. *IMP/IMS.*   The IMP (integrated master plan) includes all key costs, schedule, and quality information to serve as the project plan. The IMP includes project goals and objectives, customer requirements, scope of work, schedule and budget, risk assessment, a description of the approach to the work and deliverables, and the project team.
    e. The IMS (integrated master schedule) is the highest summary level schedule for a project, depicting the overall phasing and all major interfaces, contractual milestones, and key elements. The interfaces are shown as milestone reviews in the project schedule.

2. *Network logic diagrams.*   The network logic diagram is an arrow diagram showing the basic independencies in the project.

    Having identified the basic tasks of this summary task, one builds a network diagram and time based network of this summary task, which is later integrated with other summary task diagrams to create the whole project network, as shown in Fig. 5.1.

3. *Line of balance.*   Line of balance is a method of keeping track on key milestones on the way to satisfy multiple deliverables. The "line" in the line of balance is actually the goal for meeting intermediate milestones, say, *full*

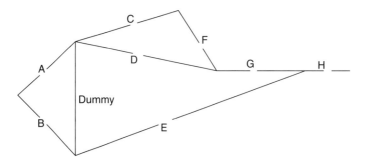

Project paths:

A, C, F, G, H = 6 + 50 + 35 + 3 + 3 = 96 (critical path)
A, D, G, H = 6 + 30 + 3 + 3 = 64
B, E, H = 3 + 25 + 3 = 31

Time-Based Network Diagram

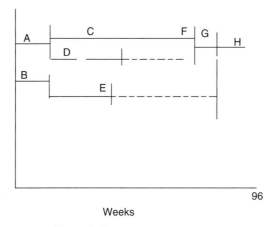

Weeks

Figure 5.1   Network diagram

assembly in a manufacturing process for a high volume of products. The line is the goal and is matched against actual performance. For instance, the manufacturer may be meeting 80% of the line of balance (LOB) goals for full assembly, thus can be anticipated to miss outcome goals as well without some corrective action.

In sum, this New Orleans program would need political, private sector, and community support to succeed. But it is clear that the integrated program management approach would make sense as the structure for rebuilding.

6

Technical Program and Project Integration Tools

An essential tool of project integration is the master schedule. Figure 6.1 shows the integrated tier concept and relationships between master schedule, program element, team production, and work packages at the lowest work breakdown structure (WBS) level.

Top-down integration builds a master schedule to drive the work breakdown to tier 4—the work package level. Vertical integration, or "bottom up" planning, builds the cost estimate and schedule linkages from the lowest level up, rolling up to the master schedule. In practice, this is an iterative process. Bottom up also addresses the validation of the process, aligning lower-level tasks with upper-level activities in the master schedule. Status reports begin at the work package level, along with revisions of work package and level of effort tasks.

The horizontal integration occurs as tasks are outlined against a calendar and linked, as in a Gantt chart. Project integration occurs when baselined schedules and actual work are monitored with horizontal and vertical issues in mind.

Project Management Integration Activities

Once an integrated master schedule (IMS) has been created and approved, there are many management activities that must occur to achieve full integration.

Set the baseline.   The baseline establishes a "benchmark" of the program plan, thereby allowing the initiation of schedule performance measurement, and risk evaluation, to begin. That benchmark is also tied to the customer requirements.

Recurring schedule status.   The status determines the amount of work that has been started completed, or how much work in progress (WIP) has been completed of an ongoing task. Earned value assessment is a part of this process along with the determination of the earned value (EV) or budgeted cost of work performed (BCWP).

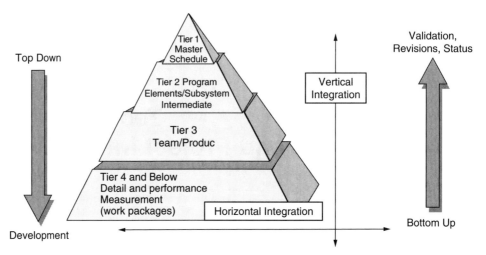

Figure 6.1   The integrated tier concept.

Performance analysis from status.   Performance analysis from status reviews earned value BCWP and SPI and CPI, critical path method, "what if" scenarios, schedule risk assessment, lead time/duration analysis, and capacity planning.

Schedule reporting.   Schedule reporting provides the customer with schedule information that is required to manage the project. It establishes a reporting frequency that meets the customer requirements. Timeliness and accuracy are the keys to a quality schedule report. Reports are generated in various forms depending on the contract.

Develop contingency/recovery plans based on risk matrix.   Contingency plans are based on risk assessment and completion of the risk matrix, which includes the development of a contingency plan for each task, judged to be medium or high risk. Contingencies are alternate plans that provide a means for recovery of a project, impacted by a risk event. The following is an example of a risk matrix.

Risk Matrix Sample

Task	Risk	Probability	Impact	Severity	Contingency plan
Filing US DOT application	Application incomplete or missing required information	25%	Delay projected commencement date	Showstopper	Resubmit application with DOT
Pass DOT fitness test Part 1	Sufficient business and aviation experience	25%	Delay projected commencement date	Showstopper	Ensure that management team is experienced

(Continued)

Risk Matrix Sample

Task	Risk	Probability	Impact	Severity	Contingency plan
Pass DOT fitness test Part 2	Review of operating and financial plans	25%	Delay projected commencement date	Showstopper	Ensure that "seed" and "bridge" funding are in progress or completed. Backup funding programs
Pass DOT fitness test Part 3	Applicant's history of compliance record with DOT rules and regulations	10%	Delay projected commencement date	Very high. Would have to realign management team	Should not pose a problem with intensive background check of management staff
FAA Preapplication Statement of Intent	FAA Preapplication not on file before US DOT reviews application	20%	Delay certification	Medium	Ensure that this application is filed first
Incorrect data on DOT application	Markets served, frequency of flights, aircraft type inconsistent with first year revenues and expenses	30%	Delay certification	Showstopper This will cause DOT to reject application	Ensure that this application is in alignment with financials

DOT—Department of Transportation

A key tool in correcting a schedule for risk is "risk-based scheduling."

This is the process of "scrubbing" the schedule to alter durations to offset delays and reflect risk. Some tasks will be longer and others shorter. The risk-based schedule process is as follows:

The purpose is to use risk assessment and analysis information to calculate a risk-based project schedule in Microsoft Project. The risk-based schedule is calculated from the original project schedule, but uses weighted estimates of three possible task durations (expected, pessimistic, and optimistic) to come up with a new project schedule. The new schedule is calculated for individual tasks and "rolled up" to the whole project.

The risk-based schedule is usually a better schedule estimate than the original one because it reflects the best estimates of what could go wrong (risk) and what could go right (controlling risk).

Procedure

1. Prepare regular project schedule using Microsoft Project and best estimates of task durations and linkages. This project schedule does not reflect any risk assessment.
2. Prepare a risk matrix. Using the WBS and the project schedule, rank all project tasks in terms of risk, designating them "high, medium, or low."

   a. A high-risk ranking shows a high probability (>50%) of the risk actually occurring, and that the risk will have a relatively severe impact on schedule, cost, and/or quality.
   b. A medium-risk ranking implies less probability (<50%) of happening and less schedule impact.
   c. A low-risk ranking implies very low probability (<10%) that the task will occur and low impact.

3. Select the five highest task risks (or more if you have more tasks that present risks that you want to reflect in the risk-based schedule).
4. Calculate the risk-based schedule. The objective now is to calculate a risk-based schedule by taking into account each of the five highest-risk tasks and calculating a risk-based duration for each. Using Microsoft Project, here are the steps:

   d. Pull the PERT Analysis Toolbar up from "View."
   e. Highlight one of the high-risk tasks on the Gantt chart.
   f. Go to the PERT Entry Form and enter duration estimates for that task for three scenarios—expected (use the duration in the original schedule), pessimistic (worst case impact if risk occurs), and optimistic (best case, all risk controlled with no impacts).
   g. Then use the PERT Weight button to set the weights for each scenario (weights reflect the probability that a given risk and impact will happen). Microsoft Project uses a total weight scale of six points; the job is to divide the six points up among three scenarios—expected, pessimistic, and optimistic. Note that the Microsoft Project "default" is four for expected (based on the high probability that the actual duration will fall somewhere between the two extremes) and one each for pessimistic and optimistic. But you may want to change those weights based on the estimate of the relative probability that a given scenario is going to happen.
   h. Once you have entered weights, go to the PERT Calculation button and calculate the risk-based duration for that task, based on inputs.
   i. Now click the PERT Entry Sheet and you will see the newly calculated, risk-based duration for the task compared to the three scenario durations (expected, pessimistic, and optimistic).
   j. Now repeat this procedure for the remaining high-risk tasks.
   k. The resulting "rolled up" schedule is now a risk-based schedule, reflecting a new project duration.

A note on Microsoft Project PERT and risk matrix terminology

Microsoft Project uses the terms *pessimistic, expected, and optimistic.* Expected usually means the duration you originally estimated without concern for risk. Optimistic means the risk and impact are low and you think you might be able to "beat" the expected—you are optimistic about it. Pessimistic means that the risk and impacts are high and you don't think you will be able to "make" the expected duration—you are pessimistic about the expected duration based on risk.

In the risk matrix you use the terms high, medium, and low for risk rankings. In general, high is over 50% probability and high severity; medium is less than 50% probability and moderate severity; and low is less than 10% probability and low impact.

Here is a table comparing the terms from risk matrix and PERT analysis.

Risk ranking in risk matrix		
High (risk severity is high and probability is high that it will happen)	Medium (risk is moderate and impact not so severe)	Low (risk is low and impact low even if it occurs)
Microsoft Project terminology		
Pessimistic (duration reflects concern based on probability that risk will occur and will have major adverse impacts and will slip the schedule)	Expected (original estimate of duration without considering risk, unless there is a reason to change it)	Optimistic (duration reflects low risk and therefore "hope" that the risks can be controlled by contingency plans and the task can be completed quicker than expected)

- Task linkages are also reviewed to generate more concurrency in the work, more parallel tasks and interdependencies.

- Off-load or outsource activities that are slipping in order to assure more control. This activity involves sharing the risk of delayed work with contractors or partners and creating contractual incentives to bring the work back to plan.

Change control tools

Items that cause a change include:

- Modifications to scope statement of work (SOW)

- Customer requests

- Performance variance

Change impacts analyses can be used to anticipate the impacts of a given change on a wide variety of project outcomes, and sensitivity analysis can be used to identify major impacts of single variables. An integrated change impact analysis looks at cost, schedule, quality, team performance, customer requirements, and general business impacts.

Change control documentation must include:

- Formal change documentation
- Description and reason for the change
- Change coordination/authorization
- Risk assessment

Schedule Structures: WBS and IMP

The WBS is a product-oriented structure and describes that product as program deliverables providing vertical integration to that product of the program. Generally speaking, the WBS rolls from the total program down to the parts and provides the structure for cost collection.

The integrated master plan (IMP) on the other hand is a high-level, event-oriented structure that divides the program into major phases and then tracks those phases to completion. Programs are sets of related programs and portfolio projects, and are managed at the upper levels of the organization by a program manager or business officer.

Supplier Data Integration

Contractors often play important roles in project integration. Suppliers and vendors will be used more and more to participate and even lead integrated program teams. Internal managing techniques will need to be revised to keep pace with this new environment while suppliers become a part of the leadership team. Cost, schedule, and technical performance measures (TPM) will be increasingly linked electronically to the prime contractor's performance systems. The prime contractor will perform supplier site visits and the customers will see the entire schedule. This means that contractors will have full visibility to the project plan and schedule so that they can see the "big picture" and integrate activities related to their roles and tasks. As a result, data and information from suppliers will be framed in the whole project.

Program Networks

Networks are inherent in project integration. Networks, or linked program and project schedules, offer opportunities for "what if" analysis, facilitate schedule risk analysis, verify and accentuate horizontal integration, and ensure accurate assessment of schedule performance.

The primary elements of a project network are tasks, durations, and logic/relationships. The basics of a network are task, duration, and logical linkages or relationships.

A task can be described as an activity or event, work package, milestone, and has the following characteristics: Tasks are the building blocks of a network. Each task is a unit of work and has a finite duration with quantifiable progress, requires resources, and has a single point of accountability.

Durations are an estimate of the time required to accomplish a task. Scheduled (and baselined) dates are derived using duration. Good durations are required to generate an accurate estimate for a task. When estimating task duration, use expert judgment (subject matter experts), historical data, examine "intangibles," and the level of risk that may impact the duration of a task.

Schedule linkages, or "logic/relationships," are created when the analyst establishes the order in which a task must occur in order to accomplish the project and task dependencies. Those relationships are established, altered, and driven by the assigned logical occurrence of tasks, lags, predecessor, and successor relationships.

Integration occurs in the linking of tasks in terms of time, cost, and quality. Thus program and project integration is facilitated by networks that create visible images of coordination and interdependencies in a project.

Critical Path Methodology

An accurate network model allows us to focus management attention on the pacing elements of a program. Critical path method (CPM) provides the ability to compare the time needed to accomplish a path of work to the time available to do it. In order to model a program accurately, the elements that comprise the network must be valid.

Project Contract Integration:
The Federal Government Model

Government acquisition often serves as a model for contractor integration in three phases—preacquisition, system development, and production and operations.

Concept and technology development.   This is generally the preacquisition phase, where the customer is seeking technologies related to a future acquisition endeavor. Government customers will often ask potential players to invest in the technology development, with the potential tool being a future contractor.

Systems development and demonstration.   This is a first step acquisition phase, where the customer will establish significant procurement opportunities. However, many government procurements at this point will also ask the contractor for cost share concessions. As the title indicates, this time frame is dedicated to the development and demonstration of a given system.

Production and development. This phase of the model is dedicated to advanced development during prototyping, engineering, manufacturing, and development phases of a development program. Often this will also include low rate introductory production as well.

Operations and support phase. This phase of the cycle is where the product is fielded and the contractor is responsible for the logistics support of the fielded system.

Integration and life cycle

The system development life cycle is critical in understanding the relationships that need to be developed during a process where an integrated program level schedule is being developed. Please provide the understanding of this life cycle to include hardware and software development tracks.

A typical system is developed in "pieces" then integrated, for instance, software and hardware are developed as separate components and then integrated. A series of critical design reviews are conducted during component development. The integration phase includes a configuration audit and system verification reviews, where the system takes shape as a whole and individual engineers and team members put components together to test them, verify that they meet specifications in the scope of work and customer requirements, and that the product configuration, such as components documented, is assured.

Integration of external factors

Very often the most critical bottlenecks to full project integration lie outside the project itself. Dependencies on variables that are not under the control of the project manager are a special integration challenge. For instance, project manager in charge of a technical product development process in the avionics business depends on the availability of an aircraft for testing and integration but cannot control when and where the aircraft is available. The business itself controls the aircraft, from the public relations and marketing department, thus aircraft serves several business purposes. External factors such as these often make project success difficult, even if they are within the parent company's capacity to control.

Functional integration depends on team integration

Experience in product integration indicates that the successful functional integration of product components depends on the successful integration of team members. This means that software, mechanical, and electrical engineers must think of themselves as interdependent and on the same wavelength. Team cohesion then becomes the platform for successful integration. If team members do not feel for each other's challenges and outputs as they work and communicate, they will not design with product integration in mind.

Team relationships in integrating a complex product: avionics example

Systems engineering teams in the avionics business monitor key program milestones through design reviews. Figure 6.2 shows that key integrative activities are associated with key schedule milestones; integration cannot occur until there is agreement on what points in the schedule integration *should occur*.

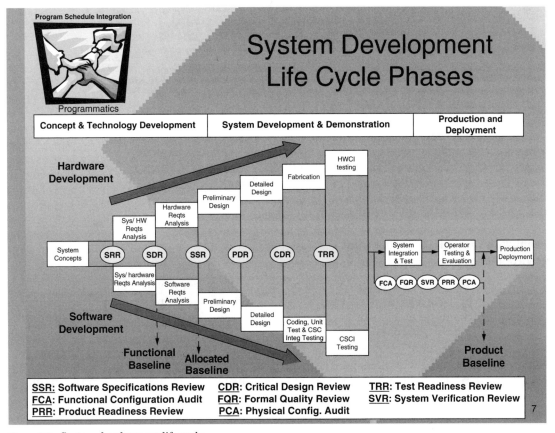

Figure 6.2   System development life cycle.

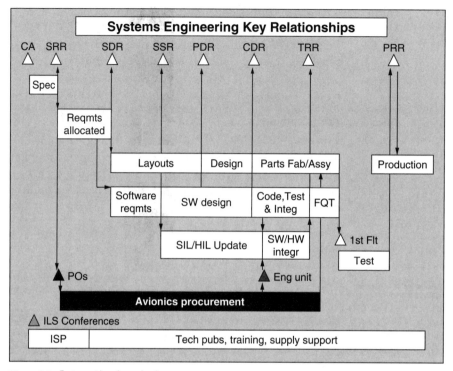

Figure 6.3 Integration in avionics.

Because software, electrical, and hardware integration in an avionics product development process is typically managed by engineers, the process has a
heavy technical flavor. As shown in Figure 6.3, the "forward integration" focus
is on test results and performance aspects of components, data collection and
analysis, and documentation.

Teamwork Difficult in Engineering Environment

What is often lacking in this process in the working world of complex technical
projects such as avionics is the social and functional integration of the engineers
themselves, simply because engineers *are often trained and inclined to deal
with things and performance and not with each other.* This becomes a major challenge to program and project management because the necessary parallel and
concurrent work necessary to ensure effective integration does not happen automatically. Review meetings and team exercises are necessary to tie engineers
together to encourage integrated development.

IMP and IMS Relationships

Transition of the IMP to the IMS requires an integrated scheduling organization, sometimes also serving as a project management office. This function

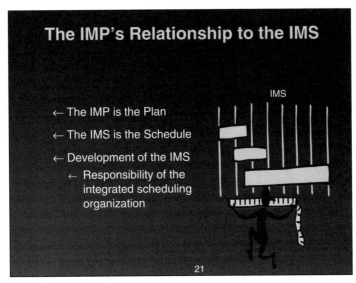

Figure 6.4 Relationship of IMP to IMS.

of integrating a program plan (including objectives, scope of work, and a multiple-project portfolio) with a master schedule of related projects, all integrated across projects and tasks, is a formidable challenge. As Figure 6.4 suggests, vertical integration requires that the scheduling process keep one "eye" on the IMP while developing WBS structures, generic task definitions, linkages resource assignments, and cost estimates.

Integration of the Business Plan, Product Development and Production

The integration of the corporate business plan, product development plans, production plan, master production schedule, material procurement plan, and production control involves the role of a general manager with accountability across the whole process. It is difficult for a project manager to look beyond the project deliverable and it is difficult for the manufacturing control manager to see the project inputs and outputs and their impacts on production scheduling. The linkage of business plan, product development, and manufacturing is made even more challenging when configuration management serves as the basic linkage between the two. In other words, configuration management often works at the interface of designed products and production schedules; if the production department does not know what is being designed and released by project managers who are conducting product development, and therefore do not know what they are going to produce. If they have no access not to bill of materials, inventory issues, or assembly issues, they can not schedule production. To fill that void, typically, configuration management is the review point for the transition of product design to manufacturing.

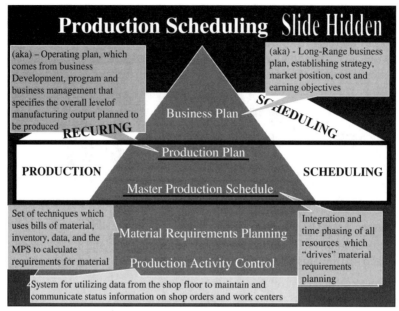

Figure 6.5 Production scheduling.

Material resource planning (MRP) assures that resources necessary to support planned manufacturing are available, when needed (Fig. 6.5). Configuration management ensures that the components of the product to be manufactured are well defined; manufacturing inventory ensures that parts are available when necessary—just-in-time.

Integrating monitoring and customer reporting

In order to keep the customer informed *on the issues of interest to the customer*, a regular, virtual reporting system is provided to him. Customers are typically interested in schedule variances, quality problems, and lessons learned during the development and manufacturing of the product. Therefore, using Microsoft Project Central, project managers can keep customers and stakeholders informed even if they do not have the MS Project software. Indicators reported to the customer include

- 60 to 90 day look ahead report
- Late items report
- Total late item trend metric
- Performance reporting
- Line of balance for recurring programs

Integrated performance analysis and earned value

Earned value allows monitoring the work from two related perspectives—schedule and cost—and since they are often independent, the two views provide an integrated look at progress.

Integrated cost control focuses on aligning actual costs of the work performed with what it should have cost to do the work performed, according to the original cost estimate. Thus, costs are not looked at against the planned budget, but rather against the work actually done to date. This approach integrates cost control with the work performed, e.g., it is OK to be over the original cost estimate by $100,000 if you have done $100,000 worth of work and you are that much ahead of schedule.

Cost variance (CV) = budgeted cost of work performed – actual cost of work performed

$$CV = BCWP - ACWP$$

Schedule variance measures the work performed against what it should have cost to the work performed. Earned value is essentially the value of the work you have done, enabling you to invoice the customer.

Schedule variance (SV) = budgeted cost of work performed – budgeted cost of work scheduled

$$SV = BCWP - BCWS$$

Quality is integrated into the performance-monitoring system by assuring that reports on completed work are based on doing it right the first time. Team members understand in an integrated monitoring system that when they report %complete, work is indeed complete according to the quality standards in the scope of work and technical specifications for the work.

The integrated program schedule

An integrated program schedule is a set of project schedules that are synchronized, making the best use of resources and time in the management of all the projects in the portfolio. That means that available resources are utilized consistently over time across projects (including contract resources) and that unanticipated demands on resources that might be costly and disruptive to the company are minimized.

Integrated program, project, and process teams

As we have indicated earlier, the degree of successful integration of the work and products of a project is often determined by the degree of integration of the team's actual work. People who work in contact with each other on separated components or elements of a product are more likely to be able to integrate their products into a functional whole.

More on Stage Gate Process as an Integrating Function

Integration implies coming together, both in the project planning and implementation process. This means not only to bring the team together with stakeholders, but bringing in the final arbiter, the final "integrator," the customer. How this is done varies with companies and industries, but in most successful companies you are going to find a defined process, with frequent interaction with the customer as a part of the decision to proceed to the following stage or phase of the project.

The process is a system of disciplined stages and control points which provide the basis for an integrated project review and go or no go decisions. Key decision points are established at the end of each stage or phase, with gate or design reviews scheduled to monitor progress and decide whether to proceed. This system gives the program manager a way of integrating cost, schedule, quality, product, and customer data at the end of each phase using earned value. This process allows management to avoid continuing unnecessary or low-performing projects at each stage. Moving to the next stage is approved by some kind of top management, program committee or approval council.

Figure 6.6 shows a typical product development process with five stages and preliminary, critical, and final design reviews at periodic milestones at the phase, system, and task levels.

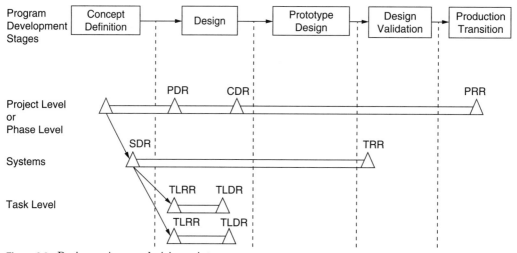

Figure 6.6 Design reviews as decision points.

Gate decisions in this process are based on an integrated look at project progress in terms of earned value, risk management, and customer satisfaction. Earned value reviews schedule and cost variance separately. Schedule variance reviews how well the project is performing against the baseline plan; cost variance reviews how well the *actual cost matches with the work performed.*

Risk enters the picture as risk events are anticipated and contingency plans are prepared for all major risks. The integration of risk contingencies with scheduled work is the key. This involves the development of a risk matrix as follows and then the insertion of contingency tasks into the schedule as baseline activity.

Quality and Project Integration

Quality and integration are inextricably linked. In the case of new product development and other projects that face technical issues, project integration management takes on a special meaning, one focused on integrating product components into quality systems and products in a highly technical environment. In the end, however, technical integration does not occur without team integration, without trusting relationships among different project team members and functional departments.

This chapter contains the following integrating tools and techniques:

- Concurrent engineering

- Quality function deployment

- Robust design

- Statistical process control

- Cost of poor quality

- Miscellaneous other methodologies

System integration focuses on the design of system components, first by work breakdown from the top down, then designing and building components from the bottom up. A configuration management system is typically used to document the product breakdown as it is designed for testing and manufacture.

The system can be as complicated as an F-16 or a car, or as simple as a flight control surface or a car door. The system improvement tools and techniques can be used for any system—a system, subsystem, or a part. In fact, some of the tools, like statistical process control (SPC) and quality function deployment (QFD), have been used successfully for the continuous improvement of entire organizational systems.

The integration tools and techniques described in this chapter have specific application in the product design, process design, and production processes. However, these tools and techniques can be used to improve any system in the organization. They are applicable for improving whole systems, subsystems, or parts.

System Development/Improvement

System integration starts with the customer. The voice of the customer carries through the product design and integration process to the actual production and marketing of the product. Within the product design, process design, and production processes, specific tools are useful for ensuring customer satisfaction. The specific tools are concurrent engineering (CE), robust design (RD), quality functional deployment (QFD), statistical process control (SPC), and cost of poor quality (COPQ).

Concurrent engineering is useful during the product and process planning and design phases for integrating functions and subsystems. Parallel work leads to cross-functional consultation and improves communication on integration issues. Such an approach also reduces the cycle time and cost of product development. Quality functional deployment is beneficial for clarifying the voice of the customer throughout the entire process. Robust design focuses on designing quality by eliminating loss through integration. Statistical process control is a technique for measuring process behavior during project management, testing, integration, and production. Cost of poor quality emphasizes eliminating waste in all the processes.

Concurrent Engineering

Concurrent engineering (CE) is a philosophy and set of guiding principles where product design and process design are developed concurrently, with some product design and process development overlapping. This includes production and support planning. Unlike sequential engineering, concurrent engineering involves parallel work and dynamic integration. Software, electrical, and mechanical engineers are in constant contact on integration issues as they design and build prototypes.

Concurrent engineering requires an integrative management and cultural environment, matrix teams, and an improvement system focusing on customer satisfaction as the final "arbiter" of quality.

The concurrent engineering philosophy emphasizes on customer focus. It advocates an organization-wide, systematic approach using a disciplined methodology. It stresses the never-ending improvements of product, processes, production, and support. It involves the concurrent, simultaneous, or overlapping accomplishment of the phases of the project. For instance, the concept and design phases are accomplished concurrently with a design-build approach. The design and development phases are performed simultaneously. The development and production phases are done with some overlapping activities. In most cases of concurrent engineering, all the phases contain some overlapping activities. Concurrent engineering requires upper management's active leadership and support to be successful. It focuses on robust design that decreases loss. It aims at reducing cost and time, while improving quality and productivity. It uses the latest engineering planning initiatives, including automation. Concurrent engineering forges a new reliance on multi-functional teams using tools and techniques such as quality function deployment, design of experiments, Taguchi approach, and statistical process control.

If concurrent engineering is a systematic approach to the integrated, concurrent design of products and their related processes, including manufacture and support, then project integration management involves the "scrubbing" of project schedules in order to maximize concurrency and integration. This means that project schedules are characterized by overlapping task dependencies. This approach is intended to cause the developers, from the outset, to consider all elements of the product life cycle from conception, through disposal, including quality, cost, schedule, and user requirements.

Concurrent engineering steps

The concurrent engineering steps are as follows:

1. Establish a multifunctional team. Ensure representation from all required disciplines. The team should include representatives from such functions as systems/design engineering, reliability and maintainability engineering, test engineering, manufacturing engineering, production engineering, purchasing, manufacturing test and assembly, logistics engineering, supportability engineering, marketing, finance and accounting.

2. Use a systematic disciplined approach. Select a specific approach using appropriate tools and techniques.

3. Determine customer requirements. Be sure to communicate with customers.

4. Develop product design, process design, and the planning of production and support processes together.

Quality Function Deployment

Quality function deployment (QFD) is a disciplined approach for integrating customer requirements, the voice of the customer, into product development requirements, in effect, integrating customer requirements with scope of work. Too often, scopes of work and functional requirements are not integrated with customer expectations, thus successful completion of functional requirements on time and within budget can be unsatisfactory to the customer. QFD is a tool for making plans visible and then determining the impact of the plans. QFD involves all activities of everyone at all stages from development through production, with a customer focus.

The four phases of QFD are product planning, parts deployment, process planning, and production planning. During phase 1, customer requirements are transformed into design requirements. In phase 2, design requirements are converted into a system (part) or concept design. Phase 3 examines candidate processes and selects one. Phase 4 looks at making capable production processes.

Robust Design

Robust design means designing a product having minimal quality losses. There are several methodologies associated with robust design. The major ones are traditional design of experiments (DOE) and the Taguchi approach. Traditional design of experiments is an experimental tool used to establish both parametric relationships and a product/process model in the early (applied research) stages of the design process. However, traditional design of experiments can be very costly, particularly, when it is desired to examine many parameters and their integrative effects. Traditional DOE examines various causes of performance for their contribution to variation, with a focus on arriving at the most influential causes of variation. Traditional design of experiments may be a useful tool in the preliminary design stage for modeling, parameter determination, research, and establishing a general understanding of product phenomena.

A major approach to robust design is the Taguchi approach. The Taguchi approach focuses on quality optimization. "Quality optimization" is based on Dr. Taguchi's definition of quality. Taguchi (2004), in his book *Introduction to Quality Engineering*, states that any failure to satisfy the customer is a loss. Loss is determined by variation of performance from optimum target values. Loss, therefore, in the form of variability from best target values, is the enemy of quality. The goal is to minimize variation by designing a system (product, process, or part) having the best combination of factors, i.e., centering on the optimum target values with minimal variability. By focusing on the bull's-eye, the product, process, or part is insensitive to those normally uncontrollable "noise" factors that contribute to poor product performance and business failures. The Taguchi approach is not simply "just another form of design of experiments." It is a major part of the successful total quality management (TQM) philosophy.

Robust design phases

Product or process designs have three phases:

Systems (part) or concept design.   This phase arrives at the design architecture (size, shape, materials, number of parts, and the like) by looking at the best available technology. Gate reviews focus on design and performance against customer and functional requirements.

Parameter (or robust) design.   This stage focuses on making the product performance (or process output) insensitive to variation by moving toward the best target values of quality characteristics.

Tolerance design. This stage focuses on setting tight tolerances to reduce variation in performance. Because it is the phase most responsible for adding costs, it is essential to reduce the need for setting tight tolerances by successfully producing robust products and processes in the parameter design phase.

Statistical Process Control

Statistical process control (SPC) is a statistical tool for monitoring and controlling a process. SPC monitors the variation in a process with the aim to produce the product at its best target values.

The major elements of SPC is a process chart consisting of data plots, upper control limit (UCL), lower control limit (LCL), and the mean for the process.

Variation is the result of both common and special/assignable causes. Common causes produce normal variation in an established process. Special/assignable causes are abnormal causes of variation in the process.

Statistical process control steps

There are four steps in SPC:

1. Measure the process. Ensure that data collection is thorough, complete, and accurate.

2. Bring the process under statistical control. Eliminate special/assignable causes.

3. Monitor the process. Keep the process under statistical control.

4. Improve the process toward best target value.

Cost of Poor Quality

Cost of quality is a system, providing managers with cost details often hidden from them. Cost of quality includes both the cost of conformance and the cost of nonconformance to quality requirements. Cost of conformance consists of all the costs associated with maintaining acceptable quality. The cost of nonconformance or the "cost of poor quality" is the total cost incurred as a result of failure to achieve quality. Historically, organizations looked at all costs of quality. Today, many excellent organizations are concentrating strictly on the nonconformance costs. This highlights the waste, or losses, due to deviation from best target values. Once these costs are determined, they can be reduced or eliminated through application of the continuous improvement philosophy.

Typically, the cost of nonconformance includes items such as inspection, warranty, litigation, scrap and rejects, rework, testing, retesting, change orders, errors, lengthy cycle times, inventory, and customer complaints.

Cost of quality can often be traced to lack of early integration of system parts and functions. When the deliverable is planned in parts, with little interaction between project team members, quality usually suffers and the cost of inspection, testing, integration, and rework increases.

Just-in-Time

Just-in-time (JIT) is a method of having the right material just in time to be used in an operation—the integration of inventory and manufacturing. JIT reduces inventory and allows immediate correction of defects. This methodology is used for reducing waste, decreasing costs, and preventing errors.

Total Production Maintenance

Total production maintenance (TPM) is a system for involving the total organization in maintenance activities. TPM involves focusing specifically on equipment maintenance. TPM emphasizes involvement of everyone and everything, continuous improvement, training, optimum life cycle cost, prevention of defects, and quality design. This methodology is effective for improving all production maintenance activities.

Manufacturing Resource Planning

Manufacturing resource planning (MRPII) is an overall system for planning and controlling a manufacturing company's operations. MRPII is used as a management tool to monitor and control manufacturing operations.

Computer-aided design, computer-aided engineering and computer-aided manufacturing

Computer-aided design, computer-aided engineering, and computer-aided manufacturing (CAD/CAE/CAM) are automated systems for assisting in the design, engineering, and manufacturing processes. CAD/CAE/CAM are used to improve systems and processes, enhance product and process design, reduce time, and eliminate losses.

Computer integrated manufacturing

Computer integrated manufacturing (CIM) is the integration of computer-aided design and computer-aided manufacturing (CAD/CAM) for all the design and manufacturing processes. The CIM methods improve on the CAD/CAM weapon system by eliminating redundancy.

Computer systems

Computer systems include a wide range of items such as hardware, software, firmware, robotics, expert systems, and artificial intelligence. Computer systems are a major integrating methodology.

Total integrated logistics

Total integrated logistics (TIL) is the integration of all the logistic elements involved in the inputs of the organization, all the processes within the organization, and the outputs of the organization to ensure total customer supportability at an optimum life cycle cost. This method aims at total customer satisfaction by supporting the operations of the organization and the customer. TIL can be a major differentiator.

**System development/improvement
methodologies within the DoD**

There are many methodologies that are used specifically by the Department of Defense (DoD) that have application in the commercial world. Many of the CDPM tools and techniques described in this book can be originally attributed to the DoD or government agencies. The methodologies mentioned in this section are in addition to the tools and techniques described in other parts of this book. Some examples of the more specific DoD TQM methodologies include computer-aided acquisition and logistics support (CALS), in-plant quality evaluation program (IQUE), reliability and maintainability (R&M 2000), and value engineering (VE). This is not an all-inclusive list. The DoD has many TQM methodologies being used in all its agencies to continuously improve its processes, focusing on customer satisfaction.

**Computer-aided acquisition
and logistics support**

The CALS program is a strategy to institute within DoD an industry and integrated "system of systems" to create, transmit, and use technical information in digital form to design, manufacture, and support weapon systems and equipment, and apply communication and computer technology to acquisition and support of major weapon systems and information systems. CALS focuses on integrating automation between the DoD contractor and the DoD. This is a program to acquire, manage, access, and distribute weapon systems information more efficiently. This includes all acquisition, design, manufacturing, and logistics information. CALS focuses on an increase in reliability, maintainability, and availability through integration of automation systems. In addition, CALS seeks improvement of the productivity, quality, and timeliness of logistics support while again reducing costs.

In-plant quality evaluation

The in-plant quality evaluation (IQUE) program changes the method by which in-plant government people evaluate contractor controls over product quality. The IQUE program changes some of the traditional methods of evaluation with a TQM approach. The IQUE approach focuses on measuring and continuously improving processes with the aim toward quality (customer satisfaction). It concentrates on the "what" versus the "how." The government provides the "what" and the contractor determines the "how." IQUE implements a cooperative team concept between government and contractors.

R&M 2000

The reliability and maintainability (R&M) 2000 approach is geared to increasing combat capability while reducing costs through R&M practices. It stresses improvements in R&M to increase combat availability and reduce logistics support requirements. The R&M 2000 principles build on the TQM approach. R&M 2000 stresses the need for management involvement (leadership), requirements (vision/mission, involvement of everyone and everything focused on customer satisfaction), preservation (continuous improvement of processes and years of commitment and support), design and growth (training and ownership), and motivation (rewards and recognition).

Value engineering

Value engineering (VE) is an organized effort directed at analyzing the function of systems, equipment, facilities, services, and supplies for the purpose of achieving essential functions at the lowest life cycle cost consistent with performance, reliability, maintainability, interchangeability, product quality, and safety. This definition comes from DoD Directive 4245.8. This specific DoD weapon system for TQM again stresses the need to improve quality and productivity of DoD and DoD contractors while reducing cost.

Integrating quality into project management through customer-driven project management

Customer-driven project management's foundation is in the integration of the project management and TQM approaches. Customer-driven management merges the proven methodologies, tools, and techniques of project management and TQM under a single customer-driven management approach. Customer-driven project management expands the boundaries of both TQM and project management by using the customer (customer's voice) to drive an organization to complete a project focusing on total customer satisfaction.

Historically, a project manager's primary purpose was to use the organization's resources to meet the objectives set by the organization's management. Production was normally the most important objective of the organization. This naturally places management's emphasis on completing projects emphasizing internal operations. They focused on the management functions of planning, organizing, staffing, coordinating, directing, and controlling. In most organizations, directing and controlling were the primary functions of management. This traditional management approach stresses strong task-oriented management, especially at the top of the organization, to meet organizational goals. Often, these goals are driven by schedule and cost rather than quality.

This process requires the customer to use the organization's resources to achieve customer satisfaction. The customer must take the initiative to work with project teams in integrating customer requirements. The customer-driven project leader's purpose is to optimize the use of all resources through the use of people in customer-driven teams to meet objectives set by the customer. Total customer satisfaction is the most important objective of an integrating project organization. This places management's emphasis on internal operations focusing on the customer. This requires a greater concentration on all the management functions. In addition, this makes leadership essential to guide the teams. In customer-driven project management, strong people-oriented leadership and effective task-oriented management throughout the organization are both necessary to satisfy the customer.

In traditional organizations, production was usually more important than people. People were viewed as just another resource. They were just "slotted" into job functions as part of the organizing and staffing function of management. In the day-to-day operations of the project, the human resource like all other resources was to be minimized to maximize profit. In fact, as most organizations concentrated on the directing and controlling functions of management, they viewed people as just another commodity to be controlled by structuring, eliminating, and specializing.

In customer-integrated project management, people are the most important resource. People are the primary means to add value to a deliverable that is necessary when striving for total customer satisfaction. People are used on customer-driven teams, where they can best contribute. People not only need to perform the process, they are expected to continuously improve it. People are viewed as a valuable asset adding value to the product. This people resource must be developed by coaching, facilitating, training, and supporting.

These basic changes to traditional and project management, that form the foundation of customer-driven project management, evolved from a wide range of earlier management practices, manufacturing productivity enhancement, quality improvement efforts, and project management methodologies. Customer-driven project management uses the concepts that provide an organization the means to meet the many challenges of today, while ultimately moving the organization toward the future.

History of Project Integration Management and Quality

Integrated project management has its roots in the experience of managing complex technological and system developments during World War II. During WWII, traditional management approaches proved deficient in integrating the many aspects of the development and production of complex weapon systems. After WWII, the need to manage large and complex undertakings increased the interest in project management approaches. This was fostered by successful efforts, such as the Manhattan project. In the early 1950s, project management started to evolve into a more systematic approach to completing programs. Project management became necessary as industries took on specific jobs, usually defense-related or civil engineering-related. These programs were typically for the management of major space, weapons, and construction projects through the stages of design, development, manufacturing, testing, and production. In the 1960s, project management began to be implemented in many organizations besides defense, space, and construction industries. Project management became essential in the computer industry. By the 1970s, project management was recognized as an established management approach for many organizations involved in government, education, and private endeavors. Today, project management has continued to progress into a management approach—essential to producing many deliverables. Further, project management software helps perform many of the project management tasks.

As it evolved from the management of complex projects, project management, usually involved the management of defined, nonroutine activities aimed at distinct time, financial, and performance goals for a system development project. Through the years, project management has been refined through the application of a wide range of industrial and service organizations. The most well-known use of project management is within the DoD industries to develop weapon systems. Weapon systems such as the B-2 aircraft, with its state-of-the-art design, would not be possible without highly sophisticated project management techniques. Modern construction projects could not be built without using project management. Today, computer companies, the movie studios, small businesses, and even the music industry uses project management.

The basic project management techniques have remained fairly standard over the years. However, the greatest impact on project management has been with the use of technology. Technology, especially automation and telecommunications, has allowed project management techniques to expand in breadth and scope.

What is integrated project management?

Integrated project management is the coordinated management of an activity that has a defined start and finish. Because project management is usually viewed with a definite finish, the focus of project management is on completing the project as scheduled. The objective in project management is to complete the project before or on time, at or below cost, and within technical performance specifications.

Project management can be called program management, product management, and construction management to relate to the major areas where it is used. Program management is usually the term used in the DoD. Product management is the term used to manage a product in a commercial industry. Construction management is used in a building industry.

The uniqueness of project management

Project management is unique because of the following:

- It has a defined specification, deliverable, and end point.
- It borrows and integrates resources.

Each of these unique factors presents its challenges to an organization. First, since the focus of project management is on completing the project at its defined end, there is always a focus on the time element. This frequently results in a constant battle between the three basic competing elements of project management: time, cost, and performance. Balancing these three parameters while striving to complete the project requires constant attention to ensure that the priority is not on just getting the deliverable out of the door. This constant consideration for time, cost, and performance trade-offs requires developing positive internal coalitions. It also makes the relationship with the customer critical to success.

Second, the borrowing and integration of resources from functional departments constantly creates the potential for conflict between functional resources and project resources. Collaborative unions between functional managers and project managers are essential to resolve issues relating to the dual responsibilities of project team members.

Time, cost, and performance trade-offs

Traditionally, there are three factors that are key to the success of integrated project management, time, cost, and performance. Each of these factors is fundamental to successful project management because they represent three of the most important project management characteristics as follows:

1. Completion of the project within allocated resources. This is the cost factor of project management

2. Completion of the project within allocated schedule. This is the time factor of project management

3. Completion of the project within explicit criteria, standards, and specifications. This is the performance factor of project management. This is also sometimes called the quality factor

These factors are not considered equal in every project. In some projects, it may be critical to have the product on time. For instance, a weapon system may be required to perform a certain military mission or a computer program may be required to build the rest of the computer system or a new registration system must be ready for students. In other projects, cost might be critical. For example, only a specific amount of funds is allotted to the project. In this case, a fence or limit may be put on the budget of a project. In some cases, quality may be the most important characteristic and resources are essentially unlimited. Traditionally, the project management organization focuses on planning and controlling time and cost, while assuming its functional departments will ensure quality through a focus on specifications.

Integrated matrix organization

Project management requires integration of function and project delivery. Success relies on the technical expertise in each one of the many functions at varying times during the project. This requires a matrix organization to share resources between functional management and project management. This use of a matrix organizational structure for project management presents a major management challenge. To comprehend this challenge, the differences between the traditional organizational structure and the matrix organization must be known. In a traditional organization, the organizational structure is based on functional organizations. For example, on the chart engineering, production, marketing, and support are functional organizations. These functional organizations perform all the activities in the organization within their specific areas. This type of organization depends on each separate function performing within its specialty. There is little emphasis placed on cross-functional coordination or on communication with the customer. Each functional organization is responsible for the technical capabilities of its processes and people.

In a matrix organization, the project managers use resources (people, equipment, and material) from the functional organizations. This requires using the same resources in both functional management and project management. It also means the distribution of resources among various projects. In a matrix organization, responsibility, authority, and resources flow vertically through the functional organization and they flow horizontally from the project manager. Project managers influence the "what," "when," and "how much." These are the essential elements of the project. Functional managers direct the "how." The "hows" are the processes in the organization. In today's organizations, the functional managers are the overall process owners. They decide on how the process will operate.

Project management requires a full appreciation of the complexity of behavior in organizations. It also recognizes that successful work in an organization is not guaranteed, or even facilitated, by a traditional organization structure. Project work concentrates on pulling diverse activities together into short-term projects. It emphasizes communication and coordination of effort among functional departments such as planning, engineering, production, and marketing. Project management stresses functional departments focusing on distinct short-term outputs and products while performing their traditional continuous long-term operations. Project management facilitates successful negotiation of scarce time and resources. This strengthens the organization's ability to share responsibility and accountability throughout the organization. Rather than encouraging isolated work in each departmental setting, the project management approach encourages people to aim their functional expertise toward the organization goal (the project). This ensures that the organization can produce products and services on time, within budget, and performance standards, meeting and satisfying the needs of the customer.

Project management philosophy

The project management philosophy incorporates the following fundamental beliefs:

The project is the primary focus for organizational activity with specifications and project tasks driving the work.

Resources and responsibility can be shared between the functional organization and the project.

The organization's matrix team completes projects on time, within cost, and performance specifications.

Planning and control are the principle techniques for achieving the project objectives with task completed sequentially through critical path networks.

Technology is usually the main method to make improvements.

Coordination of all project activities is the key to effective use of resources.

Teams in a matrix are the organizational structure for project management.

Authority, responsibility, and resources can be spread throughout the functional and project organization.

Numerous product lines and projects can be managed at the same time.

An adequate reservoir of functional specialists can be maintained.

Growth is encouraged through the project management process.

Project management principles

The principles of integrated project management target the successful completion of the project. The emphasis is on the project, production, technology, control, responsibility, cost, schedule, and performance parameters, matrix and team organization, and customer satisfaction.

The project management principles are:

- Provide a project focus.
- Reward production.
- Involve functional organizations.
- Nurture rapid technological change.
- Control and plan all activities.
- Include authority, and resources with responsibility.
- Provide time, cost, and quality objectives.
- Let functional organizations perform processes.
- Encourage teamwork and cooperation.
- Satisfy the customer.

Integrated project management cycles

Project management involves a cycle of processes. These cycles for defining, designing, developing, and delivering a deliverable vary according to organization.

The classical project management approach and DoD cycles provide two examples of most widely used project management cycles. The classic project management cycle has been described by many authors. For instance, David I. Cleland (2002) in *Project Management, Strategic Design, and Implementation* discusses a generic project management life cycle including conceptual, definition, production, operation, and divestment. This approach is also detailed by Harold Kerzner (2003) in *Project Management*. The five phases generally involve the following functions:

1. *Conceptual.*   This is the phase in which objectives and goals are set and specifications determined. It is in this phase that projects are outlined and modeled to assure that the project deliverable is understood. Often the assumption is that the customer—the sponsoring agency or firm has already determined the priority and need for the project deliverable, and that the basic role of the project team is to deliver it within schedule and budget. Traditional project management does not make much room for involvement of the project team with the customer in selecting the project, much less assuring that it results from a quality improvement process performance within the customer's organization and environment.

2. *Definition.*   This is the process of defining the project deliverable in terms of a work breakdown structure (WBS), a budget and schedule, and a critical path network. This is where the WBS provides an organizational and hierarchical look at the project, showing basic interdependencies and interrelationships with the project task structure. A scope of work, budget, and schedule is drawn up in this phase, and the project team is developed around the tasks.

3. *Production.*   It is in this phase that the project deliverable is actually produced or "prototyped," so that testing and measuring can proceed. Production involves lining up all the required resources and integrating them according to their interdependencies as shown in the WBS.

4. *Operations.*   Here the project deliverable is installed, tested, and measured in operation, with the customer or user. Operations assure that the project deliverable, whether a system, product, or a new service, conforms with the original specifications.

5. *Divestment.*   Divestment involves documenting the project and closing it down. Here the team members are typically selected for other project teams and the project books are closed.

Within the DoD, the project management cycle is described as the seven phase acquisition cycle. The seven phase acquisition cycle as described in James V. Jones's Integrated Logistics Support Handbook (2004) includes:

- Preconcept
- Concept
- Demonstration and validation

- Full-scale development
- Production
- Deployment and operations
- Disposal

The preconcept phase begins the acquisition cycle. In this phase the need is identified through an analysis of missions and/or systems. This triggers the identification of operational deficiencies, operational needs, system or equipment development, modifications, and improvements.

The concept phase involves developing alternative approaches to satisfying the need identified during the preconcept phase. During the concept phase, all possible alternatives are analyzed to determine the alternative or alternatives best capable of satisfying the need.

During the demonstration and validation phase, the alternative or alternatives developed during the concept phase are evaluated to determine feasibility to actually accomplish the requirement. The demonstration and validation phase has two purposes: (1) demonstrate that the concept can actually work, and (2) validate that the alternative can meet the need defined earlier.

Once an alternative passes the demonstration and validation phase, full-scale development begins. During full-scale development the deliverable is designed.

The production phase involves the actual development and/or manufacturing of the deliverable.

The deployment and operation phase begins after the item is delivered to the customer. During this phase the customer assumes ownership with the support of the supplier.

Eventually the item may need to be replaced. This is when the disposal phase begins for the old item. The disposal phase involves removing the item from inventory.

Whichever traditional project management cycle is used, the thrust is the same, producing a deliverable. The deliverable is essentially already identified by the sponsor or customer. This project management approach is based on traditional quality control. Its innovation was the matrix team that integrated internal functions to complete a project.

Generating Commitment and Purpose in the Integrated Project Team

We believe the essence of project success in most organizations lies not in teamwork, per se, but in individual performance focused on integration, inspired by the team and by the customer. Like any joint effort, it is the combined effect of individuals with common purpose that produces success; it is too easy to describe this simply as teamwork. It is in fact individual effort and integrity that produces success. Both individual proficiency and integrity as well as teamwork are needed, but in a mix unique to each enterprise and created by the project manager to match the project situation.

Again, keying off some of Tom Peters' ideas, we stress the new dimension that individuals with unique perspectives—not team-dominated, consensus-driven groups—can bring to the field to accept a new "rainbow" team. We deal with "brand you" concepts in a project environment. We hold that individual creativity sparks most successful projects, and most breakthroughs occur not as a result of teams brainstorming, but of individuals simply thinking through implications and impacts in the context of their own experiences.

The chapter describes a brand new chapter on women in project management and elaboration on Tom Peter's rainbow team concept.

People are the key to success in customer-driven project management. People make are the ones who perform and improve the project. Customer-driven project management aims to maximize the potential of the human resources in an organization. This is accomplished by fostering both individual and team contributions to the organization. Customer-driven project management relies on individuals working smart and taking pride in their work accomplishing the project mission. In addition, these individual's contributions are multiplied through customer-driven teams. People involvement tools and techniques include: individual involvement, teamwork, communication especially listening, focus setting, meetings, brainstorming, and presentation.

Integration and Individual Involvement

Individual involvement concerns each person's contributions to the organization. In customer-driven project management, individuals work to continually perform their work and improve the processes in the organization, focusing on total customer satisfaction.

Each individual is unique and valuable. This diversity is a distinct advantage in today's economic environment to the organization that learns to use this to improve their competitive position. People have a variety of attitudes, beliefs, perceptions, behaviors, opinions, and ideas. These are potential sources of creativity. Innovation can be gained from different competencies, abilities, knowledge, and skills of the work force. Each person's culture, background, and personality fosters an individuality that can be used for the good of the organization. Creativity, innovation, and individuality can be the edge needed for growth. Therefore in a customer-driven project management organization, individual differences are valued as an important resource.

Although each person is different, people generally want some of the same basic things. They want to be safe and secure, trusted, and appreciated, need to belong, feel important, have pride in work, be involved and have advancement and personal growth opportunities. The organization that provides a work environment where all of these wants can be achieved by the individual will be rewarded with high individual productivity.

In an integrated project management environment, the goal is the actual empowerment of everyone in the organization. Empowerment means all individuals in the organization have the authority to do what is necessary to perform and improve their work. Empowerment does not just happen. The organization cannot simply announce that the people are empowered and expect it to work. Typically, empowerment comes in stages. First, people must trust the organization. Typically, most organizations have developed many adversarial relationships over the years. This has led to mistrust between management and workers, organizations, and unions, and one department or function and another department or function. These barriers must be removed before an individual will become involved in any extraordinary effort. Restoring trust may take some time depending on the organization. This can only be accomplished by the actions of management working through structure activities. These activities should foster honest and open communication, leading to some specific actions that build the trust.

Once trust is restored, people will start becoming involved in assuming more ownership in their work. At this point, the resources must be available to allow the person to take pride in work. When pride in the work is the norm, people can be completely empowered to provide total customer satisfaction.

With the added emphasis on human resources, people must work smarter to perform and improve their work, with a focus on customer satisfaction. People have always known best how to do things right, and do them better. However, neither the organization nor the people knew how to tap this resource for the benefit of the organization, the individual, and the customer. The organization must be transformed to provide an environment where individuals can maximize their potential. At the same time people must be trained in a systematic process that provides them the capability to influence their work. When this is accomplished, individual involvement can reach its maximum potential.

Individual involvement is fostered by the following:

- Instill pride of workmanship.
- Nurture individual self-esteem.
- Develop an atmosphere of trust and encouragement.
- Involve everyone.
- Visualize a common purpose.
- Improve everything.
- Demand effective and open communications.
- Use rewards and recognition.
- Allow creativity and innovation.
- Lead by example.

Individual involvement steps

1. Establish a people-centered environment.
2. Provide development opportunities.
3. Provide experiences with expected behavior.
4. Reward and recognize appropriate behavior.

Teams

A team is a group of people working together for a common goal. Teams should not be confused with groups. A team shares responsibility, authority, and resources to achieve their collective mission. They feel empowered to do whatever is necessary within their defined boundaries. Action through cooperation is practiced both within the team and when acquiring support. Problem solving and decision making are natural activities. Effective, open, and full communication, especially listening, is prolific. The leader and the members possess a positive "can do" attitude even during difficult times. Team members motivate, respect, and support each other. Team members manage conflict. Team members build self-esteem and motivate other team members. They all contribute their technical competence in their specialty as well as all other skills. They acquire many skills to accomplish the mission and build and maintain teamwork. Effective teams realize diversity, individuality, and creativity are their greatest advantages. Individual and team contributions are rewarded and recognized appropriately. The team takes ownership and pride in their performance. Everyone is totally committed to cost, schedule, and quality standards of excellence with total customer satisfaction being the primary focus of all team activities.

Types of teams

Teams can be either functional or multifunctional. A functional team consists of members from the same discipline or organization. For example, an engineering functional team would be a team in which all the members work in the engineering department. A multifunctional team would have members from engineering, manufacturing, marketing, and other fields as appropriate.

Teamwork

Teamwork is the technique where the individual team members work together to achieve a common goal. This involves cooperative relationships, open communications, group problem-solving and consensus decision-making. Teamwork can only be effective in an environment of honesty, trust, open communications, individual involvement, pride of workmanship, and commitment. Specifically, effective teamwork involves the following:

- Trust
- Effective communication, especially listening
- Positive "can do" attitude
- Motivation to perform and improve
- "We" mentality
- Ownership of work with pride
- Respect and consideration for others
- Remaining focused on total customer satisfaction

Benefits of teamwork

Teamwork provides the responsive workforce required to survive in today's environment. Cooperation toward a common goal is essential for success. Some of the benefits of teamwork include:

- Better decisions and motivation
- Everyone can participate
- Nurtures improved working relationships
- Encourages rewards in work itself
- Freer contribution of information
- Increased communication
- Thrusts an organization toward common focus
- Supports an organization-wide perspective

Principles of teamwork

In order to build and maintain teamwork, the team must obey some principles. The key principles of teamwork involve the following:

- Keep focused on the mission; not on the person
- Encourage open communication and active listening
- Yearn for constructive relationships

In addition to these key principles, there are basic principles that every team must observe to build and maintain teamwork over the long term. The team must be continuously developing and maintaining teamwork. The individual team members and the team must receive appropriate rewards and recognition to maintain interest in teamwork. Further, all members must be involved in team activities to maximize the true potential of the team. Team members must have enough self-esteem to actively contribute. Communication is essential in any team activity. In addition, the strength of the team lies in the individuality of each of the team members. Constructive cooperative relationships are critical, both within and outside the team—between team members and with customers, suppliers, and other teams. All the members, especially the team leader must set the example. Team members can develop the behavior necessary to work as a team through observation. Ideas are the power of the team. All team members must be encouraged to continually contribute toward innovative and creative ideas. Above all, focus on the mission—not the person. It is not personal. Teamwork demands an unrelenting devotion to a common purpose. The basic principles of teamwork can be summarized as follows:

- Pursue team environment.
- Reward and recognize the individual and the team.
- Involve all team members.
- Nurture the self-esteem of all team members.
- Communicate freely and openly.
- Include individuality.
- Pursue constructive relationships.
- Lead by example.
- Encourage all team members' ideas.
- Stay focused on the mission.

Building teamwork

Team building requires continual diagnosing and improving the effectiveness of the team. In order to build the cohesiveness and effectiveness of the team, it is important to pay particular attention to the mission, roles and responsibilities, group dynamics, and interpersonal relationships within the team.

The following are essential to build teamwork:

- Identify the team mission.
- Establish team roles and responsibilities.
- Understand team dynamics.
- Manage conflict.
- Provide motivation.
- Build individual self-esteem.
- Develop the team.

Identify the team mission

The mission is the intended result. It provides the focus for all team activities. It gives the expected outcome(s) of the project. The mission provides an indication of the magnitude of the project. It should state the boundaries of the project to include specific process(es). It is important for the mission to define the authority of the team. Further, the team's resources to accomplish the mission must be identified. Normally, the mission originates from outside the team. It comes in general terms from variety of sources, i.e., management, customer. This general mission must be negotiated and clarified by the team.

The mission must be written in a mission statement. The clarification of the mission should be the first outcome-related activity of the team. The mission statement must be understood, clear and achievable. The team must reach consensus on a mission statement before doing any other team activity. Teamwork requires unrelenting devotion to a common purpose for success. The mission provides the common purpose.

Establish roles and responsibilities

Roles and responsibilities are the specific contributions expected from each team member to accomplish the mission. These contributions can include any formal or informal offerings, each team member brings to the team. Formal contributions include the expected roles and responsibilities of a specific discipline, function, or organization. Informal offering are the contributions a team member can add as a result of personal strengths. Each team must develop their own unique roles and responsibilities based on the requirements of the mission and the capabilities of the team members.

Roles and responsibilities must be defined in a "living document" developed by the team. Each team member must have distinct responsibilities with corresponding accountability. The roles and responsibilities change as the team develops and the project progresses. Developing the initial roles and responsibilities should be the next team activity after agreeing to the mission statement. The roles and responsibilities should include:

- Results—expected outcome(s) from each team member
- Ownership including the amount of control
- Limits of resources—funds, equipment, and people
- Empowerment with amount of authority
- Standards focusing on customer satisfaction

The roles and responsibilities should include the expected outcomes from each team member. These should be stated in terms relating to the contribution to the mission. If possible, it should be stated in terms of metrics. In the initial stage of a project it may not be possible to include specific measurement, but performance measurements must be included as soon as possible. This lets team members know exactly what they need to do.

Another part of roles and responsibilities involves ownership. The roles and responsibilities must state which processes each team member owns. This provides each team member a statement of what they do.

Critical to performance of roles and responsibilities is the amount of resources available. Again, this should be detailed. This provides each team member a statement of what is available to do it.

Empowerment involves having the responsibility, authority and resources to do whatever is required to satisfy the customer and achieve the mission within defined boundaries. The key to empowerment is defined boundaries. Each team member must know the boundaries. These boundaries will change as the team develops and the project progresses. In the beginning of a project, team members usually do not have the capability to be fully empowered. As they are trained and gain new experience, the team can assume more empowerment. Eventually the team can be fully empowered. This is when the maximum potential of the team can be realized through the creativity and innovation of the team members. This provides each team member a statement of what they can do.

Standards are an essential part of roles and responsibilities. These are the accepted norms for all team members focusing on customer satisfaction. Standards must be a clear definition of what is acceptable under all situations. This provides each team member a statement of what they all should do.

Specific team roles and responsibilities

The team consists of a team leader, team members, and sometimes a team facilitator. Each of these team players has a specific role. The team leader guides the team to mission accomplishment. The team members contribute toward achieving the mission. The team facilitator assists the team with focus, teamwork, methodology, tools, and techniques. Detailed roles and responsibilities for team leader, team member, and team facilitator are contained in Chap 6.

The team leader and team members' roles depend on the category of team. The first category of team is the traditional directive organization with a manager. The role of the manager in this team is to get the task accomplished. The role of the team member is to strictly perform the directed job. The second category of team is a participative organization. A leader guides the team to a common goal through a process involving all team members. The team members provide their expertise and cooperation. The third category of team is a collective self-led organization. In this team, ownership is shared by all team members. A team facilitator creates and maintains teamwork. The fourth category is an empowered organization. In an empowered organization, teams have the total responsibility, authority, and resources to perform and improve their process(es). In this category of team organization, a coach and/or resource person advises the teams.

Understand team dynamics

Each must understand that although they are unique, all teams normally go through four distinct stages before they are truly performing as a team. The four stages of team development are orientation, dissatisfaction, resolution, and production. Each team must go through all four stages of team development before they reach synergy. There is no short-cut. The duration and intensity of each stage varies with each team. It is important to maintain the focus and a positive attitude throughout all the stages; the team will achieve its mission.

A general description of each of the stages of team development follows.

Stage 1: Orientation.   During the first stage, the team is becoming acquainted to each other and teamwork. Members are building rapport, honesty, trust, and open communication. They are trying to determine what it takes to fit in. The team members usually have great enthusiasm for the project. However, they do not know how to work as a team to accomplish it. During this stage, the team is deciding: what they need to accomplish and who needs to accomplish it.

Stage 2: Dissatisfaction.   Stage 2 is characterized by being overwhelmed by the information and task. Sometimes power struggles, emotions, and egos become evident. This stage is the most difficult to overcome. Some teams never progress past this stage. If this happens, they should be disbanded. To move forward to the next stage, the team must find some small success as a group. Once the team understands they can perform as a team, the team usually progresses to the next stage.

Stage 3: Resolution.   During Stage 3, the team moves toward the mission. In this stage, customer contact and measurements can help the team members to start assisting each other and focus on the mission. This is the first stage where the team is actually working as a team. Here the team knows how to operate as a team.

Stage 4: Production.   Finally, in Stage 4 the team becomes effective. The team members work together to achieve the mission.

Manage conflict

Conflict can exist whenever two or more people get together. Differences exist in every organization. These differences are an advantage to any organization that has learned to control conflict. Conflict is positive and agreement may be negative.

Differences exist in every organization. Our diversity is one of our major strengths. In teams, we must take advantage of differences to be successful. There are major benefits to be gained by difference. For example, an organization can use the people in its organization of different cultures and backgrounds to research a potential new market or product targeted toward a specific culture or background. Further, the organization can gain new ideas from a diverse workforce. These new ideas can lead to improved operations, decreased cost, and/or reduce time. The following is a list of potential sources of conflict that can be beneficial to an organization:

- Cultures and background
- Opinions
- Needs and expectations
- Facts and perceptions
- Levels, departments, and organizations
- Interests, personalities, and egos
- Competencies, knowledge, and skills
- Targets, missions, goals, and objectives

Conflict can be controlled. Cooperate rather than compete. Orient toward the issue; not the person. Negotiate win/win solutions. Take an organization-wide perspective. Recognize conflict as natural. Observe empathy with other's views. Limit perceived status differences.

Conflict can be positive. Conflict leads to the pursuit of win/win solutions. It allows the team members to observe other team members' point of view. Conflict displays the team working through open communication. It forces the team to take an organization-wide view. By focusing on mission, any conflict takes personalities out of issue. Conflict invites trust and involvement, while viewing the entire issue. It provides the opportunity to examine different sides of an issue. All this leads to effective consensus decision making which establishes and maintains teamwork.

Agreement can be negative. This is commonly called groupthink. Groupthink is the tendency of the group to agree that may have an adverse effect on the effectiveness of the team to achieve the mission. Groupthink comes from many sources. Sometimes, groupthink results from the good intention of maintaining the cohesiveness of the team. In other cases, groupthink stems from fear. The team members may be afraid of losing their job, losing face, offending the leader, management, or other team members. Regardless of the source, groupthink must be identified and controlled. The following are some specific actions to overcome groupthink:

- Appoint a devil's advocate.
- Get open discussion on all issues.
- Recognize impact of status differences.
- Examine all agreements without resistance.
- Evaluate all views/sides of the issue.

Conflict symptoms

The first step in managing conflict is recognizing that conflict exists. Everyone in the team including the team leader, team members, and especially the team facilitator must be constantly alert to the symptoms of conflict and groupthink. Some of the symptoms of conflict and groupthink are as follows:

■ Stopping open communication

■ Yielding to win/lose solutions

■ Making little movement toward solution

■ Pressure to stop challenges

■ Taking sides (we/they)

■ Observing no action on suggestions

■ Members silent

■ Stopping any resistance

Conflict management actions

Conflict can be managed during the day-to-day operations of the team. First, avoid any face losing situation. If honor and pride are at stake, people will defend their position even when they themselves realize they may not have the answer. Second, continuously self-examine attitudes. Sometimes, a person may develop an attitude triggered by some emotional response. This may be detrimental to teamwork. Focus on the mission and maintain a positive attitude throughout all team activities. Third, target win/win solutions. This allows the team to avoid a we/they situation. Fourth, involve everyone in all team activities. People do not agree with their own contributions. If all team members participate they will support the decision. Fifth, observe the limits of arguing. Arguing is useless. It does not lead to positive solutions. Sixth, nurture differences of opinion. Everyone is right in their own mind. There are no right and wrong answers. Differences of opinion can be used to stimulate other ideas. Seventh, support construction relationships. Relationships are the key to all teamwork. Build long-term relationships on a foundation of honesty and trust. This allows open and free communication which is the real key to conflict management.

Provide motivation

Motivation is the behavior of an individual whose energy is selectively directed toward a goal. Performance is the result of having both the ability and motivation to do the task. Motivation influences team members to certain behavior. Motivation depends on satisfying the needs of the individuals. Traditionally, motivation equated to extrinsic rewards. Extrinsic rewards are compensation, promotion, and benefits. This aims at satisfying the basic needs of individuals for housing, food, and clothing. Today, people need to be motivated by a higher order of needs such as sense of belonging, feeling of accomplishment, improved self-esteem, and opportunities for personal growth. Teamwork, especially customer-driven teams, provides intrinsic rewards.

Rewards and recognition for individual and team performance is essential for teamwork. The intrinsic rewards are usually sufficient to start teams. Once a team is established, team members covet higher level intrinsic rewards. An example of a reward that is effective in today's environment at that stage is personal development workshops. During all the stages of team development, recognition is particularly effective to reinforce positive behavior. Praise and celebrations are necessary to maintain teamwork. Some examples of recognition include letters of appreciation, pizza party, coffee and donuts and public announcement. Particularly effective is a pat on the back with a "you did a good job" comment. In the early stages, extrinsic rewards have a short-term effect and they may be actually a negative motivator for long-term teamwork. Extrinsic rewards are important for long-term teamwork, but they must be appropriate for the desired outcomes. Before any rewards are instituted, they must be thoroughly analyzed to ensure fairness to everyone.

Besides rewards and recognition, the team can provide motivation to team members. The following are some specific actions the team can use to motivate team members:

- Make clear that goal is shared.
- Orient, develop, and integrate team members.
- Think and speak.
- Institute internal team rewards and recognition.
- Value individual contributions.
- Avoid frequent changes of team members.
- Take time to develop relationships.
- Encourage sense of belonging.

Build individual self-esteem

An individual's self-esteem affects his/her performance of organizational tasks as well as his/her relationship with others on the team. There are actions each team member can do to maintain and build the self-esteem of team members. They are as follows:

- Establish an environment in which an individual feels his/her self-worth is important to performance.
- Stay focused on mission; do not make it personal.
- Treat each person as you want to be treated.
- Encourage individual contributions.
- Ensure individual reward and recognition.
- Motivate, communicate, involve, and develop.

Teamwork critique

Periodically, the team should perform a periodic self-assessment of their development as a team. Each team should develop their own critique based upon their criteria of a successful team. This critique should be completed individually, the results tabulated, and evaluated and discussed as a team. The teamwork critique should be performed on a regular schedule.

Communication

Communication is the most important tool in integrated project management. Communication involves exchanging information and customer-driven project management demands a free flow of information. The success of customer-driven project management demands communicating with and among all team members. It also requires frequent and effective communication with people and teams outside the team. The customer-driven team needs information to understand the needs and expectations of the customer. They need information from each other to complete and improve the project. They rely on information from support teams. There must be constant communication between customers, process owners, program managers, suppliers, other support teams, and the functional organization. Communication coupled with the sharing of the right information is vital.

Communication of the right information is a complex process including many verbal and nonverbal forms. These include speaking, listening, observing, writing, and reading. Because of this complexity, the information may not be communicated correctly. Even in the simplest communication model with just a sender, messenger, and receiver, there are many obstacles to effective communication. For communication to be effective, the sender must be credible, the message must be clear, and the receiver must interpret it the way the sender intended. For example, if the sender is not trusted by the receiver, the sender may not be able to communicate with the receiver. Regardless of the message, communication will be ineffective.

Communication gets even more complex if we add reality to the model. Rarely do we communicate with just a sender, messenger, and receiver. Normally, there are many distractions. We are influenced by our work environment—political pressure and fear. We are thinking about other things at home and in the workplace. We have different values, cultures, perceptions, and the like. The communication can be improved by the following:

- Clarify the message.
- Observe body language.
- Maintain everyone's self-esteem.
- Make your point short and simple.
- Understand others' points of view.
- Nurture others' feelings.
- Involve yourself in the message.

- Comprehend the message.
- Attend to the message of others.
- Talk judiciously.
- Emphasize listening.

Because of the possibility of ineffective communication, it is critical to ensure through feedback that the right information is communicated. It is always the responsibility of the sender to ensure effective communication. Feedback involves providing information back to the sender to verify the communication. Feedback can indicate agreement, disagreement, or indifference. Feedback like communication can be verbal and/or nonverbal. Some guidelines on effective feedback follow:

- Foster an environment conducive to sharing feedback.
- Encourage feedback as a matter of routine.
- Establish guidelines for providing feedback.
- Discuss all unclear communications, paraphrase and summarize.
- Be direct with feedback.
- Ask questions to get better understanding.
- Consider "real" feelings of team members.
- Keep focused on mission.

Listening

Listening is a technique for receiving and understanding information. Listening skills are critical to effective teamwork. Listening is one of our most important communication needs but it is the least developed skill. Effective listening requires an effort to understand the ideas and feelings, the other person is trying to communicate. An effective listener hears the content and emotion behind the message. Expert listening requires active behavior. It requires an effort. It requires attention to the person and the message. An active listener attends to not only what the person is saying, but also to gestures, posture, and vocal qualities. It means actively communicating that you are listening and trying to understand the other person. It requires discipline, concentration, and practice. Effective listening requires the following:

- Let others convey their message.
- Involve yourself in the message.
- Summarize and paraphrase frequently.
- Talk only to clarify.
- Empathize with others' views.
- Nurture active listening skills.

Let the other person convey his or her message without interrupting or forcing your own views. This is accomplished by letting the other person know you are interested in what they are communicating without displaying an opinion or judgment.

Involve yourself in the message by actively listening to what the other person is communicating. Establish and maintain an eye contact. Keep an alert posture. Look for verbal and nonverbal cues.

Summarize and paraphrase frequently to show an understanding of the message. By listening carefully and then rephrasing in your own words the content and feelings of the other person's message, the exact meaning of the message can be determined.

Ask questions to clarify points you do not understand. Points can be clarified by using open-ended questions. This type of question with an answer other than yes or no provides a more detailed explanation.

Understanding the other person's views is essential to effective listening. Set aside your opinions and judgments and place yourself in the other person's place. Show the other person you understand by requesting more information or by sharing a similar feeling or experience you've had and how you think it helps you understand the other person.

Nurture listening skills to improve communication. Listening skills must be practiced daily.

Benefits of active listening

Active listening is a skill that provides many benefits. These benefits are in the best interest of any person to develop active listening skills. Here is a list of benefits.

- Better understanding of the communication
- Engage in effective communication
- Nurture personal growth
- Earn trust in the organization
- Find improved self-esteem
- Increase competence
- Thrust yourself into influence
- Save time

Focus Setting

Focus setting is a technique to achieve a specific outcome. The focus should be on the output of the process satisfying the customer. The focus is a vision, mission, and goals. The vision is the overall view of the organization for the future. The mission is the intended result. The goal is a specific desired outcome. In order to achieve results, customer-driven teams must focus on their specific purpose within the overall vision of the organization. This purpose must always strive for excellence while satisfying the customer. The purpose of the team is the focus. This focus for the team is the mission. To achieve the mission, the team needs to accomplish goals.

Vision

A vision is the long-range focus for the organization. The vision is usually the organization's leadership's view for the future. Although leadership creates the vision, it must be instituted throughout the organization. To be instituted, it must have meaning and be shared by everyone in the organization. It must be more than a slogan. It must foster some definite course of action. These specific actions must be displayed by the leadership in the organization. To have meaning on where the organization wants to go, the vision must be oriented toward the customer. The vision must communicate both inside and outside the organization a long-term future for the organization. This vision must be constantly communicated to build the loyalty and trust necessary to develop a workforce committed to its achievement. The following are some guidelines for a vision:

- View the future.
- Institute the vision in the organization.
- Set the example through leadership.
- Include where you want the organization to go.
- Orient toward the customer.
- Nurture through constant communication.
- Vision examples.

"GenCorp will be one of the most respected diversified companies in the world." GenCorp
"To have the most effective fighting force." U.S. Department of Defense

Mission

The mission is the intended result. It should be stated in a results-oriented form. Specific details on missions for customer-driven teams is contained in Chap. 6.

Mission examples.   Examples of a mission statement for customer-driven teams are as follows:

- Provide a deliverable, meeting the customer's total satisfaction.
- Continuously improve the deliverables value to the customer.
- Eliminate errors in order processing.

- Decrease cost of manufacturing.
- Improve assembly workmanship.
- Reduce failure rates of circuit boards.

Goal

The goal is the specific desired outcome(s). It should be specific, measurable, attainable, results-oriented, and time bound. Set reasonable goal(s) but do not set sights too low. Set a goal that will be a challenge. Orient goals to specific measurable results. Link goals to customer requirements.

Gear to specific results.   Define within specific parameters.

Observe by measurement.   Check through identified system of measurement.

Attain success.   Challenge yourself, but include a high degree of success.

Limit to a specific time period.   Define within a specific time period.

Set by an individual or the group.   Determine by the people who make it happen.

Goal example.   Some examples of goals are as follows:

- Reduce manufacturing cycle time for assembly X from 6 to 2 hours within 1 month.
- Decrease errors in quantity required block on order processing sheet from 10 per month to 0 in 3 months.
- Reduce rework on process A from 50% to 20% in 2 months.
- Produce a training program for customer-driven project management tools and techniques within 4 months.

Focus setting steps

1. Create the vision.
2. Define the mission.
3. Determine improvement opportunities or benchmark.
4. Select an opportunity or benchmark for improvement.
5. Analyze the opportunity or benchmark.
6. Set goal(s) to accomplish the mission.
7. Use improvement methodology to achieve goal.

Meetings

Meetings are a technique of bringing a team together to work for a common goal. Effective meetings are an important aspect of customer-driven project management to get the team to develop improvements that an individual could not come up with. By bringing together people in a meeting to develop improvements for a common goal, better decisions can result. The key is making the meeting effective. Effective meetings require an action-oriented focus. All the members of the team must have a common focus and a common methodology geared toward specific actions.

Meetings can be effective through the use of meeting tools. The meeting tools provide rules of conduct, identify meeting roles, responsibilities, and relationships, give a focus, and provide documentation of progress. The meeting tools are:

- Rules of conduct
- Meeting roles, responsibilities, and relationships
- Focus statement
- Agenda

Rules of conduct

Rules of conduct provide guidance for the team's conduct. The code of conduct considers "how" meetings will be conducted. Each team makes their own unique rules of conduct. These rules are determined during the first team meeting by consensus. The rules of conduct open communications for the team in a non-threatening situation. They are posted during every team activity. Although they are established during the first team meeting, these rules can be changed at any time the team determines it is necessary. However, the rules are established by consensus in the first meeting to help build rapport in a nonthreatening task.

The code of conduct considers the following:

- *Commitment of team members.* A rule on the amount of participation by the team member might be appropriate.
- *Owners of meeting roles.* The rules of conduct may identify the specific meeting roles of the team leader, team members, team facilitator, and meeting recorder.
- *Negotiation process.* A rule for outlining the negotiation process might be appropriate for some teams.
- *Decision-making process.* The process for decision making is a must for most teams.
- *Unity issues.* Rules for maintaining the team's cohesiveness are usually a good idea for the rules of conduct.
- *Communications procedures.* Procedures for allowing all members an opportunity to communicate on all issues is always appropriate.
- *Time management.* Rules for the start and end of the meeting are sometimes needed. Also, rules for conformance to the agenda may be needed by some teams.

Rules of Conduct Examples

- Rely on facts, not opinions.
- Understand others' points of view.
- Listen actively to all ideas.
- Encourage others.
- Submit assignments on time.
- Open communication of all issues.
- Focus.
- Come to meetings on time.
- Orient toward customer satisfaction.
- Never gossip about the meeting or team.
- Decide everything by consensus.
- Use and build on everyone's ideas.
- Conduct the meeting using an agenda.
- Take time to self-critique the meeting.

Roles, responsibilities, and relationships

Besides normal team functions, team meetings involve additional roles, responsibilities, and relationships. These must be defined. The team leader guides the team to mission accomplishment and the team leader may guide the team during team meetings. Team members are expected to prepare, participate, and perform for team meetings. The team facilitator helps the team focus and apply methods, tools, and techniques during the meeting. In addition, for team meetings a recorder is needed. The recorder prepares all the administration documentation for the meeting. This could include such items as agenda, minutes, assumptions, and list of definitions.

In addition to roles and responsibilities, each team member must understand the relationships that exist. These relationships could affect the team meeting. The relationships involve the team as a whole, other team members, the organization as a whole, the functional organization, and self. A conflict in any of these relationships could cause a team meeting to be canceled or ineffective. These potential conflicts should be resolved as early as possible to ensure maximum participation by all team members.

Focus statement

A focus statement provides the purpose of a meeting. Each team meeting must have a written focus statement. If the team cannot write a focus statement, there is no need to hold a meeting. The focus statement should provide the following:

- Focus for an entire meeting
- Output expected from the meeting
- Clear, concise, simple statement
- Understanding for everyone on the team
- Start for the agenda

Agenda

An agenda acts as the meeting guide. It gets the team to focus on the meeting's desired outcomes. An agenda encourages effective and efficient meeting because it provides a target for the meeting. It documents key team activities and acts to stimulate progress.

Team meetings in action

In addition to the meeting tools mentioned, action must be taken before, during, and after the meeting to ensure proper preparation, conduct, and follow-up.

Initial meeting actions

It is important to get the team started correctly. During the first meeting, the following should be accomplished:

1. Establish rules of conduct.
2. Understand the mission of the team.
3. Establish roles and responsibilities.
4. Develop next agenda.

Before the meeting

The success of the team depends on the active involvement of all the team members. Team members should participate fully in all meetings. The following are some meaningful guidelines to assist the team in conducting an effective meeting:

- *Brainstorm ideas.*   Review the focus statement and write your ideas on everything you know about the focus.
- *Evaluate what you know.*   Start with ideas you brainstormed and gather any additional information you may need. Analyze the information trying to determine the specific opportunity, problem, or root cause.
- *Formulate alternatives.*   Generate a list of alternatives to accomplish the focus.
- *Orient toward one alternative.*   Determine one alternative you can support. This is your starting position based on the information you know. During the

meeting, you may change your alternative based on additional information provided by other team members.

- Review agenda to ensure you are prepared with information, status, or assignments.

- Ensure you complete any assignments. The team depends on you to accomplish your specific actions. Even if you cannot make the meeting, try to make sure your assignments are on-time.

During the meeting

During the meeting, speaking, listening, and cooperation are the key activities of all team members. Speak to make your point, present and clarify ideas. Listen actively. Cooperate with all other team members. During the meeting, do the following:

- Display teamwork
- Understand viewpoint of others
- Remain focused
- Involve yourself
- Nurture others' ideas
- Go for win/win solutions

Speak.   During the meeting, speak to share information but be short, simple, and concise. Plan what you are going to say before you say it. This will help you focus and save the team time. Encourage building of ideas. This stimulates interest and involvement. Although you or others may not have anything to contribute initially, many people can add their ideas to others. Avoid personal remarks. Remember, it is not personal. Keep remarks focused on the mission, goal, problem, and issue. Also, avoid any words that may trigger an emotional reaction. These types of words may refer to race, sex, religion, politics, and the like.

Listen.   Again listening is essential during a meeting. Let another person convey his/her message. Do not interrupt the other person while he is speaking. Involve yourself in the message. Look for ideas you can support. Determine the central theme or concepts. Summarize and paraphrase frequently. This provides the speaker with feedback on the success of the communication. It is also the only way to confirm your understanding of the information. Further, there may be another team member who does not understand. All critical ideas must be repeated by another member and discussed to ensure clarity of ideas necessary for consensus decision-making. Talk only to clarify while you are listening. Effective listening requires your full concentration. Empathize with other people. In other words, put yourself in their shoes for a while. You do not have to sympathize with them. Empathy helps you understand; sympathy may actually be a barrier. Nurture active listening skills. Active and effective listening is not natural. It requires dedicated concentration of effort.

Cooperate.   Cooperation makes a meeting work. Consider the self-esteem of others. This will give them the confidence to participate. Operate with the team—give others a fair chance. Do not go outside the team to seek action or talk about other team members. Observe others' reactions. This provides feedback on true reactions. Use this to find common ground for negotiations for win/win solutions. Pursue a common focus. As long as the team focuses on a common goal, the team can work. Many times a common focus overcomes many conflicts as peer pressure to achieve a shared result overshadows the personal needs of team members. Establish open communications. This is necessary for any cooperative effort. Recognize individual contributions. This helps stimulate more participation. Allow positive conflict. This leads to consensus decision making. The team will support a decision better if positive debate was endorsed during the meeting. Trade-off ideas with the group. This distributes ownership to the whole team. Encourage trust. This is the most important ingredient to developing and keeping cooperation on the team. Without trust, there can be no real cooperation during the team meeting.

After the meeting

Once the meeting is over, the real team actions are performed. This is when the team members act to perform assignments and action items. Finding support and resources may be necessary after the meeting. A team member coordinates with management or a support function to ensure the team can complete actions or implement a solution. All team members must talk up team activities to develop pride for their team in their organization. This gives all team members a feeling of belonging to a worthwhile team. It also helps promote teamwork throughout the whole organization. Further, it is necessary to maintain team integrity. Team members do not gossip about team activities or other team members. Finally, the team member must review the agenda of the next meeting to start preparation before the next meeting.

Meeting critique

Some teams find it useful to perform a self-assessment meeting at the end of the meeting. This is particularly beneficial when just starting a team. It provides a means to develop the skills required for effective team meetings while also fostering teamwork through finding success working on a nonmission related activity. The more successes a team has as a team, the easier the team can develop and maintain teamwork. The team needs to design its own meeting critique. This critique should be completed as a team at the end of the meeting. It should take no longer than 5 to 10 minutes. The critique should address the following:

- Communications
  - Was communication effective?
  - Was there discussion on all items?
- Results
  - Was focus statement accomplished?
- Involvement
  - Did everyone participate?
- Training
  - Does the team require any specific training?
- Individuals
  - Were individual contributions recognized?
  - Does any team member require more attention?
- Questions
  - Are there any items requiring further research?
- Unity
  - Did the team work together?
  - Was there any evidence of conflict? Groupthink?
- Escalate
  - Are there any issues requiring management resolution?

Brainstorming

Brainstorming is a technique used by a group of people that encourages their collective thinking power to create ideas. The purpose of brainstorming is to stimulate the generation of ideas. It adds to the creative power of the team. The value of brainstorming lies in the fact that there may be more than one way to look at a problem or handle it. Through brainstorming, not only are individual ideas or thoughts brought out, but they may spark new ideas or thoughts from others, or improve on an idea already under consideration. The more ideas a team has, the greater the probability of finding an opportunity or solution.

- Brings out the most ideas in the shortest time.
- Reduces the need to give right answers.
- Allows the group to have fun.
- Increases involvement and participation.
- Nurtures positive thinking.
- Solicits varying ideas and concepts.
- Tempers negative attitudes.
- Omits criticism and evaluation of ideas.
- Results in improved solutions.
- Maximizes the attainment of goals.

Rules.   For brainstorming to work effectively, the group leader must make sure that the principles of brainstorming are followed. Thus, each member must know the rules and follow them.

It's a good idea to review them before each meeting until the group has established its brainstorming approach. The rules are as follows:

- Record all ideas.
- Use free-wheeling ideas.
- Limit judgment until later.
- Encourage participation by everyone.
- Solicit quantity.

Let's look at each of these rules in more detail.

   a. *Record all ideas.*   Team members learn over and over the importance of recording things. This is the only way you can recapture what has happened. With brainstorming, it is easy in the excitement to be careless about recording ideas. Be sure someone is appointed to see that everything is recorded. Remember, do not allow judgment on ideas during the recording process by letting the recorder omit any ideas. It is best to display every idea in full view of all members on a flipchart or whiteboard, or similar device. After the brainstorming session, all ideas should be recorded on a sheet of paper so the ideas can be preserved for use at a following meeting.

   b. *Use freewheeling ideas.*   Freewheeling has value in that while an idea may be unsuitable in itself, it serves as a stimulus for other members of the group. Even wild or exaggerated ideas have thought-provoking value that should never be underestimated.

   c. *Limit judgment until later with no criticism allowed.*   Keep the ideas flowing. Criticism will shut off the flow. All ideas are encouraged and accepted. Remember, there are only right ideas. All ideas are right in each individual's mind.

   d. *Encourage participation by everyone.*   Good ideas are not necessarily in the minds of a few individuals. Give each member a turn to speak; don't miss anyone. It's important to give ample time for each member to speak.

For example, solicit responses clockwise around the room. If a member has no idea at the moment, the member says "pass." By this remark, there is added assurance that no one is missed. Furthermore, a team member that passes on one round may very well have an idea on the next round.

Encourage participation by building on other ideas.

Solicit a large number of ideas. Ideas build on ideas. They can be the combination or extension of other ideas. Ideas are thought-provoking and stimulating. Work toward a large number of ideas. Postpone judgment on ideas; that comes later.

Steps.   The step to brainstorming are as follows:

a. *Generate ideas.*   Follow the rules given above.

b. *Evaluate Ideas.*   During the evaluation step, the team examines each idea for value. This is the point at which to offer constructive criticism or analysis of the ideas presented. Again, it is important that only the idea and not the generator of the idea is criticized. The ideas and alternative combinations of ideas are compared and examined. At this time, some ideas may be eliminated or combined with other ideas.

c. *Decide using consensus.*   There are a number of ways to develop a consensus.

Brainstorming methods

There are three primary brainstorming methods:

1. Round robin
2. Free-wheeling
3. Slip

Each has advantages and disadvantages that the group or discussion leader will have to weigh before determining which one would be best to accomplish desired results. In some cases, the best method may be a combination of the various brainstorming methods. For instance, the brainstorming session may start with a round robin or slip method and move into a free-wheeling method to add more ideas.

Round robin.   Each group member in turn contributes an idea as it relates to the purpose of the discussion. Every idea is recorded on flip chart or board. When a group member has nothing to contribute, he or she simply says "pass." The next time around, this person may offer an idea if they wish or pass again. Ideas are solicited until no one has anything to add.

Advantages

- Difficult for one person to dominate the discussion.
- Everyone is given an opportunity to participate fully.

Disadvantage.   People feel frustration while waiting their turn.

Free-wheeling.   Each team member calls out ideas freely and in a random order. Every idea is recorded on a flip chart or board. The process continues until no one has anything else to add.

Advantage.   Spontaneous and no restrictions.

Disadvantages

- Some individuals may dominate.
- Quiet team member may be reluctant to speak.
- Chaotic, if too many people talk at the same time.

Slip.   Team members writes all their ideas on an issue, a problem, or an alternative on a piece of paper. Then the slips are collected and all the ideas are written on the board. A variation to this method is the Crawford Slip method where each idea is written on a separate slip of paper. The slips are then put on a board and arranged in categories.

Advantage.   All ideas are recorded and all contributions are anonymous.

Disadvantage.   Some creativity may be lost due to the inability of the other team members to react to the contribution of others.

Brainstorming example

Advanced brainstorming techniques.   There are many advanced brainstorming techniques beyond the basic three mentioned above. Two of the most popular of these advanced techniques are nominal group techniques and affinity diagrams.

Nominal group technique.   Nominal group technique is a refinement of brainstorming. It provides a more structured discussion and decision-making technique. The nominal group techniques allow time for individual idea generation. This can be anytime. Sometimes, if the subject is not too complex, the team may only have 5 to 10 minutes. For a complex issue, the team may be asked to generate their ideas between team meetings. Once the ideas are generated, the nominal group technique then allows the leader to survey the opinions of the group about the ideas generated. Finally, nominal group technique leads the group to set priorities and focus on consensus. The nominal group technique steps can be summarized as follows:

1. Present the issue and give instructions.
2. Allow time for idea generation.
3. Gather ideas via round robin, one idea at a time. Write each idea on a flip chart or board and post.
4. Process or clarify ideas. Focus on clarification of meaning, not on arguing points. Eliminate duplicate ideas; combine similar ideas.
5. Set priorities.

Affinity diagram

The affinity diagram is another idea generator. It starts with the issue statement. Once the issue is presented, it continues like the nominal group technique with some time for individual idea generation. The difference is with an affinity diagram each of the ideas are written on an index card or post-it note. Each idea is recorded by the individual on one card or post-it. All notes are then posted on a wall or put on a table. The team members then put the cards or post-its into similar groupings. This is all complete without discussion. Next, the team decides on a theme for each group of notes through discussion. The team creates a header card for each group of notes from the theme. The cards are arranged under the issue with the header card and each of the notes relating to the grouping under the header card. Next, just like nominal group technique the items are prioritized for action.

Presentation

Sometimes a presentation may be necessary to provide information, obtain approval, or request action. The presentation may be formally or informally given by the team. Involve as many team members as possible in the actual presentation. The presentation provides the opportunity to inform about team activities and accomplishments, and recognize team members for their contributions.

Presentation steps

Step 1: Gain support. Gaining support requires identifying and involving key people early in the improvement process. Ensure support for recommendation from owners, suppliers, and customers by stressing benefits to the organization.

Step 2: Prepare the presentation.

- Anticipate objections
- Rehearse the presentation
- Arrange the presentation

Step 3: Give the presentation.

- Build rapport
- Make the recommendation
- Stress the benefits
- Overcome objections
- Seek action

Step 4: Follow up on the presentation.

■ Follow up to ensure that the recommended action is implemented.

■ Reduce post decision anxiety by repeating and summarizing benefits.

■ Stress the benefits of early implementation.

Prepare the presentation

Once the team knows they have sufficient support for a recommended course of action requiring management approval, the team must prepare the presentation. Preparing the presentation involves the activities as listed above. To accomplish these activities, the following processes must be performed:

■ Develop presentation materials.

■ Produce the presentation materials.

■ Arrange for the presentation.

■ Practice the presentation.

Develop presentation materials

Development of presentation materials involves developing a specific objective for the presentation and preparing a presentation outline to accomplish the objective. The presentation objective should state specifically the expected outcome of the presentation. The objective should be stated in terms of who, what, and when.

Presentation objective example

The organization development and training manager will analyze within 3 months the specific needs of the organization to implement customer-driven quality improvement teams throughout the organization.

In this example, the who is the organizational development and training manager. The "what" is to analyze the specific needs of the organization to implement customer-driven quality improvement teams throughout the organization. The "when" is within 3 months.

The outline of the presentation should be geared to accomplish the objective. When preparing the presentation outline, consider the audience, understand how the recommendation affects others, and outline the organization-wide benefits. The audience may be supportive or unreceptive. Conduct a force field analysis to determine the restraining forces and driving forces of the audience. At the same time, consider how the recommendation affects others. Anticipate objections. Again, conduct a force field analysis to determine driving forces of any known objections to your proposal. Further, outline the organization-wide benefits through brainstorming and data collection.

Now you are ready to prepare the presentation outline. The presentation outline should contain an introduction, body, and conclusion. In the introduction, tell them what you are going to tell them. In the body, tell them. Tell them what you have just told them in the conclusion.

Presentation outline

The introduction

- Establish rapport with introductions.
- Get the audience's attention by giving benefits.
- Tell them what you are going to tell them.

The body

- State your mission.
- Describe the process using process diagram.
- Significance of the process.
- Inputs with suppliers.
- Process itself.
- Output(s) with customer(s).
- Owner(s).
- Identify the underlying cause.
- Describe data collection.
- Discuss results.
- Detail the action requested.
- Alternatives considered.
- Solution selected.
- Plan for implementation.

The conclusion

- Reinforce benefits.
- Tell them what you told them.
- Get agreement on what you want.
- Summarize actions.

Prepare presentation materials

Presentation materials can be as simple or complex as required to get the requested action from the audience. Presentation materials are used to attract and maintain attention on main ideas. They illustrate and support the team's recommendations.

They focus on minimizing misunderstanding. Presentation materials could include handouts, overhead transparencies, flipchart, video, and computer-based visuals. As a minimum, the presentation material should consist of a handout for all participants. Normally, the presentation material consists of a handout and some form of visual aid for the group to observe. In most organizations, this is either flipchart or overhead transparencies. Specific tips for preparing the most common presentation aids of handout, flipchart, and overhead transparencies are as follows:

Handout. The handout supports the presentation by providing critical information and/or supplemental detail. The handout should follow the presentation, if given prior to the presentation. If the handout only provides supplemental or reinforcing information, the handout should not be provided to the audience until it is appropriate during the presentation or given at the conclusion of the presentation.

Flipcharts. Flipcharts enhance the presentation. They should emphasize the key points or graphically show concepts. Some specific tips for the design of flipcharts are:

- List main points as bullets.
- Limit bullets to six or less per chart.
- Keep bullets short around six words or less per bullet.
- Chart should be readable from every seat in the room.
- Multiple colors can be used to stress key words.
- Leave a blank sheet between flipcharts.
- Should reflect the professional pride of the team.

Overhead transparencies. Overhead transparencies are the most frequent material used to aid in the understanding of information in a presentation. The overhead transparency is used the same as a flipchart. However, with today's computer technology, especially graphic capability, the overhead transparencies should be used to reinforce ideas graphically. Since people have different styles for understanding, this is supported by dominance of the right or left brain. It may be appropriate to use both words and pictures to convey your message. The words appeal to the more logical (the left brain preference) people and the graphics focus on the creative right brain dominant people. The same tips for flipcharts apply to overhead. In addition, you should not attempt to show large amounts of data or complex processes on one overhead. Reduce the information to show trends, relationship, or overall processes. If detailed information is necessary, provide this information as a handout.

Produce the presentation material

Depending on the situation, the team may produce the presentation itself or the team may have to rely on various support services to produce the materials.

If the team produces the materials, ensure the presentation meets the standards of the audience. If the team has support services the presentation materials, planning and coordination are important. Many organizations have support services such as word processing, editing, graphics, and printing. When using these services, the team must plan enough time to allow for professional workmanship. This means determining all the tasks to be accomplished with appropriate time period allowed to meet the team's scheduled presentation date. Ensure there is enough time to use the presentation materials for a dry run before the actual presentation. Also it is wise to periodically coordinate with the support services people to ensure progress toward meeting the schedule.

Arrange for the presentation

Administration details can have an effect on how the presentation is received. Ensure that the following administration details are accomplished:

- Schedule presentation time and place.
- Ensure all the right participants can attend.
- Set up the room.
- Have presentation materials.

Practice the presentation

Rehearse the presentation prior to the actual presentation. If possible, practice the presentation one time to an audience that provides a representation of the actual audience.

Give the presentation

Giving the presentation involves presenter preparation and the actual conduct of the presentation. The best way to ensure a successful presentation is by adequate preparation. This is enhanced through the development of some basic presentation skills. These skills can be grouped in the following categories:

- Presenter's preparation
- Presenter's style
- Presenter's delivery

Presenter's preparation

Depending on your experience, you will be more or less comfortable presenting to a group. Your level of comfort can be improved with time spent preparing. Specifically, the following techniques can be used to enhance your comfort level:

Practice.   Practice the presentation enough to get very familiar with the flow of ideas. Do not memorize the presentation. Practice enough to allow you to present the information naturally.

Plan for objections.   Perform a force field analysis to determine objections and your response.

Visualize success.   Prior to the presentation, spend some time alone picturing yourself and accomplishing a successful presentation.

Presenter's style

Although presenters have their own style, the following guidelines will help any presenter become more successful:

- *Act naturally.*   Make the presentation as natural as possible. Try to avoid doing anything that would appear faked, forced, or flaky.

- *Maintain positive attitude.*   Display a positive attitude by showing enthusiasm. Above all be sincere in your commitment and support for the presentation goal.

Presenter's delivery

There are several nonverbal and verbal presentation tips to improve anyone's presentation. Most people concentrate on the verbal communication aspects of the presentation, although nonverbal behavior communicates much of the meaning. Nonverbal communication skills enhance your ability to effectively communicate to the audience. These nonverbal communication behaviors include eye contact, body movement, and gestures.

- Eye contact shows interest in the audience. Look directly at your audience and include everyone equally. Good eye contact results in enhanced credibility.

- Body movement is another important physical behavior for a presenter. It helps hold the audiences' attention, and puts the speaker at ease by working off excess energy that can cause nervousness. You can use body movement as punctuation to mark a change in your presentation. Moving from one spot to another tells the audience you are changing the line of thought. Some body movement can be distracting. Pacing back and forth, rocking from side to side, or "dancing" serves no purpose and tells the audience that you are nervous.

- Gestures can clarify, emphasize, or reinforce what is said. Make gestures by using your hands, arms, shoulders, and head. Fidgeting with your watch and scratching your ear are not gestures. This type of behavior usually distracts from the presentation. Gestures take practice to use effectively.

Conduct the presentation

During the presentation, the team does the following:

- Builds rapport by developing a friendly, but professional relationship with the audience.

- Makes the recommendation using the results of the customer-driven project management improvement methodology. Support the recommendation with facts.

- Stresses the benefits of implementing the team's recommendation. The benefits should emphasize the tangible measurable gains of the solution. In addition, show intangible advantages.

- Overcomes objections by using the driving forces driven from the force field analysis. Remember, focus on the issue, never make it personal.

- Seeks action for implementation. The conclusion must provide a definite course of action.

Follow up on the presentation

After the presentation, the team should do the following:

- Follow up to ensure that the recommended action is implemented.
- Reduce post decision anxiety by repeating and summarizing benefits.
- Stress the benefits of early implementation.

Creating a Quality Organization in the New Millennium

Perhaps as a commentary on our modern age, we could very well conclude that "systems, processes, and integrated technology do not a project make." Alas, we have found that all the quality tools and techniques and all the available project management systems and support personnel do not sum—simply by definition—to a quality product or service that satisfies the customer. Countless examples of failed projects testify to the need to build project quality management from the bottom up, starting with the individual. Unlike the work breakdown structure (WBS) that starts at the high-level view and drills down, a quality organization starts at the work package and individual level of effort level and builds up. The battle will be in trenches, not in the boardrooms, and the weapons of war will be undergirded by the individual will to excel, one by one.

Creating an organization that inspires individual project quality and professionalism will require new energy and new strategies. This new need stems from the forces for change, which have themselves changed.

Five forces will shape the future quality organization:

Serious rededication to the work ethic and the individual will and passion to make a difference

Flexible organizational structure with purpose and direction

Full cycle customer involvement

Embedded quality and the slow disappearance of a separate quality culture

The coming of age of the Internet

Individual Work Ethic

The collectivist philosophy that focused on teams and teamwork for such a long time has been an important ingredient to building project success, but we know that the team itself is not the secret to integration and quality work. It still remains that unless individual team members understand customer requirements and their role in accomplishing customer satisfaction, quality will remain an elusive and increasingly foreign concept. The movement back to the individual places accountability for integration where it belongs; with each team member whose tasking derives directly from the work itself.

That is why it is important to see the tools and techniques in this book as *individual, even personal* tools of success, applied by team members, sometimes in teams but always in the privacy of their own work and job setting. Quality function department is a tool to transform customer requirements to product specifications on a broad systems scale, but the same technology can be applied by individuals trying to pin down how to meet their "downstream" customer's needs in the value chain of the daily work process.

Flexible Organization

The flexible organization of the future that can respond to integrated programme will create the conditions of success for project quality management. New telecommunication networks and techniques will allow the development of virtual groups who work together without the need to meet regularly in one place. Customers will be fully integrated into the project process, helping to make key decisions and participating and learning as team members. Jobs will be defined in terms of the deliverables themselves, not in terms of longer term, recurring function job descriptions with little meaning in the real world of project deliverables. The individualization of information will focus large amounts of project information in the hands of individuals, without the middle man and without system delays, thus empowering individuals to act on project information rapidly and responsively.

Full Cycle Customer Involvement

While the wide debate continues on the role and function of the customer in project quality management, there will be no such debate in the future as the customer becomes a full and assimilated partner in the project team. Instead of self-directed team, a new concept will surface which might be termed, "customer-directed team." The customer will be able to drive the project quality process by direct decisions on specifications, design issues, change, and project team performance.

Embedded and Integrated Quality

Quality will be fully embedded into policies, processes, and procedures, and corporate and team/group practices will increasingly reflect quality assurance and control principles. In the project management field, we will see quality fully reflected in goal setting task. While the light can be seen at the end of the tunnel, the issue of embedding quality into individual practice will remain a difficult challenge.

Related to the individual practice issue described above, this issue has to do with building quality professionals in projects who have a detailed grasp of their industry sectors and their business, who know and use project planning and control techniques, and who practice in their daily work habits the concept of doing things right the first time.

The Internet

The coming of age of the Internet is changing project quality management by gathering project information through the Web and providing real time, personalized project information that will not only present relevant project data, but also translate that data into impacts, individual and team tasking, and follow up action lists. In other words, the Internet will enable the capture of decision rules and protocols which will automatically assess project performance, come up with optional corrective actions, choose the most cost-effective tool, and advise the team member. Likened to artificial intelligence, this new system of project quality management will anticipate quality issues based on current project data, address corrective actions, and build documentation for lessons learned.

The Internet will enable this new planning tool to operate without substantial cost because "Project" firms providing such services will increasingly gain revenues from avoiding project penalties and realizing incentive awards.

Universal Avionics, Inc. integrated quality into its product development process through a number of test and safety related protocols that are an integral part of the government's certification of its products for use in aircraft. A good example of meeting customer requirements by adhering to regulatory and industry standards practices, this approach defines quality as the successful completion of the procedures, tests, and exercises described in the customer's lexicon, in this case the Federal Aviation Administration's avionics certification requirements. This is a good example of the use of an industry standard such as failure assessment protocols as third party guidance for quality that both the customer (a corporate aircraft owner) and the project firm (Universal Avionics, Inc.) could support. In this case quality is not an external process (although the company has an external quality function largely focused on documentation and ISO compliance), but rather quality is embedded into the product development process itself. Their design verification and validation process, which address the question of whether the designed product will meet specifications (verification) and whether the product will work (validation), are part of the generic WBS for all company products.

The mere presence of the Internet will have substantial impacts on the field of project management, but the most important impacts will be in the field of product development, engineering, and information technology. Project quality management cannot be seen out of context from the industry sector and product development/engineering issues involved. Therefore, project management as a generic approach to cost, schedule, and quality is a hollow effort, until combined and integrated with technical and product specific processes. Therefore, the Internet's impacts on project management will funnel through the impacts on various product groups such as electronics and various functional groups such as software engineering.

Tracking Change and Integrating Midstream Correction

In this chapter, we take a rather unconventional approach to scheduling, budgeting, and monitoring project progress. We start with project goals and the monitoring process and work backward, a sort of backward mapping of the project process to give perspective to what is important up front. Our discussion is based on the rule of thumb, most notably demonstrated in Europe than in the United States, that the front end planning of a project should normally represent at least 50% of the whole project process. We key the discussion of monitoring on the use of modern project management software, not only to flag earned value and lessons learned, but also to look ahead regularly and intensely to project completion with a new tool, which we term "the future value indicator." The future value indicator is the extent of new value to be added to the project in the remaining cycle time, largely a function of the value added to date, plus a prediction of new technology and marketing opportunities to be opened by the project.

Today, teams are the organizational structure of choice to meet the challenges of the global environment. People working together for a common goal in teams are absolutely essential to success. Teams maximize the use of human resources in the organization. In project management, functional, process, and multifunctional teams ensure that all aspects of the project are integrated to achieve the desired end result satisfying the customer(s). Teams provide better decisions and the motivation to carry them out. Everyone can participate in a team. Relationships are nurtured for improved working coordination. Working together for a common goal leads to increased job satisfaction and rewards in the work itself. Teams foster freer contribution of information through more active communication. Further, the organization is thrust toward a common goal and an organization-wide perspective is fostered through teamwork. Teams provide the rapid, responsive organizational structure that is necessary for any organization to compete successfully in the ever-changing economic environment of today and the future.

Traditional organizations in government and private industries, usually are not geared to using teams, especially project teams, to their full advantage. They do not structure project teams to both perform and improve the project. Normally, the project team is only responsible for completing the project. Thus, there is much inefficiency and redundancy in the kind of organization that uses one kind of team to perform the project and in some of the more progressive organizations another kind of team to seek out quality improvements and build a customer-driven culture. In a traditional organization, management concepts typically focus on outputs and profits. The focus is on cost, schedule, and quality, usually in that order. Quality in the traditional sense only means that the product or service meets technical acceptance. Traditional organizations do not empower teams with the responsibility, authority, and resources to continuously improve their processes geared toward customer satisfaction or "quality" in the total quality sense. In these organizations, it is difficult to compete in the global marketplace because productivity and quality are separate and suppliers and the customer are isolated from each other.

Customer-driven teams are the preferred organizational structure for performing a project as efficiently and effectively as possible to satisfy customer's expectations. The customer-driven team focuses on both—working on a project and continuously improving the project. Customer-driven teams strive to marry productivity and quality through all phases of a project. In addition, customers and suppliers are linked from the external customer throughout the organization by supplier and customer relationships. Only through customer-driven teams, empowered to perform and improve all aspects of their project, can an organization use project management for true success in satisfying the customer, whether the customer is external or internal to the organization.

Traditional Project Teams

Traditional project management teams place accountability for results in one manager—the program manager who uses a disciplined planning, direction, control, and evaluation approach. That project manager is a member of the supplying organization, not the customer's organization. The basic function of the traditional project manager is to control quality, cost, and schedule; to manage the team's work; and to assure the effective and efficient delivery of a project deliverable, acceptable to the customer within schedule and budget constraints. The traditional matrix project group borrows people from the functional departments of the organization, such as, engineering, manufacturing, logistics/supportability, marketing, finance, human resources, and the like, and pulls them into a project organization. The project manager focuses the team on the project specifications and requirements, and keeps the customer informed as necessary.

This structure has presented major problems for many projects, mainly because the customer is typically uninvolved in the key decisions in the project life cycle. Once a contract is signed, the supplying organization project manager is likely to feel "in charge" to the point that the team's creative and innovative efforts are too rapidly and too narrowly targeted on building the specification, instead of developing a fuller understanding of the customer's performance issues and expectations as the project "learning" progresses.

This tendency to isolate the project manager and the team from the customer too quickly is rooted in the propensity of project managers and project management organizations to drive projects by schedule and cost rather than by quality. This is due to the project manager's need to be "in control." Usually the project manager can establish some control of cost and schedule within its organization. However, since quality is defined by customer satisfaction, quality can be a changing requirement. Therefore, project managers place extreme pressure on the customer to lock in on customer needs early in the concept phase of the project through quality standards and specifications, with little assurance that any adjustments can be made once the project proceeds into definition. In addition, customer satisfaction requires full communication between the supplier and the customer. This is difficult when the project manager emphasizes specifications, statement of work, schedules, and budgets instead of the customer's needs. Further, traditional project managers ignore the "learning curve" in both the supplier's and customer's organization during the life cycle of the project. Without continuous improvement based on customer satisfaction, the project deliverables often do not meet the customer's needs and expectations in a changing environment.

The Texture of Integration

The texture of the integrated project management organization differs from the traditional organization in many ways. The focus on integration gives the organization a responsive tone that creates a constant impetus for defining and scheduling work, resolving problems, and getting tasks accomplished. Integration is a broader, deeper concept than simple teamwork. In the project firm, the support functions are lean, and the role of supervisor is shared between project managers and functional managers, each observing and monitoring the work of project team members. The project organization is characterized by flurries of activity, crashing projects, and accelerating milestones with a view toward on time performance. And perhaps most of all the project organization is intensely aware of the customer and the customer voice.

Unfortunately, all too often the customer is seen as a negative influence, a source of change and "scope creep" that interferes in the accomplishment of carefully scheduled tasks performed in a critical path of interdependence and handoffs. Ironically, the project organization, so close to the customer, often disengages from the customer at critical points in the project simply to avoid complications toward the end of the project cycle.

Integration and Ethics and Internal Control Management

Project integration supports accountability and ethical behavior because integration tends to increase the visibility of program and project operations to a wider variety of stakeholders. Thus, the better the various perspectives are reflected in the work, thus requiring project work to be visible to all the levels of the organization, the more that accountability problems can be uncovered early and often. Sarbanes-Oxley requirements for CEO level awareness of costs generate a new impetus for reporting earned value to top management as part of the monitoring process. Cost control is now seen as a key aspect of projects, which heretofore has been viewed only in terms of on-time delivery.

Vertical Integration of Businesses: Another Application of Integration

Gareth Morgan in *Images of Organization* (Sage, 2d ed., 1996, p. 65) hints at the integrative nature of organizations, now a clearly predominant model for partnering at the global level:

Examples of day-to-day collaborative relations between organizations in different industries or in different parts of the same industry are also very common. For example, firms often cultivate interlocking directorships to create a measure of shared decision making and control, engage in joint ventures to pool expertise or share risk in research and development, strike agreements with suppliers or manufacturers to achieve a measure of "vertical integration" of production, and engage in numerous kinds of informal networking. Sometimes, they also establish informal joint organizations to link firms that have an interest in special problems or lines of development. For example, in the financial services industry it is not uncommon for banks, trust companies, insurance firms, and other interested agencies to offer joint services, in effect creating a new form of organization at the level of the industry. Similar developments can be seen in many other areas as well.

Project Integration Lessons Learned

One way to learn about the consequences of the lack of integrated project management is to hold a lessons learned meeting in the close-out phase. This meeting explores the extent to which integration was effective in the project. The following questions would be asked.

Was the team focused on a single set of goals and deliverables?

Did the scope of work change without anyone documenting it?

Were resources (e.g., test equipment) allocated to resolve problems quickly?

Were contingency plans in place when necessary?

Was documentation integrated with project progress, for instance, were software outputs and others documented as the team progressed?

Was communication across disciplines good, and were functional and project activities synchronized?

Did corporate heads communicate a consistent priority status to the project and was the project aligned with business plans in practice?

Were team members responsive to each other so that downstream integration issues were avoided?

Did the scheduling and monitoring process focus on the right integration issues?

Was the program manager open to change and was he flexible in responding to team issues?

Did company process and procedure requirements, and differing interpretations of document requirements, sometimes act as barriers to necessary work?

Were policies and procedures integrated with project work?

Was the document numbering system integrated with project codes?

Was training integrated with the real skills necessary to complete the project work?

Was effective integration inhibited because the team did not have the "big picture" on the project; sometimes the big picture helps to facilitate doing your job.

Were meeting agendas integrated with the current status of the project and real issues being faced by the project team?

Risk and Project Integration

The integration of risk into project planning is a major challenge. Risk management planning is ineffective unless made an integral part of the project cycle. Successful integration of risk requires a proactive approach. The following is a risk integration checklist suggesting key points of interface with project decisions in the following categories: business culture, business strategy, project selection, project plan, formal risk management planning, project manual, product/technical process development, customer risk tolerance, and lessons learned.

Action	What?	Why?	When?	Output?	Who?
Business culture					
Create risk management policy	Create business intent to manage risk	Confirm that it is important and back it up	Part of business plan; underlies project process	Policy statement on how the business will handle risk	Executive and program management level
Assess organization awareness	Find out how aware workforce is on risk and risk response impacts	Survey workforce	Every six months	Workforce awareness of risk management report	HR/project team
Deliver training program	Design training around practice planning tools; use to introduce business risk	Workforce will implement if they understand tools	Every year with refresher	Certification	All PM, teams, and technical personnel
Reward effective risk management	Provide rewards for good risk management effort and effectiveness	Incentives motivation	During project	Compensation reward	Project managers and team members

(Continued)

Action	What?	Why?	When?	Output?	Who?
Business strategy					
Risk component of business plan	Provide for a risk section in the business plan and communicate it	SWOT analysis; threats = risks Translate to product line risk exposure	Annual update of business strategic and business plan	Risk-based business plan; integrate with financial and profitability analysis	Executives and program managements
Strategic objectives	State objectives in terms of risk	Measurable strategy goals	Part of plan; communicate to workforce	Set of 10 long-term objectives	Executives and program managers
Project selection					
Do risk assessment of candidate projects	In developing business portfolio of projects, use risk as one criterion for project selection	Use PMBOK process; broad-brush risk assessment	Each time project portfolio pipeline is updated	Rank order projects using composite risk, alignment, cost and revenue assessment	Program managers and functional managers
Weigh risk against revenues and alignment	Demonstrate that risk has been embedded in business and financial analysis	Trade off risk with opportunity for profitability and taking advantage of business core competence	Each time pipeline is updated	Analysis, data, and documentation	Project management office, project team, business planning staff
Project plan					
Requirements	State customer requirements in terms of customer risks	Risk that customer requirements do not reflect risk, or mis-understanding customer perspective and expectations on project risks	During initial concept phase, part of project plan	Requirements document stating customer requirements and risks	Project manager, functional manager, and customer
Work breakdown structure (WBS)	Include risk contingencies from risk matrix in WBS work activity	Because there is inherent risk in missing major parts of the deliverable in initial planning; WBS assures coverage of major "chunks" of work	During development of the deliverable, the "work" should include initial contingencies identified in risk assessment	WBS in organization chart form and outline in MS Project	Project manager

Action	What?	Why?	When?	Output?	Who?
		Project plan			
Task list	Include risk tasks and contingencies in baseline schedule	Task list should include all anticipated contingency actions if risk events occur	After WBS is prepared, do task list and link; there is inherent risk that linkages will be too "hard;" allow for "soft" linkage	Task list in MS Project Gantt chart or spreadsheet	Project management office and/or project manager
Network diagram	Show risk in network diagram with three scenarios, expected, pessimistic, and optimistic	Arrow diagram shows critical and noncritical paths; risks inherent in focusing on critical path when resource constraints in noncritical tasks may serve as bottleneck—theory of constraints	During translation of WBS to Gantt chart, prepared to show dependencies and paths	Arrow diagram in MS Project or other software	Project management office template, or project manager
Calendar-based diagram	Relate network to time to begin to see schedule impacts and milestones	Histogram using arrows and calendar	During translation of WBS to Gantt chart	Graphics software or word document	Project manager
Risk-based schedule	Do risk-based schedule using MS Project PERT analysis tool	MS Project Gantt chart showing calculated risk-based duration after weights and three scenarios are entered	During initial scheduling, then any time risk is identified and contingency prepared	MS Project schedule file showing calculated durations for high risk tasks	Project management office or project manager
		Risk management process (see PMBOK)			
Risk identification	Using input from business plan, identify and rank project tasks in terms of risk	Using data, information and past experience, rank summary tasks in WBS using risk matrix	During business planning, project and portfolio selection, and project WBS scheduling	Risk matrix	Project management office or project manager

(Continued)

Action	What?	Why?	When?	Output?	Who?
Risk management process (see PMBOK)					
Risk assessment	Assess risks using risk matrix format	Complete risk definition, impact (schedule, cost, quality, business growth); make probability estimate (25%, 50%, 75% probability), severity on project outcome, and contingency	During business planning, project selection, and project planning and control	Risk matrix updated monthly	Project manager
Risk response	Prepare contingency actions and include in baseline schedule	Response is planning through definitive contingency plans and tasks which are embedded in project schedule as regular tasks, triggered if risk event occurs	During project planning, responses and contingencies are designed to address specific risks and recorded; this is where the team anticipates what might happen to slow or delay the project, what can be done to prevent it or address it, and schedules contingency tasks into the project	Risk contingency actions	Project manager
Risk matrix	Prepare risk matrix as basis for scheduling	The risk matrix is the basic checklist item for risk throughout the process; it is the guide for action	During project planning a basic risk matrix file is established and appears with all project planning and project review documents	Risk matrix following prescribed format	Project manager and team or task managers

Action	What?	Why?	When?	Output?	Who?
		Risk management process (see PMBOK)			
Decision tree	Do decision tree analysis to expected value of optional decisions	This is the way project managers anticipate decisions they will have to make based on risk, and what alternative paths and expected values will follow each decision path	During project planning, decision tree analysis is applied to high risk tasks	Decision tree diagram with expected values calculated	Project manager
		Integrate risk into project manual			
Basic project manual	Assure that risk is not treated separately, but seen as part of the way projects are planned and controlled	Because risk should not be treated separately from project management process; manual captures how risk is integrated into process	Business establishes a system of basic project manuals as part of "projectizing" the organization	Online and hardcopy manual including basic project planning and risk management tools and templates	Project management office (PMO)
Provide software tools	Train and provide software analysis tools in manual	Much of the risk analysis can be done through spreadsheets and decision tree analysis software; workforce needs to know how to use them	Business establishes a support system of risk management application software and trains appropriate staff	Software library	IT and project managers

(Continued)

Action	What?	Why?	When?	Output?	Who?
Product/technical process development					
Define product/ technical development process in generic WBS	Assure that business has defined the core, product development, and technical processes which it uses to produce products and services, such as engineering, construction, system development, standardizing where possible	Because project risk management cannot be successful unless both technical and product development/ testing requirements are conducted to control risk, and management impacts, such as schedule and cost, are applied to the real industry processes that create customer value	Business establishes a generic WBS of technical processes; these are recorded and updated so that all project WBS and schedule information, and risk data, are taken from the generic model and tailored	WBS file	Functional managers
Project codes	Provide for coding actions in WBS so that costs can be captured	Because once you have identified all tasks and risk contingencies, you will want to capture costs against those codes to build a history of risk management and mitigation costs	When generic WBS is set up, codes are added at the appropriate level to capture costs	Coding system integrated with time sheets and accounting system	Accounting, project management
Identify customer risk tolerance					
Assess customer perspective on business and project risk and how much risk customer is willing to assume	Solicit customer input on customer risks and uncertainties	Because customer may have different and valuable insight on business and project risks that have been part of the customer expectations but not reflected in real planning	When requirements are being written	Customer risk analysis	Customer representative and functional and project managers, jointly

Action	What?	Why?	When?	Output?	Who?
		Lessons learned			
Risk audit	Do a project risk audit following selected projects to evaluate success in anticipating and managing risk	Because insights and documents that can lead to better risk management in the future will be lost unless a risk audit team builds a history of the project, how risk decisions were made, and how effective risk management was	At project close-out	Risk audit report to project manager	Project management office, audit staff, project and functional managers
Lessons learned meeting and report	Prepare and communicate short report on what project team members and customers learned in the project that would reduce risks in a similar future project	Because the best lessons and insights are going to be lost unless someone facilitates a lessons learned session and report	At close-out	Lessons learned report, referencing systems, decisions, risk, outcomes, but no names	Project manager

Earned Value: A Risk Integration Indicator

The earned value management system (EVMS) is a method used to *plan, schedule, and monitor cost and schedule* performance. Earned value systems are used to ensure that risk of schedule and cost variance is monitored.

EVMS:

Measures work progress to the plan, identifying potential risk impacts

Integrates cost, schedule, and technical performance

Leads to root cause analysis to identify risk causes

Aids in making informed decisions on corrective action to mitigate risk

The Risk of "Unaccountability"

Here we discuss some organizational and management tools that facilitate risk integration: responsibility assignment matrix (RAM), the organization structure, and the cost account manager.

The RAM is the document that integrates the organizational structure and the WBS into a usable matrix for assigning work responsibilities within any given organization working on the program. The RAM may be referred to as a single point verification of authority for a given organization to expend effort on an assigned program task. Without the RAM, there is risk of performance breakdowns because of unclear accountability.

The cost account manager (CAM) concept stresses accountability for work performance and cost control at the work package level. The CAM and the support team are responsible for planning, managing, and tracking technical, schedule, and cost performance for one or more control accounts. Risk impacts are cost overruns and cost variance.

The CAM:

Participates in the identification of scope

Is responsible for schedule and budget development

Reports status cost and schedule performance

Explains and documents variances to the plan

Develops work-around and recovery plans

Reviews and updates estimate at completion (EAC)

Supports internal and customer reviews

Responsible for maintenance of EVMS reports

Identifies, tracks, and mitigates technical, schedule, and cost risk

Is responsible for budgeted cost of work scheduled (BCWS), budgeted cost of work performed (BCWP), and actual cost of work performed (ACWP) of control account

Project Manager Integration Roles

The project manager is responsible for integration of risk into the project decision making process. The project manager:

Integrates project work scope, schedule, and cost objectives

Provides for an objective assessment of accomplishments against the prospect of risk impacts

Summarizes risk data to higher levels (roll-ups) for management, critical path analysis, and decision making

Enables analysis of significant variances from the plan forecast impacts

Project managers use vertical and horizontal traceability to verify integration.

Vertical traceability occurs when all subelement tasks that support a summary element start and complete ontime.

Horizontal traceability occurs when a stated milestone or event from one schedule is identified and coordinated with another schedule. This is also referred to as project interface management, for instance, the mitigation of risk through coordination of similar milestones across projects.

Integration Issues in Budgeting

Undistributed budget.   Budget that has been authorized by a contract but as a result of an incomplete related task, has not been released to the contract team for use.

Management reserve.   Stated amount of the authorized project budget that is being held in reserve by the project/program office for contingencies and unknown unknowns. Sometimes referred to as the buffer in critical chain management, it is a "tap" on the project budget that the project manager uses to offset risks and resource bottlenecks.

Work package.   Time phased and budgeted tasks that are assigned to a specific work group, team or other entity to be accomplished. Typically the work package contains the lowest level of identifiable and budgeted tasks within a given project.

Planning package.   Planning package represents tasks that have not been planned in detail and is typically a holding package for budget that is yet to be identified in discrete tasks.

Rolling wave.   Technique for providing a plan of action and discrete budgeting and scheduling once a better definition of how to accomplish the effort is known. Typically the rolling wave is accomplished in six-month modules.

Why Integrate Risk?

Risk management is an organized systematic decision-making process that efficiently identifies risks, assesses or analyzes risks, and effectively reduces or eliminates risks to achieve program goals. Risk assessment should not be a separate process but rather an integrated part of the project planning and management process.

The purpose of risk management:

- Spans all phases of the project
- Provides an iterative process
- Is not an option or a project add-on
- Should be developed to the specific project

Integrating question. The key risk issue is "what could go wrong in the project and how can contingencies, e.g., mitigation actions be developed and integrated into the schedule so that should the risk occur, the actions to offset the risk are an integrated part of the project plan and schedule?"

Risk management planning.   The process of setting up the organization to do risk management as an integral part of the project planning process.

Risk identification.   Risks are identified during development of the WBS, in the definition of tasks in a generic WBS "data dictionary."

Risk analysis.   Assessing the qualitative and quantitative characteristics of the risk occurs during the planning process.

Risk planning/mitigation.   Contingencies to deal with risks are integrated into the WBS task structure and corrective actions scheduled into the program and project.

Risk tracking.   Earned value indicators are used to monitor risks, e.g., those risks identified in planning that will have schedule impacts are monitored when negative schedule variance indicates their impacts.

Integration and Sensitivity Analysis

Sensitivity analysis is the process of looking at what variables—project tasks, costs, materials, fixed costs, are most likely to affect project outcomes such as on-time delivery or cost control. Sensitivity analysis is integrated into project scheduling by identifying key variables in the project and their impact on costs and schedules. It can be useful to use MS Project to model a trial and error process, making changes in task durations to quantify impacts on project due dates.

Monte Carlo Risk Analysis : Quantitative Risk Integration

Here is a listing of expectations from Monte Carlo analysis.

1. How likely is any date, but particularly the critical path method date or any imposed date, to occur given the current plan?
2. Which activities contribute the most to schedule overrun risk in the project?
3. What is the exposure to risk, which is the same as asking, "How much schedule contingency do I need to drive the risk to an acceptable level?"

Four distinct steps in a Monte Carlo analysis are required in order to gain the benefit of a network:

Create a solid network.

Apply most likely optimistic and pessimistic durations for activities.

Run the Monte Carlo simulation.

Interpret results.

Special Challenges of Integrating
Risk into a Software Project

Integration of risk takes on a special meaning in the case of software development projects simply because the performance record for software projects is not good. Software presents particular integration obstacles in designing and testing.

The risk in software development is that failures turn up too late to resolve. Risk integration in software development requires that testing and verification be integrated in the design phase. This means that software engineers must be trained to iterate their designs early into the customer platform and "setting." Further, unless software engineers document their designs and communicate them early, software integration typically fails.

Third party intervention is sometimes necessary to "force" integration issues early. Text cases using customer requirements are used in such cases. In addition, change impact analysis is used to evaluate integration impacts of code and design changes.

A good integration plan includes a scheduled integration phase with gate reviews at particular milestones, including design, coding, and testing. In addition, the project team is made aware of the need to communicate across functional areas to make sure that software engineers, certification engineers, quality assurance engineers, electrical engineers, and mechanical engineers are all talking during software development.

Errors detected in integration are often difficult to address. Thus, a parallel verification process is managed to identify errors early in design, usually by another software engineer acting as a quality assurance reviewer. The purpose of verification activities is to detect and report errors that may have been introduced during the software development process. Verification activities consist of developing requirements-based test cases and procedures; executing test cases and procedures; and reviewing and analyzing requirements-based testing, structural coverage analysis, and formal qualification testing. The software engineer may serve the role of a certification engineer, generating test procedures and running tests when independence is not required.

Finally, verification should include requirements-based test cases and procedures, carried out by third party "certification" engineers. This ensures an objective integration process later in the project cycle.

Strategic Integration: The Eastern Case

The risk of inadequate integration of business strategy and program development is inherent in the nature of a business itself. Business planning, aimed at developing a business strategy considers various risks and threats to its success in the planning process. But often, the work of developing and implementing a portfolio of projects to improve the business does not align with the business priorities and plans.

This discussion uses the case approach by addressing how a typical company, the Eastern Company for purpose of this case, handles integration of strategy and programs in its business planning process. Eastern is a global manufacturer and distributor of aluminum products.

Typically, the Eastern company faces major competition and challenge from a global aluminum market and from foreign manufacturers who regularly "dump" aluminum into western markets at very low prices. Thus, there is continuous risk in the business from forces out of the control of internal company and project management. To address the risks of integration failure inherent in its business, Eastern prepared a risk-based strategic plan.

Eastern faces eight integration risks and has developed eight strategic goals to address them.

Risk 1. Required electric power will not be available at an affordable price

Strategy 1. Secure economically priced power to reduce the risk of power shortage

Risk 2. Cost increase in aluminum manufacturing will increase faster than margin

Strategy 2. Secure other resources at reasonable costs to offset the risk of cost escalation

Risk 3.   Customers will not be satisfied with Eastern's products

Strategy 3.   Cultivate customer awareness and promote customer satisfaction to avoid customer satisfaction risk

Risk 4.   Eastern's working environment will prove to be unsafe and the company will experience substantial loss of workforce and finance as a result

Strategy 4.   Create a safe working environment to control the risk of worker injury and associated costs

Risk 5.   The Eastern workforce will not grow with the technology available for continuous improvement

Strategy 5.   Build a responsible and knowledgeable workforce to avoid the risk of workforce instability

Risk 6.   Eastern will not act to improve the technology of manufacturing in time to keep ahead of competitors

Strategy 6.   Improve technology and plant equipment to produce products more efficiently to control productivity risk

Risk 7.   Pollution from Eastern facilities will lead to noncompliance with government environmental requirements

Strategy 7.   Improve Eastern's impact on the environment to avoid the cost of pollution and noncompliance

Risk 8.   Increasing waste in the manufacturing process and workforce will lead to uncontrolled costs

Strategy 8.   Reduce waste and non–value-added costs to control the risk of wasted effort

Eastern recognized the need to directly take action to sustain its ability to successfully compete on a continual basis in the world aluminum marketplace. The assumption was, despite the fact that Eastern employees—in general—were dedicated to providing the highest quality products and services to the customer at a competitive price, and to providing a positive return for our owners' investment, they were heavily unionized. The company committed to the principle that:

> We will not be able to step up to those challenges unless our employees—and the union—can see where we are going and why, and have the opportunity to "buy-in."

It is through this strategic plan and its communication plan that they saw they could accomplish alignment and reduction of their considerable risk exposure.

The strategic plan was being communicated continuously throughout the plant through special meetings and focus groups to ensure that all employees understand it and can relate their work to achieve it. Employees were being encouraged to document actions they or their teams were taking to accomplish or support particular initiatives. This process would continue as we update the plan annually and realign our policies, procedures, and organizational structure to accomplish the plan.

This strategic plan was developed by the directors of Eastern with support from area managers.

Commitment and Partnership

Eastern management and United Steelworkers of America stated directly that they were committed to this mission for the organization. It was clearly recognized that by working together to accomplish this mission, the interests of all participants would be served. All management and employees were to benefit from long-term job security, job enrichment, and the monetary rewards that result from a successful business, which was able to manage its risks. Eastern's stakeholders and owners would benefit from the product recognition and profitability gained by producing superior goods and services. Eastern's customers would benefit from the high quality and service levels delivered to them. Finally, the community was to enjoy a stable revenue base from the success of Eastern and from the skills and services individual employees offered.

Stakeholder Relations

The company stated that Eastern's "stakeholders" were people, organizations, or groups of people who have a vested interest in the success of the company. Our major stakeholders were:

Employees, who seek continued employment and income, quality of work life, and opportunities to learn and develop; their perceived risk was related to job security and lack of growth, development and marketability.

Customers, who seek quality products at low cost and reliable delivery; their perceived risk was related to product price, quality, and timing, but mostly price. Cost was a major issue as competitors dumped quality aluminum at lower prices.

Owners, who seek return on investment and continued viability; their risk was grounded in stock value.

Regulators, who seek compliance with laws and regulations; their risk was in noncompliance with regulations and the cost of enforcement and litigation.

Community, who seek contributions through taxes and service, and minimal environmental impact; their risk exposure was in losing the industry tax base but having to pay pollution and environmental control costs.

Suppliers, who seek to meet Eastern requirements and continue business with Eastern; their perceived risk lies in their inability to meet Eastern contract requirements and having to share more of the risk in contracted work than they can handle.

To illustrate the documentation of a risk-based strategy, the following document contains an executive summary, situation analysis, and a detailed description of eight key strategies. The situation analysis provides a framework for the strategies including mission and goals, management direction, SWOT analysis, and linkage to the parent company strategic plan. The eight strategies are supported by specific initiatives and a system to measure achievement of those initiatives.

This strategic plan for Eastern Aluminum Company covered a five-year period, from 1996 to 2000, and thus will help to guide the company and its employees into the twenty-first century. As the general long-term pathway to growth and profitability, the plan presents the company's approach to achieving Eastern's central strategic goal: to compete successfully on a continuing basis in the world aluminum marketplace. The plan served a wide variety of purposes, including support to ownership decisions; support to budgeting and resource allocation; guidance for management and employee planning, training and education; and support to long-term capital investment planning. A major element of the strategic planning process that produced this document is the communication of the plan and its underlying vision, assumptions, and values to our employees.

The plan explored Eastern's current strengths, weaknesses, opportunities, and threats, and presented and discussed eight basic key strategies, initiatives, and measures to accomplish the central strategic goal.

Eight Strategies

Within the overall framework of the basic strategic goal to compete successfully in the world aluminum marketplace, and to be consistent with the parent company's strategic objectives, eight key strategies were at the heart of this strategic plan:

1. *Secure economically priced power.*   Eastern would find ways to lower its power costs through a variety of strategies, including building stronger partnerships with power companies and state and local governments, and through exploration of independent options for generating less expensive power.

2. *Secure other resources at reasonable costs.*   As the cost of materials rises, Eastern planned to find low-cost sources for raw materials as well as to explore approaches for using lower graded materials. Eastern would take the initiative to assure that effective partnerships are built with quality suppliers.

3. *Cultivate customer awareness and promote customer satisfaction.*   Eastern would work to educate employees about customers and their requirements and promote closer ties with customers. Greater appreciation of customers would give employees more incentive for addressing future customer requirements and connecting their daily work more clearly with the "value chain" to the customer.

4. *Create a safe working environment.*   Eastern was working to improve its safety record through enforcement of safety and health rules and regulations. Employees would be better educated and trained to understand safety

implications of their work. Safety compliance would be considered a major performance standard for all employees.

5. *Build a responsible and knowledgeable workforce.* Facing a major workforce turnover in the next five years, Eastern placed special emphasis on strategies to build a more responsible and skilled workforce, to improve the partnership with the United Steel Workers, to improve performance and productivity, to lower labor costs, and to find better ways to work together through teamwork. They recognized that if this strategy grounded in the commitment to building a team-based organization is not accomplished, Eastern could not thrive and grow even if other strategies were accomplished.

6. *Improve technology and plant equipment to produce products more efficiently.* Eastern prided itself on its leadership in technology and technical innovation and plans to continue this industry leadership. Eastern was managing several capital improvement projects to make major breakthroughs in productivity and quality. Eastern felt it was demonstrating to its customers and its employees through these improvements that major investments are being made in the plant to meet the challenges of the future global marketplace.

7. *Improve Eastern's impact on the environment.* Through strict compliance with federal, state, and local environmental standards, Eastern would continue to respond to and anticipate environmental impacts and address them. Special emphasis were being made to meet new clean air requirements.

8. *Reduce waste and non–value-added costs.* Eastern continued to pursue quality and process improvement initiatives to eliminate unnecessary costs due to accidents, rework, and scrap, outdated positions and job requirements, and equipment damage. Employees would continue to be trained and educated in process improvement and reengineering to streamline the way work is accomplished.

Overview on Integration Issues

Eastern had already been turned around from a high-cost swing plant, with a confrontational labor atmosphere, to a much more competitive operation practicing effective and efficient management and supervision, worker empowerment, and self-directed team concepts. However, there was new urgency to integrate employee views with the business strategy, to assure that all employees understand that the plant would grow only "by permission" from future customers, and only if it continuously improved its productivity, quality, and internal cohesion and teamwork across departments. Below, we discuss how they were positioned to compete in the future.

Strengths, Weaknesses, Opportunities, and Threats

The following discussion covers Eastern strengths, weaknesses, opportunities, and threats.

Strengths

Eastern had made a concentrated effort to retain its competitive position in the marketplace through technology. Its major strength is its ability to produce quality products continuously, focus on technology and capital improvement, and keep wages and salaries relatively high for its employees while controlling costs. Capital improvements and improved management and team practices have made it possible to achieve record premium production in the recent past. Eastern continued to demonstrate its leadership in technological improvements and plant capital investment.

Eastern had experienced the longest run at full capacity in its history, remaining one of the few North American smelters not curtailed due to the recent metal surplus caused by the flow of aluminum into the world market from the Commonwealth of Independent States. Eastern continued to show resilience and responsiveness in the face of changing market conditions.

Eastern was working hard to empower our workforce, improve their knowledge, skills, and responsiveness. They sought to align their incentive and reward programs, partnership practices with hourly employees, performance appraisal systems, and quality and process improvement initiatives with our key long-term strategies. They faced the future turnover of the workforce with a strong commitment to use the opportunities that changes bring to build a leaner, more integrated and productive plant team.

At the heart of its strength was Eastern's traditional core competency to choose, operate, and improve process technology effectively; to produce a variety of difficult-to-produce premium products; and to understand and meet customer needs. Whatever initiatives Eastern undertook, it knew it had to continuously improve these drivers of success.

Weaknesses

Eastern's products (primary, slab, billet, tee, and foundry pig) were priced by the worldwide commodities market. High quality and excellent service of these products would ensure a positive customer relationship, but Eastern could not control the selling price of the finished product.

Eastern knew that it was a high cost plant, compared to other producers, primarily because of the age of the facility and technology, and because of high wages, salaries, and fringe benefit levels. Because Eastern had little or no control over the market price, the cost of producing aluminum became a key determining factor in remaining globally competitive. In fact, 75% of all aluminum in the world was being produced at a cost lower than Eastern.

Eastern faced major challenges in turning over its workforce and creating a more energetic and knowledgeable workforce team; past practices had not always inspired employees to align themselves with the plant's best interests and commit themselves to continuous improvement through teams.

Eastern needed to improve its ability to learn and document its successes; in short, to become a "learning" organization. Past practice had not always taken advantage of what the organization had already learned through the years.

Opportunities

Demand for aluminum was continuing to rise; supplies of aluminum had increased each year with primary aluminum products now sold on a worldwide basis.

Eastern had the opportunity to position itself at the midpoint on the world cost scale, the point at which 50% of world production costs would be higher than Eastern's. In achieving this position, Eastern could take more advantage of its high quality products and services and its improving productivity.

A reduction of 4 cents per pound by 1999 would have placed Eastern in that competitive position, keeping in mind that other aluminum plants are also attempting to reduce their costs.

Eastern's major opportunity was to improve its process efficiency and productivity through a combination of technology and capital improvement, building a more efficient workforce, and reducing labor costs. The 4 cents per pound cost reduction could be achieved by:

1. Conversion of potlines (production lines) to a new "point feed" technology, already underway.

2. Reduction of man-hours per ton by 15% from 1996 to 2000.

3. Reduction of non–value-added costs, wherever possible, through process improvements, total quality management, ISO 9000 certification, and other quality initiatives.

Eastern had a major opportunity to improve its human resource practices and programs as the plant transitioned its workforce in the coming five years, both through better training and development of supervisory and hourly employees, and better, more effective assessment and hiring practices.

Threats and Risks

If Eastern did not reduce costs continually, their position would worsen, because:

1. New plants with lower costs would open.

2. Existing competitive plants would reduce cost and improve their cost position.

3. Other plants with higher costs would close, worsening Eastern's position.

The most critical of these risks was the possibility that power costs would continue to rise beyond Eastern's capacity to absorb them. This scenario represented the most significant threat to Eastern's continued growth and had to be avoided. In addition to power costs, the long-term cost of coal could be another important threat to Eastern growth, as well as unanticipated environmental regulations, particularly from the federal Clean Air Act.

In addition, although Eastern had made major progress in building a more team-based culture, the process could not be slowed by resistance to change and failure to be clear about new roles and functions. Therefore, one source of threat and risk was clearly from within the threat of slow deterioration of the momentum of teamwork and process improvement already underway. Such a step backwards could always happen as a result of neglect and a lack of trust and respect in the organization.

Eastern's Strategic Plan

Eastern's strategic plan was an integrated set of strategies, initiatives, and measures supporting an overall goal of competitiveness. Figure 10.1 presents a graphic depiction of the company's eight key strategies. Each strategy was seen as serving the central goal of world competitiveness, but each strategy was also tied to the others inextricably, indicating a strong interdependency of all plan elements. If any one strategy and risk reduction plan was not accomplished, overall achievement of the goal suffered.

The plan describes plant strategies, initiatives, and measures of success. Initiatives are programs and projects, now underway or planned to help accomplish a particular strategy. Measures are indicators of progress and will be used to monitor achievement of the eight key strategies.

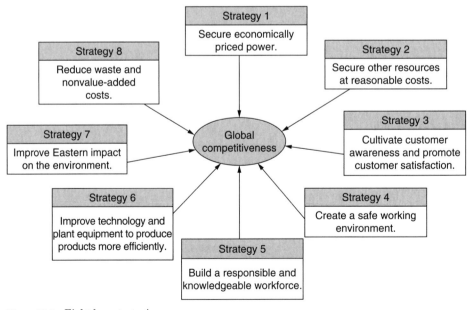

Figure 10.1   Eight key strategies.

Underlying elements of the risk-based strategic plan

Five major elements formed the basis for this risk-based strategic plan; mission, commitment and partnership, driving forces, core competencies, and stakeholder relations. They are discussed as follows.

Mission.   Eastern's mission was to be the most cost-effective producer of the highest quality primary aluminum products, shipped on time to its customers, with optimum utilization of resources. They placed special emphasis on employees and their role in defining mission, and on good community relations. They recognized that accomplishing our mission involved a never-ending journey of continuous improvement.

Commitment and partnership.   Eastern management and United Steelworkers of America indicated that they were committed to this mission for the organization. It was clearly recognized that by working together to accomplish this mission, the interests of all participants were best served. All management and employees would benefit from long-term job security, job enrichment, and the monetary rewards that resulted from a successful business. Eastern's stakeholders and owners would benefit from the product recognition and profitability, gained by producing superior goods and services. Eastern's customers would benefit from the high quality and service levels delivered to them. Finally, the community would enjoy a stable revenue base from the success of Eastern and from the skills and services individual employees can offer.

Driving force: production capability.   An underlying element in this strategic plan was the single most important driver of company success: its capability to convert resources effectively into products through highly organized and managed production processes. Their value added for the future will continue to be their capacity to produce products continuously.

Core competencies and risk contingencies.   Three core competencies separated Eastern from its competitors:

1. *Capacity to effectively choose, operate, and improve process technology.*   Its ability to keep up with technology change was rooted in its ability to anticipate technology risk stemming from out-of-date technology.
2. *Capacity to produce a variety of difficult premium products.*   Its ability to change its production systems quickly was rooted in its ability to anticipate the risks of change in product requirements and plan for them.
3. *Capacity to understand and service customer needs.*   Its capacity to understand its customers and especially to anticipate and manage customer services to reduce the risk of failed customer service expectations.

Eastern would strive to maintain and build on these core competencies.

Eight Key Strategies

Eastern identified eight key strategies to carry out its central strategic goal of global competitiveness. Each strategy was being carried out through several initiatives and was being monitored by the measures shown.

They are presented and discussed in the following.

Strategy 1. Secure economically priced power

The cost of power was a major factor in Eastern's strategic plan. In its partnership with the community, power companies, and state and local government, Eastern would develop support for its efforts to continue to compete in the world aluminum marketplace. Eastern planned to negotiate lower power costs and to explore independent options for generating less expensive power.

Initiatives	Measures	Risks
Address power pricing issues by: Maintaining relationships with Potomac Edison, Public Service Commission, People's Council, local and state government Investigate power wheeling sources and benefits Develop alternative power sources, including self-generation Increase community support for reducing Eastern's power costs Eliminate power modulation	Reduced power costs by 2–4 mills per kilowatt hour (approximately $6–12 million/year) Favorable public response and concern for Eastern's power pricing issues	That relationships with stakeholder agencies would deteriorate That power wheeling sources (independent sources of power created by deregulation) would not provide lower prices That self-generation of power would fail either from technology problems or cost That the community would not support Eastern That power modulation—the practice of energy providers to reduce power—could not be anticipated

Power costs became the key factor in maintaining competitiveness because of impending major increases in costs from new sources. Eastern management was working closely with utilities, government officials, the community, and other power sources to assure that it can achieve independence in power generation, should that be necessary. Power wheeling sources and benefits were being pursued as well as self-generation options.

While this issue is beyond the scope of any one employee, special attention was being given to communicate the power cost issue to all employees so that they could understand the urgency of the situation and help Eastern to achieve power independence.

Strategy 2. Secure other resources at reasonable costs

The cost of materials continued to rise and had the potential to erase savings created by increased productivity and reduced power costs. Eastern planned to find low cost sources for raw materials as well as explore approaches for using lower graded materials. Eastern would continue to manage human resources costs through employee attrition and retirements.

Initiatives	Measures	Risks
Obtain raw materials such as petroleum coke, pitches, alumina, and hardeners Secure high-quality supplies from the most economical sources	Maintain or decrease current raw material costs	That raw materials would not be available on a just-in-time basis
Manage human resource (labor) costs through attrition and retirements	Reduce man-hours per ton by 15% by the year 2000 Contribute to overall efficiency and productivity	That human resource costs would inflate and attrition goals would not be achieved
Explore innovative approaches to using lower-graded materials, such as calciner fines and lower grades of petroleum coke	Maintain or decrease current raw material costs	That lower-graded materials would be acquired

Key raw materials (alumina, aluminum fluoride, petroleum coke, and liquid pitch) were purchased for all parent company smelters by the same parent office. These costs were rising to a point such that the Eastern's overall cost effectiveness was threatened.

This issue challenged the company's capacity to find and use lower graded materials, such as calciner fines and lower grades of petroleum coke. The company would continue to acquire both raw materials and supplies from the most efficient sources, while assuring quality. This involved forming partnerships with suppliers to limit the number of such sources. This would accomplish two objectives: holding down costs and minimizing purchasing and warehousing requirements.

As a major cost element, labor costs had to be controlled while productivity was enhanced through capital improvements and better management, team, and individual performance. Reduction of man-hours per ton by 15% by the year 2000 was a major measure of success in reducing risk exposure.

Strategy 3. Cultivate customer awareness and promote customer satisfaction

Eastern continued to provide consistent and high-quality products and services to end-users and customers. The company would work to ensure that all employees were aware of customers and their needs. Emphasis on the customer would encourage the development of new products and services, and help Eastern establish a larger market niche. Eastern would look to external stakeholders to verify gains made in employee customer awareness and customer satisfaction.

Initiatives	Measures	Risks
Enhance employees awareness about customer and end product satisfaction	Third party assessment of employees' customer awareness Recognition through accreditation and quality audits (American Association for Laboratory Accreditation, etc.)	That employees were not able to connect their success with company's success in end product quality
Selectively diversify products and services to support market expansion	Capacity to change products Number of customer assists through the Metal Quality Group	That its product mix could not be diversified
Support parent company marketing strategy Market services to make customers aware of Eastern's capabilities	Alumax Inventory Management System (AIMS) data Customer team visit comments Customer satisfaction data	That the parent company's strategy was not consistent with Eastern's strategic plan and core competence
Focus on individual customer demands in metallurgy, product chemistry, packaging and delivery requirements through process improvement Develop a long-term cast house plan and monitoring systems	International Standards Organization (ISO) 9000 registration QS 9002 accreditation Monitor customer claims and contacts about technology services and products Review customer satisfaction survey results Improve product turnaround indicators	That Eastern's process improvement efforts were not successful because of personnel and union disincentives
Set up cross-functional teams to increase awareness on internal customers	Internal customer satisfaction surveys Extent to which internal customer requirements are met	That cross functional teams would not work because of internal conflicts and role definitions

Eastern had to establish a market niche in high-quality, premium products to remain a viable company and successfully compete. To meet this demand, Eastern had to work closely with its ownership to identify future customer needs. Eastern would continue to work with parent company marketing teams in the areas of initial order processing, customer team visits, and customer surveys.

Eastern would also make it easier for customers to deal with the plant. Increased use of bar code systems and electronic data interchange would be planned, establishing a "seamless" electronic relationship with prospective customers. More attention would be paid to promoting our laboratory and metallography capabilities.

The continuing move to improve quality worldwide was having its impact on the company. More customer inquiries, e.g., from the automotive industry, were expected regarding our quality standards. This development prompted efforts to maintain registration and refine documentation to both ISO 9000 and American Association of Laboratory Accreditation, and for attaining QS 9000 and 14000 certification as well. Increased cycle time was becoming a major customer expectation, generating internal plans to develop systems to measure order entry, production scheduling, and shipping performance.

Finally, because many employees did not have a direct relationship with customers and customer needs, the company was undertaking a program to enhance employee appreciation of customer needs. This program included use of a third party organization to monitor employees' understanding of these issues.

Strategy 4. Create a safe working environment

Eastern had significantly reduced accidents in recent years, and needed the support of employees and management to continue these safety efforts. In addition to developing and implementing state-of-the-art safety procedures and guidelines, the company needed to enforce safety and health rules and regulations consistently.

Initiatives	Measures	Risks
Eliminate safety and health hazards by: Upgrading engineering standards, safety features, and ergonomics consistently Promoting employee awareness Updating joint safety and health committee guidelines Enforce rules and regulations Increase team and employee accountability for safety and health	Decrease accident incident rate Stay within accident and safety scorecard budget Improve safety severity ratio index Rate of completion of items on safety list and audits Improvements in efficiency and job performance Improved plant safety performance record Increased safety gain sharing payout	That safety initiatives would not be accepted and implemented by employees and managers That safety guidelines and regulations would shift substantially

Eastern recognized its responsibility and accountability for the safety and health of each employee and for the preservation of property and equipment. The company would continue to incorporate into the design and operation of all facilities, safeguards, and procedures, which will minimize risks of personal injury and loss of property and equipment. Management was responsible and accountable for the safety and safe work conduct of all employees who report to them. Employees were equally responsible and accountable for safe practices as well as assisting in the ongoing safety program by reporting unsafe practices, procedures, or conditions when they were observed.

As indicated in the initiatives underway under this strategy, Eastern was giving special priority to upgrading engineering standards to reflect safety requirements and criteria. In some cases, this could have meant added cost and time constraints on planned capital projects, an expense well worth the investment in a safer working environment.

Strategy 5. Build a responsible and knowledgeable workforce

By increasing the skills and abilities of individuals, teams, and supervisors and empowering them, Eastern would be able to increase productivity, reduce operating costs, solve personnel problems, and increase teamwork across the entire plant. Initiatives in support of this priority included training and developmental opportunities in support of self-directed work teams.

Initiatives	Measures	Risks
Develop or continue: Continuation of empowered, self-directed work team development (decision making and responsibility) New performance appraisal system for salaried employees Development planning Knowledge and skills training for bargaining unit employees Supervisory development program Strategic plan communication process Conversion to parent salary structure New bargaining unit job classification (stemming from the labor contract) HR strategic plan	Better communication and coordination within team members and between supervisors and teams Innovative, timely, and sound employee and team decision making Better use of tools, equipment, and raw materials Employees will be prepared to assume new responsibilities as a result of developmental exposure Enhanced partnership agreement Increase in ideas and solutions from employees Reduce man-hours per ton	That self-directed teams would not work in the unionized work setting That employees would not act on incentives to train and develop new skills That the strategic plan and communication plan is not effective in improving employee support of company's goals.
Offer developmental opportunities to sustain employee education and growth through: Mentoring Inside training Outside technical managerial training Opportunities to manage	Successful development planning Track progress through training records Enhanced employee performance	That the plant could not implement mentoring and training initiatives because of the company culture

Strategy 5 held the key to successful achievement of the balance of the other strategies—the building of a workforce and organization that: (1) was aligned with the strategic direction of Eastern; (2) was structured, capable, and motivated to improve performance; and (3) worked together across departments to provide a "seamless" process of production and quality.

In building a flatter, more streamlined workforce, the company's strategy in the past had been to press for reduced manning and more teams and teamwork. As a result, many teams had been generated and trained to take responsibility to solve problems and make decisions necessary to keep their process operating at peak efficiency. Supervisory and hourly positions were reduced and roles and functions were changed.

Now in the spirit of building the total Eastern organization, the company's strategic emphasis would go beyond reduced manning and generation of teams. The strategy would be focused on organizational effectiveness: building the whole organization through a stronger linkage and alignment between management, supervisors, and bargaining unit employees. The opportunity before company management was to build new supervisory roles and functions into new team-based organization, requiring development of leadership skills, better business and productivity management and monitoring skills, and more support for technical supervision and cross-department process improvement. Support services, such as human resources management were to help to lead the effort. Organizational barriers to effective supervision would be identified and eliminated. Organizational and training initiatives were underway to help supervisors function as the guiding force for day-to-day operations.

Development tools would include business and productivity management, process improvement, facilitating and mentoring opportunities, inside training, outside development (technical and managerial), and management opportunities within the organization. To focus on incentives, Eastern would review its performance appraisal and gain sharing structure to assure that they were aligned with this strategic plan, and make improvements when called for.

To assure effective communication, quarterly plant communication meetings would continue and more information provided to employees "on line," especially in the area of human resources.

Strategy 6. Improve technology and plant equipment to produce products more efficiently

The company was managing several capital improvement projects to upgrade the condition of equipment and work processes at the plant. The company needed to continue these improvements while also employing sound capital project management skills. Eastern would work to speed up completion of these capital projects and to keep them within budget and quality requirements.

Initiatives	Measures	Risks
Complete capital program and budgets each year Conduct major maintenance projects and overhauls	Completion of capital improvements, including; Conversion of potlines to point feed technology Substation life extension Cast house continuous homogenizing furnace Rod shop anode cleaner Ladle shop ladle cleaner Bake oven rebuild Potline capacity expansion Rebuilt remelt furnace Developed stack filter systems for metal treatment Facilities expansion Completed stamper upgrades for billet and slab	That capital budgets would not be completed That maintenance projects are not completed for a variety of reasons
Conduct research to ensure that Eastern adapts or incorporates improved or emerging technologies	Completion of R&D projects within budget	That necessary research on emerging technologies is not conducted
Develop a stronger capital project management system (CPARs) through training and other developmental assignments	Improved capacity to complete projects on time within budget and schedule	That the SPARS system is not made operational

As evidenced in the partial list of capital improvements above, Eastern was heavily engaged in upgrading its technological and equipment base in order to maintain its leadership and core competency. The company was a front-runner in keeping pace with required capital improvements to aging plant infrastructure. Improvements were underway in the product production lines, carbon plant, cast house, substation, and laboratory, and in general, plant functions such as emission and noise control, and information system management.

The focus for this strategic plan was the completion of capital projects within budget, schedule, and technical requirements. This meant developing a stronger capital project management system and employing more effective project management practices.

Strategy 7. Improve Eastern's impact on the environment

The company would continue to monitor its impact on the local environment. These efforts would be directed toward reducing environmental degradation and pollution.

Initiatives	Measures	Risks
Comply with Federal, state, and local environmental regulations by: Providing proactive assistance to regulators Educating employees about regulatory requirements Promptly reporting noncompliance and correcting any violations Filing title vs. air permit application	Eliminate incidents of noncompliance Monitor response time for identifying and fixing violations	That new regulations would be enacted that Eastern could not respond to
Participating in voluntary activities on environment, safety and health issues, such as EPA greenlights, reducing greenhouse gases and PFCs, and noise nuisance reduction	Eliminate environmental, safety or health complaints about the plant or its operations	That voluntary efforts do not improve community relations
Encouraging environmentally sound industrial and agricultural growth	Partnerships with state and local agencies	That local growth objectives and dynamics would change substantially
Continuing with farm production	Farm production and maintenance of safe environmental practices	That the company's efforts on farm production around the fringe of the plant were unsuccessful

This strategy addressed the company's environmental and community relations practices. Eastern would continue to stay ahead of environmental requirements through two basic approaches: (1) being proactive in assisting regulators at all levels in developing sound and cost-effective regulations that implement both environmental legislation and meet the needs of community and the business; and (2) planning and implementing capital improvements and operating measures to comply with environmental requirements, and at the same time attempting to assure that such improvements also contribute to overall plant productivity.

Costs of compliance would increase as well in the administrative areas of record keeping, reporting, training, planning, and monitoring, and in acquisition of necessary monitoring equipment, creating the need to streamline these systems. Eastern would continue to develop the capacity to prevent pollution through technology improvements and through a multimedia approach that addresses losses of material to air, storm water runoff and solid or liquid waste streams.

Strategy 8. Reduce waste and non–value-added costs

Eastern continued to experience waste and non–value-added costs, such as safety and property costs related to accidents, rework and scrap, and equipment damage. Process improvement and problem-solving teams would continue to focus on reducing these costs.

Initiatives	Measures	Risks
Involve Q.U.E.S.T. teams in identifying and resolving quality problems in key production processes	Amount of rework and scrap by department on a monthly basis Stay within approved budget guidelines for rework and scrap costs	That the company QUEST (quality) teams were not successful in resolving quality issues
Minimize equipment damage by educating employees, monitoring equipment use, and enforcing rules for properly using equipment	Review monthly maintenance to ensure departmental account-ability for responsible equipment use Stay within approved budget guidelines for equipment expenses	That equipment damage rates continued
Eliminate duplication of effort in administrative processes Process improvement/ reengineering Encourage employee use of best practice techniques	Benchmark other processes Monitor process costs	That administrative redundancy and increase in costs of operation continued
Improve inventory management of supplies and equipment (includes maintenance, production, and raw material in-process)	Reduce inventory by at least 5%	That inventory management initiatives were not successful because of internal plant or supplier performance limitations
Minimize waste generation and increase recycling	Waste product reductions	That increasing rates of waste production would continue

This strategy was in line with strategy 5, to build a knowledgeable and productive workforce. Both were required to improve overall productivity. This strategy was key to improving the overall productivity of Eastern by eliminating waste and unnecessary work, for example, by reducing the cost of poor quality through process improvement and ISO and QS 9000 and 14000 documentation.

The company's quality and process improvement efforts started on the production floor where quality was built in through consistent practices and extensive use of statistical process control methods. Eastern was committed to being quality-driven, not cost-driven, thus the quickest route to elimination of waste and non-value added costs was "doing it right the first time." They looked to this strategy to be a major factor in lowering operating expenses by four cents per pound.

The Q.U.E.S.T. teams would continue to identify and resolve quality problems in key production processes; a new focus would be placed on administrative and support processes to assure that they were under review in the context of process improvement as well.

Communicating Strategy and Risk

The company prepared a communication program to promote the company strategy and to explain the risks inherent in the business and the local plant setting. The structure of that plan was as illustrated in Fig. 10.1.

Postscript to the Strategic Plan

The Eastern strategic plan had been designed as a guidepost for the future, a way of realizing the vision of becoming more responsive to changes going on globally, more supportive to customers and employees, and more cost effective in manufacturing processes. However, it was not a "cookbook" for success. They recognized that management and employees would continue to have to make informed judgments together each day to make the plan work. And they would have to learn from their successes and mistakes.

Acquisition and Merger

Although the strategic planning and risk reduction process was a focused and comprehensive process, and had measurable impacts on plant productivity and success in dealing with its costs and product problems, a major development was not anticipated in the process—acquisition.

During the process of developing and implementing the plan, the company was acquired by a competing parent company, creating a high degree of uncertainty and disruption in the process. Work in implementing the plan was halted until the acquisition and merger process was completed, thus tempering what payoffs could have been produced.

Integration in Global and International Projects

Global international projects inherently face difficult integration issues, simply because the normal and typical integration barriers are compounded by political, national, and language issues. Projects to assist developing countries, for instance, are typically managed by the collective of non-governmental (NGO), national, donor country managers, and local team members, who often do not agree on the purposes and goals of the project. Opportunities for fraud, waste, and abuse are again compounded because of the many *players*.

This book is intended to provide some useful guidelines for international project managers to control and deliver in their projects, not by sidestepping the *players*, but by working with them.

Postscript on Integration and the Eastern Case

The Eastern case is an interesting application of integration issues at the strategic level, e.g., how does a company integrate its strategic objectives with its program of projects, in this case the manufacturing and tooling improvements. And how does it integrate its strategies with its employees, in this case aligning key union leaders and its own plant management on the key issues. And then how do individual projects improve the manufacturing process—reducing power usage in the making of aluminum get designed and implemented.

How to Use the Integration Tools in Microsoft Project

Microsoft Project is a project integration tool and it is particularly useful in integrating task, schedule, cost, and quality.

WBS and Task Outline

As shown in Fig. 11.1, tasks are outlined to show major summary tasks, e.g., Develop Project Management, and are then broken down into subtasks, such as project scope management, that build, or roll up to the summary task. This is the beginning of integrating tasks so that the level of work breakdown is scaled to the particular needs of the project.

Linkages between tasks is accomplished through identification of predecessors. These linkages integrate tasks with each other, thus this is a second integration function of the software.

Tasks are integrated with resources next through the assignment of resources to individual tasks by highlighting the task and adding resources and percent assignment in the task information box.

Costs are then estimated for each resource after resources are assigned. MS Project allows cost entry in the resource sheet view where personnel resources are listed. See Fig. 11.2.

Then durations are estimated for each task based on the best guess or standard duration for that task, as shown in Fig. 11.3. This completes the definition of work that is the basis for MS Project assumptions—work = time × resources. Each task is measured not only in terms of the definition of the work itself in a generic work breakdown structure with deliverables, but also in terms of time and resources, such as *5 person days*. Thus the actual work of the task is defined in terms *of how long it will take, given the resources assigned to do it.*

Fixed costs, such as equipment and capital assets, are estimated and entered in a different view and table. Since fixed costs are associated with tasks, not

ID	% complete	ⓘ	Task name	Duration	Start	Finish	Predecessors	Resource group	01 Q3
32	0%		**Develop project management**	**38 days**	**Tue 11/27/07**	**Thu 1/17/08**			
33	0%		Project scope management	2 days	Tue 11/27/07	Wed 11/28/07	31		
34	0%		Generic work breakdown	2 days	Thu 11/29/07	Fri 11/30/07	33		
35	0%		Schedule management plan	2 days	Mon 12/3/07	Tue 12/4/07	34		
36	0%		Cost management plan	2 days	Wed 12/5/07	Thu 12/6/07	35		
37	0%		Quality management plan	2 days	Fri 12/7/07	Mon 12/10/07	36		
38	0%		Process improvement plan	2 days	Tue 12/11/07	Wed 12/12/07	37		
39	0%		Staffing management plan	2 days	Thu 12/13/07	Fri 12/14/07	38		
40	0%		Communication management	2 days	Mon 12/17/07	Tue 12/18/07	39		
41	0%		Risk management plan	2 days	Wed 12/19/07	Thu 12/20/07	40		
42	0%		Procurement management plan	2 days	Fri 12/21/07	Mon 12/24/07	41		
43	0%		Milestone list	2 days	Tue 12/25/07	Wed 12/26/07	42		
44	0%		Resource calendar	2 days	Thu 12/27/07	Fri 12/28/07	43		
45	0%		Schedule baseline	2 days	Mon 12/31/07	Tue 1/1/08	44		
46	0%		Cost baseline	2 days	Wed 1/2/08	Thu 1/3/08	45		

Figure 11.1 Gantt chart view, entry table.

ID	ⓘ	Task	Resource name	Type	Material label	Initials	Group	Max. units	Std. rate	Ovt. rate	Cos
1			Test eng	Work		T		100%	$70.00/hr	$0.00/hr	
2			ME	Work		M		100%	$70.00/hr	$0.00/hr	
3			Bob Smathers	Work		B		100%	$70.00/hr	$0.00/hr	
4			Bill Carter	Work		B		100%	$70.00/hr	$0.00/hr	
5			John Smoltz	Work		J		100%	$70.00/hr	$0.00/hr	
6			Ryan Brookings	Work		R		100%	$70.00/hr	$0.00/hr	
7			Ryan Brown	Work		R		100%	$70.00/hr	$0.00/hr	
8			Pete Hallings	Work		P		100%	$70.00/hr	$0.00/hr	
9	◇		**Bill Dow**	**Work**		**B**		**100%**	**$70.00/hr**	**$0.00/hr**	
10			Ben Gay	Work		B		100%	$70.00/hr	$0.00/hr	
11			Bob Harris	Work		B		100%	$70.00/hr	$0.00/hr	
12			Bart Starr	Work		B		100%	$70.00/hr	$0.00/hr	
13			Dennis Bloom	Work		D		100%	$70.00/hr	$0.00/hr	
14			Bud Manaker	Work		B		100%	$70.00/hr	$0.00/hr	
15			Bart Werrel	Work		B		100%	$70.00/hr	$0.00/hr	
16			Ben Schwartz	Work		B		100%	$70.00/hr	$0.00/hr	

Figure 11.2 Resource sheet.

ID	% complete	ⓘ	Task name	Duration	Start	Finish	Predecessors	Resource group	01 Q3
176	0%		**Performance requirements**	**95 days**	**Tue 6/3/08**	**Tue 10/14/08**	**71**		
177	0%	▦	Requirements analysis	15 days	Wed 6/4/08	Tue 6/24/08	71		
178	0%	▦	Data analysis	19 wks	Tue 6/3/08	Tue 10/14/08	71		
179	0%		Simulation studies	14 days	Wed 6/4/08	Mon 6/23/08	71		
180	0%		**Interface integration**	**70 days**	**Wed 6/4/08**	**Tue 9/9/08**	**71**		
181	0%		Electrical	16.5 days	Wed 6/4/08	Thu 6/26/08	71		
182	0%	▦	Mechanical	5 wks	Wed 6/4/08	Tue 7/8/08	71		
183	0%		Software	4 wks	Wed 6/4/08	Tue 7/1/08	71		
184	0%	▦	Powertrain	*14 wks*	Wed 6/4/08	Tue 9/9/08	71		
185	0%	▦	Wheels	0.6 wks	Wed 6/4/08	Fri 6/6/08	71		
186	0%		**Outsource controls**	**5 days**	**Wed 6/4/08**	**Tue 6/10/08**	**71**		
187	0%	▦	Contracts	0.1 wks	Wed 6/4/08	Wed 6/4/08	71		
188	0%		Supplier negotiations	2.5 days	Wed 6/4/08	Fri 6/6/08	71		
189	0%	▦	Collaboration and partnering	1 wk	Wed 6/4/08	Tue 6/10/08	71		

Figure 11.3 Gantt chart view, entry table.

ID	Fixed cost	Fixed cost accrual	Total cost	Baseline	Variance	Actual	Remaining	2001	
								Q2	Q3
67	**$0.00**	**Prorated**	**$22,400.00**	**$22,400.00**	**$0.00**	**$0.00**	**$22,400.00**		
68	$0.00	Prorated	$2,100.00	$2,100.00	$0.00	$0.00	$2,100.00		
69	$0.00	Prorated	$4,200.00	$4,200.00	$0.00	$0.00	$4,200.00		
70	$0.00	Prorated	$0.00	$0.00	$0.00	$0.00	$0.00		
71	$0.00	Prorated	$4,900.00	$4,900.00	$0.00	$0.00	$4,900.00		
72	$0.00	Prorated	$2,800.00	$2,800.00	$0.00	$0.00	$2,800.00		
73	$0.00	Prorated	$8,400.00	$8,400.00	$0.00	$0.00	$8,400.00		
74	**$0.00**	**Prorated**	**$822,860.00**	**$737,240.00**	**$85,620.00**	**$0.00**	**$822,860.00**		
75	**$0.00**	**Prorated**	**$127,740.00**	**$3,360.00**	**$124,380.00**	**$0.00**	**$127,740.00**		
76	$50,000.00	Prorated	$50,560.00	$560.00	$50,000.00	$0.00	$50,560.00		
77	$0.00	Prorated	$560.00	$1,120.00	($560.00)	$0.00	$560.00		
78	$75,500.00	Prorated	$76,060.00	$1,120.00	$74,940.00	$0.00	$76,060.00		
79	$0.00	Prorated	$560.00	$560.00	$0.00	$0.00	$560.00		
80	**$0.00**	**Prorated**	**$295,840.00**	**$191,520.00**	**$104,320.00**	**$0.00**	**$295,840.00**		

Figure 11.4 Gantt chart, cost table.

resources, but fixed costs are entered into the cost table and Gantt chart as shown in Fig. 11.4.

Figure 11.5 shows the impact of PERT analysis of one task, safety (ID153). Here, three alternative durations are estimated for this task—expected, optimistic, and pessimistic. Then weights are placed on each scenario by the project manager, depending on risk severity in that task and other information in the risk assessment and documentation in a risk matrix. Then MS Project calculates a new duration based on the weights and durations estimates. The new duration (10.8 wks) is the result of that calculation. This is risk-based scheduling,

ID	% complete	🛈	Task name	Duration	Start	Finish	Predecessors	Resource group	Apr
153	0%	🖿	Safety	10.8 wks	Wed 6/4/08	Mon 8/18/08	71		▬▬▬
154	0%		Security	14 days	Wed 6/4/08	Mon 6/23/08	71		
155	0%		Seating	2 wks	Wed 6/4/08	Tue 6/17/08	71		
156	0%		Visibility	1 day	Wed 6/4/08	Wed 6/4/08	71		
157	0%		Controls	2 days	Wed 6/4/08	Thu 6/5/08	71		
158	0%	🖿	Dashboard	3 days	Wed 6/4/08	Fri 6/6/08	71		
159	0%		Trunk	10 days	Wed 6/4/08	Fri 6/27/08	71		
160	0%	🖿	Hood	5 days	Wed 6/4/08	Tue 6/10/08	71		
161	0%	🖿	Tires	3 days	Wed 6/4/08	Tue 6/10/08	71		
162	0%		Capacity	5 days	Wed 6/4/08	Tue 6/10/08	71		
163	**0%**		**Six sigma supplier management**	**86.81 days**	**Wed 6/4/08**	**Thu 10/2/08**	**71**		▬▬
164	0%		Key processes	11.5 days	Wed 6/4/08	Thu 6/19/08	71		
165	0%	🖿	Process performance indicat	8 wks	Wed 6/4/08	Thu 10/2/08	71		▬▬▬
166	0%		Process improvement strateg	3 wks	Wed 6/4/08	Tue 6/24/08	71		
167	0%		Measures	3 days	Wed 6/4/08	Fri 6/6/08	71		
168	0%		Data collection	3 days	Wed 6/4/08	Fri 6/6/08	71		

Figure 11.5 Gantt chart, PERT chart view.

ID	Task Name	Act. Start	Act. Finish	% Comp.	Act. Dur.	Rem. Dur.	Act. Cost	Act. Work
	Critical: No	**Thu 4/17/97**	**NA**	**17%**	**9.72 wks**	**47.48 wks**	**($95,936.00)**	**849 hrs**
1	Select architect	Thu 4/17/97	NA	2%	0.77 wks	38.63 wks	$1,040.00	49 hrs
2	Recruit and train managers	Thu 4/17/97	Fri 6/27/97	100%	10.28 wks	0 wks	$5,872.00	312 hrs
5	Create production design	Tue 6/17/97	Mon 7/14/97	100%	4 wks	0 wks	$3,528.00	164 hrs
6	Building concept	Thu 5/1/97	Wed 5/14/97	100%	2 wks	0 wks	$4,312.00	88 hrs
10	Permits and approvals	Tue 8/5/97	NA	12%	0.36 wks	2.64 wks	$1,680.00	24 hrs
12	Plant personnel recruiting	NA	NA	0%	0 wks	8 wks	$0.00	0 hrs
13	Equipment procurement	NA	NA	0%	0 wks	24 wks	$0.00	0 hrs
14	Raw material procurement	Tue 7/15/97	NA	80%	6.44 wks	1.56 wks	$2,632.00	132 hrs
16	Product distribution plan	NA	NA	0%	0 wks	2 wks	$0.00	0 hrs
17	Landscaping	NA	NA	0%	0 wks	3 wks	$0.00	0 hrs
18	Truck fleet procurement	NA	NA	0%	0 wks	8 wks	$0.00	0 hrs
22	Sales/revenues	Mon 6/2/97	NA	5%	2 wks	36 wks	###########	80 hrs
	Critical: Yes	**Thu 4/17/97**	**NA**	**39%**	**######## #**	**36.11 wks**	**$228,488.03**	**707.92 hrs**
3	Select real estate consultant	Tue 7/1/97	NA	89%	1.79 wks	0.21 wks	$1,824.00	68 hrs

Figure 11.6 Tracking Gantt and tracking table.

using risk information to place weights on expected, optimistic, and pessimistic estimates of task duration.

This function integrates risk into scheduling by giving the project manager a way to reflect risk information and insight from the risk management process directly into the scheduling and planning process.

Actual costs are entered into MS Project through the tracking Gantt and tracking table (Fig. 11.6). Here the project manager can enter actual hours worked or costs incurred during a given period. But this requires the deactivation of the MS Project-automatic calculation of actuals based on work performed. The best integration can be achieved through an electronic interface between the company time

ID	Task name	BCWS	BCWP	ACWP	SV	CV	EAC	BAC	VAC
112	Vertical integration	$1,120.00	$0.00	$0.00	($1,120.00)	$0.00	$1,120.00	$1,120.00	$0.00
113	International	$0.00	$0.00	$0.00	$0.00	$0.00	$0.00	$0.00	$0.00
114	Supply internal	$5,600.00	$0.00	$0.00	($5,600.00)	$0.00	$4,480.00	$5,600.00	($1,120.00)
115	**Configuration MI**	**$2,800.00**	**$0.00**	**$44,880.00**	**($2,800.00)**	**($44,880.00)**	**$53,920.00**	**$2,800.00**	**$51,120.00**
116	Software tai	$0.00	$0.00	$44,880.00	$0.00	($44,880.00)	$52,800.00	$0.00	$52,800.00
117	Data entry	$0.00	$0.00	$0.00	$0.00	$0.00	$560.00	$0.00	$560.00
118	Change management	$0.00	$0.00	$0.00	$0.00	$0.00	$560.00	$0.00	$560.00
119	**Tooling**	**$0.00**	**$0.00**	**$0.00**	**$0.00**	**$0.00**	**$11,200.00**	**$0.00**	**$11,200.00**
120	Pre manufacture	$0.00	$0.00	$0.00	$0.00	$0.00	$2,800.00	$0.00	$2,800.00
121	Safety system	$0.00	$0.00	$0.00	$0.00	$0.00	$2,800.00	$0.00	$2,800.00
122	Drawing	$0.00	$0.00	$0.00	$0.00	$0.00	$2,800.00	$0.00	$2,800.00
123	Alignment	$0.00	$0.00	$0.00	$0.00	$0.00	$2,800.00	$0.00	$2,800.00
124	**Electrical components**	**$4,480.00**	**$0.00**	**$0.00**	**($4,480.00)**	**$0.00**	**$2,240.00**	**$4,480.00**	**($2,240.00)**
125	Component designs	$2,240.00	$0.00	$0.00	($2,240.00)	$0.00	$2,240.00	$2,240.00	$0.00
126	**Chassis assembly**	**$85,120.00**	**$0.00**	**$0.00**	**($85,120.00)**	**$0.00**	**$168,000.00**	**$85,120.00**	**$82,880.00**
127	Panels	$36,400.00	$0.00	$0.00	($36,400.00)	$0.00	$36,400.00	$36,400.00	$0.00

Figure 11.7 Tracking Gantt and earned value table.

ID	☉	Resource name	Details	Apr 12, '98							Apr 19, '9
				S	M	T	W	T	F	S	S
1	◈	**Facility Specialist**	Work		8.33h	8.33h	8.33h	8.33h	3.42h		
		Recruit and train men	Work								
		Select real estate	Work								
		Building concept	Work								
		Building design	Work								
		Site selection	Work								
			Work								
		Building construction	Work								
		Plant personnel	Work								
		Equipment installation	Work		3.42h	3.42h	3.42h	3.42h	3.42h		
		Landscaping	Work		4.92h	4.92h	4.92h	4.92h			
	📊	*Select architect*	Work								
2		Project manager	Work								
		Recruit and train men	Work								
		Select Real estate	Work								
		Select General Co	Work								
		Permits and approval	Work								

Figure 11.8   Resource usage view.

sheet and purchasing system to allow automatic entry of real-time costs into MS Project. This now allows the project manager to see true earned value at any point in the project, without entering any actual costs or hours manually.

Earned value is calculated and presented in Fig. 11.7, showing the schedule variance (SV) between the budgeted cost of work performed and the budget cost of work scheduled at any given point in the project. Cost variance, the variance between the budgeted cost of work performed and the *actual* cost of that work performed, is also shown along with estimate at completion, budget at completion, and variance at completion.

In order to keep track of actual work to be performed by resources assigned to individual or multiple projects, the resource usage view allows the project manager to see each assigned worker on the project and a breakdown of work to be performed based on the plan, by task. Note that the facility specialist is overallocated and associated work shows in red—based on an 8-hour day the specialist is over allocated by 0.33 hours during the week shown (Fig. 11.8).

Integrating Projects in Microsoft Project

One of the challenges of program management is running several projects at once, orchestrating and monitoring several projects, all with their own project

ID	% complete	☉	Task name	Duration	Start	Finish	sou Grou	20 Q2
1	0%		**Integrated Transportation System**	343 days	Mon 6/25/07	Wed 10/15/08		
243	0%	📄	**New Plant**	263.1 days	Fri 6/1/07	Wed 6/4/08		

Figure 11.9   Integrated program of projects.

ID	Resource name	Details	8/26	9/2	September 9/9	9/16	9/23	October 9/30	10/7	10/14
	Integration Gateway 3: O	Work								
	Integration Gateway 4: G	Work								
	Integration Gateway 5: S	Work								
	Business strategy	Work	40h							
	Portfolio development	Work		32h						
	Project selection criteri	Work		8h	24h					
	Demand studies	Work			16h	24h				
43	Ben Sheets	Work								
	Systems design	Work								
	Hardware	Work								
1	Facility specialist	Work	12h	10.8h	6h	8.4h	12.85h	8h	4.55h	2.4h
	Select an architect	Work								
	Select real estate	Work								
	Building concept	Work								
	Building design	Work				1.6h	8h	8h	4.55h	1.6h
	Site selection	Work	12h	9.6h						

Figure 11.10   Resource usage in integrated projects.

managers. The IMS (integrated master schedule) can be constructed using the MS Project *insert* function. Highlighting an open task below a current project, a new project can be inserted to allow for a consolidated master schedule.

In Fig. 11.9, we have integrated two projects, Integrated Transportation System (ITS) and New Plant. This was accomplished by using the ITS project as the base, then going to "insert," then "project," and highlighting New Plant from another directory, and then inserting it. This is the beginning of the process of integrating a program of projects in one schedule to allow multiproject control.

Resources from both projects can now be displayed in the resource usage view, to monitor resources committed to both projects and to identify potential conflicts, overallocations, and underallocations of personnel.

Here we can see how staff are allocated to two separate projects, e.g., Ben Sheets working in the ITS Project, and the facility specialist working in the New Plant project. The resource usage view allows visibility of resources, with all tasks by resource (Fig. 11.10).

The tasks usage view allows visibility of resources from a tasking view—each task from each integrated project is shown with all resources assigned to it. Here we can see that the prototype full integration task, build, is staffed by David Bart at 40 hours in April, while the preproduction plan task in the New Plant project is staffed by the project manager at 21.61 hours in November (Fig 11.11).

Summing up the MS Project Integration Function

No software is going to integrate projects unless the managers and project staff involved *want to integrate projects*. As evidenced above, MS Project has the

ID	Task name	Details	Nov	Dec	2008 Jan	2008 Feb	2008 Mar	2008 Apr
	Lour Bentt	Work						0h
240	Chassis available	Work						0h
	Lour Bentt	Work						0h
241	**Prototype full integration**	Work						40h
242	Build	Work						40h
	David Bart	Work						40h
243	**New Plant**	Work	########	869h	863.8h	766.4h	466h	527.2h
1	**HUNTSVILLE PROJECT**	Work	########	869h	863.8h	766.4h	466h	527.2h
2	Select an architect	Work						
3	Recruit and train managers	Work						
4	Select real estate consultant	Work						
5	Preproduction plan	Work	21.6h					
	Production specialists	Work						
	Manufacturing engineering	Work						
	Project manager	Work	21.6h					
6	Create production plans	Work	108.8h	147.2h				

Figure 11.11   Task usage view.

capacity to document and display schedule and resource information on a multi-project portfolio and provide for cross-comparisons of task, resource, and costs. But the motivation and incentive to integrate projects must come from the leadership of the organization and must be demonstrated in day-to-day project execution decisions. As implied in the new PMI PMBOK standard on integration, project execution is the "proof of the pudding" in integration. It is in execution that key project decisions are made, e.g., how scarce resources are allocated to competing projects. These decisions can be made in a vacuum by individual project managers entirely in the interest of *their own projects*, or they can be made by those same project managers in the interests of the whole organization and its business goals. This is where company leadership sets the tone; if projects are to be managed for the good of the company as a whole, then each project manager sees himself or herself as part of a collaborative management team, making judgments about company investments *beyond their own interests*. That is the integration challenge.

Tools in Building an Integrated Project Management System

In building a company or agency system to support project integration, there are 10 targets for process improvement. These are organization-wide or enterprise-wide project management systems, program portfolio system development, integrated resource management systems, information technology, technical product development including a stage-gateway review system, interface management system, project portfolio management, project monitoring and corrective action, change control, and program evaluation.

Organization-wide Project Management System

- *Integrated project management culture.* Leaders develop their organizations to accomplish integration through systems and communication. This system involves the development of a culture of defining and capturing work in terms of projects, e.g., all work of the organization outside recurring production work is considered project work with a customer and deliverables. All training and development, and incentive systems are built to encourage work to be accomplished through formal projects and plans and schedules that integrate cost, time, and quality.

- *Generic work breakdown structure (WBS).* A generic WBS is a task outline in sequence but not linked. The purpose of the generic WBS is to integrate the work, which is project coded to capture costs and task performance history, with the scheduling of any task the company takes on in any project. The generic WBS defines each task in a *data dictionary*, or task definition that covers what the task expectation is and what its deliverable is, to improve the estimation of task duration and integrating task linkages.

Here is an example of a generic task definition for a safety and testing activity associated with new product development.

1. *Functional hazard analysis (FHA).* The functional hazard assessment (FHA) is designed to assess the severity of the effects of foreseeable functional failures of the product. The FHA caegorizes the functions, possible failure modes of the functions, and associated effects; provides a classification of the severity of the failure mode; and provides justifications and assumptions for each failure classification to support the chosen failure mode severity classification.

2. *Built-in-test assessment.* Safety engineering of continuous built-in test for adequacy against safety criteria.

3. *Failure modes and effects analysis (FMEA).* The FMEA categorizes the functional block and provides a functional description; lists associated failure modes; and provides the failure rate, describes the internal and external effects of such a failure, and provides the expected detection method of the failure mode.

- *Scheduling system.* A scheduling system places all work in a project schedule software, such as MS Project or Primavera, assigns resources and estimates costs, in order to control the work. Integration of all the work of the company is accomplished through scheduling, which is seen as a process of *committing resources to work in scheduled "windows."*

- *Resource assignment.* Resources are assigned to projects and tasks so that the workforce is integrated into the work that is authorized and sponsored by the company. Projects are seen as investments in the business plan; therefore, there is a major impetus to capture the work being performed in a resource assignment system.

- *Task linkages and interdependency.* Projects are consolidated and tasks are linked to stress the interdependency of project work. No piece of work in the company is left *unconnected*, to ensure integration.

- *Matrix team structure.* The matrix structure ensures integration because functional departments and project teams are intermingled in every aspect of the company's work, from projects to process development and improvement. Project teams are staffed by functional departments in charge of the quality of work and the development of technical systems. Project managers manage assigned team members toward project deliverables and earned value.

- *Work authorization system.* Again in order to assure that work that goes on is project work, all work is authorized and directed by the project manager. Work is approved is through the baseline schedule, which defines the authorized work sequence.

- *Guidelines for project management plan.* The project management plan is defined in a company policy statement to guide the definition and control of the work. Therefore, the plan must include control points—Stage-Gateway reviews, which ensure that management authorizes advancement from one phase or stage to another. Reporting and monitoring strategies, including the use of earned value to integrate cost, schedule, and quality performance, should be made explicit.

Enterprise-wide management should also address accountability, particularly in view of the recent legislative and regulatory requirements of the Sarbanes-Oxley Act. This requirement which facilitates compliance with internal control and accounting standards is no longer optional for project managers. Compliance with Sarbanes-Oxley therefore is not a choice but a requirement, and the plan should state standards for estimating costs, tracking the costs and relating costs to work performed, and the integrity of the closeout procedure and invoices to customers for work performed.

Program/Portfolio Planning and Development System

- *Business planning system and strategic objectives.* The integrated company has a business and strategic planning process that produces a statement of strategic objectives to serve as a guide for all planning and budgeting. Such a system helps to shape the project portfolio and assures that the company invests in projects that are integrated with the direction of the business and its ownership.

- *Decision process.* Some kind of decision process supports integration because open decisions, if prolonged, can lead to waste and ineffective work. Decision trees are used to assess the commercial value of various decision paths involved in defining the task structure and sequence in approved projects.

- *Budgeting system.* A capital rationing system, or some way to allocate company resources in line with the priority of relative strategic objectives is part of integration. Once budgets are identified to carry out business plans, projects are planned and prioritized in the portfolio system, then costs are estimated. Finally, projects are funded according to their relative merit against business plans and available budget.

- *Risk management system.* Some kind of risk management planning system that identifies and assesses risks, and generates risk contingency plans, is necessary in an integrated project management system. The risk matrix is the format for developing risk information that is used in scheduling and controlling the work.

- *Program definition.* Programs are sets of projects with similarities in process, product, and customer base. Definition of longer term *product lines* will help to clarify the boundaries of a given program over time.

- *Portfolio pipeline system.* A pipeline of approved projects is maintained so that as funds and resources become available, projects are quickly initiated. Project plans and schedules are produced for projects in the pipeline so that when authorized they can proceed quickly.

Resource Management System

There needs to be a way to manage resources in an integrated project management organization simply because there is value in targeting all resources and equipment on the right project work. A resource pool can be established using MS Project that records all assignments in order to keep a running view of how people and equipment are being utilized.

- *Workforce planning.* A workforce planning system integrates the hiring and training of personnel with the needs of the program portfolio of projects. In other words, people, equipment, and systems are brought into the company to fill needs that are made explicit in the project resource allocation pool that reflects both current and planned work. Measures such as *person month needs* by project are used to predict resource needs.

- *Staffing planning.* A staffing system allocates staff to the priority project needs in order to fully integrate the core competence of the workforce with the priority needs of key projects. Staff is focused on assignments that are visible and reviewed regularly.

- Financial and accounting control is assured in a project management system that captures all project costs, both direct and indirect, and assures internal controls on project costs and equipment inventories.

- *Earned value.* Reports on work progress and costs are used to calculate earned value so that the company knows how each project is doing in terms of schedule and cost.

- *Industry standards.* Industrial cost and work standards are used to control the estimated duration of scheduled tasks, e.g., using a trade association to schedule an industry wide activity on which there are available and tested work and industrial standards.

Program Information Technology System

A program information system that documents all project work in consolidated schedules and resource pools assures that work is staffed, planned, and monitored in a uniform way. This allows comparison of project progress and supports decisions on where to focus resources.

- *Network system.* All program and project information, such as schedules, resource pools, project review and gate review data, and configuration management documents, are kept on a company intranet to allow wide ranging visibility.

- *Accessibility to key information.* Accessibility to information is controlled and focused on need to know criteria. However, customers are regularly informed on program and project progress through, for instance MS Project Central Web-based reporting systems that allow review of schedules without parent software.

- *Reliability planning.* In reliability planning, failure mode effects and functional hazard assessments, along with risk matrix documents, help to consistently design and test the reliability of product performance to conform with customer requirements and specifications.

- *Workforce training.* Workforce training is designed to meet project needs as evidenced in work performance feedback reviews and lessons learned exercises with project teams in close out.

Product/Service Development Process

Integrated project management cannot be accomplished without integrated product development processes with strong stage-gate milestones.

- *Gate decisions.* Project management is a process of managing time, cost, and quality, but the underlying strength of any project integration process is a strong, phased development process with clear controls on entry to the next stage. Gate reviews are documented and generic work breakdown structures and data dictionaries are developed for all product and service development activities.

- *Technology support and testing.* Technical support that meets industry standards assures that product integration and testing is verifiable. Designs are tested against specifications, specifications are tested against scope of work, and scope of work can be traced to customer requirements and expectations.

Interface Management

- *Matrix organization.* Interfaces procurement between functional departments, such as accounting, engineering, testing, and the project management department are assured through strong interface management. Separate departments and functions are brought together constantly through information and reporting systems and face-to-face review meetings at key milestones and gates.

- *Program review meeting formats.* Review meetings are controlled by generic meeting agendas and data and information support from a professional project management office (PMO) or staff. This way review information is objective and consistent.

- *Procurement interface.* Because of the importance of contract and outsourced work, contractor personnel and processes are integrated with sponsor company personnel and processes. Common scheduling and reporting systems are developed.

- *Financial, accounting, and internal control interface.* New impetus for strong accounting and accountability reporting now requires that project managers capture costs and be able to trace costs to work performed and equipment purchased.

- *Marketing and sales interface.*   Integration of marketing, sales, and project work is accomplished by assigning marketing and sales personnel to project teams. They attend and give input to the teams on customer developments and learn what they can and cannot commit to customers and when.

- *HR interface.*   The interface with HR is important to integrate personnel and HR policies and procedures with project work and priorities. Performance reviews are left flexible, yet are important in assigning resources to future projects.

Portfolio Management

- *Top management visibility of programs and projects.*   The whole set of projects in a multiple project system are managed consistently in an integrated project management system. All projects are monitored using common earned value and other measurement systems, e.g., balanced scorecard.

- *Uniform project management system.*   A uniform approach to projects in the portfolio is assured through a professional project management staff and PMO support system.

- Pipeline Management.
  - *Generation of projects.*   A systematic way of generating projects through brainstorming, budgeting processes, and business planning.
  - *Evaluation of projects.*   A way of reviewing portfolio projects using net present value and cash flows, weighted scoring models to score projects against business objectives, and risk management.
  - *Selection of projects*   Projects are selected using a uniform set of criteria.

Program Monitoring and Control System

- *Project management office (PMO).*   Monitoring is based on earned value reporting and quality is assured by a task planning system that relates %complete to defined milestones in the baseline schedule, all supported by a PMO.

- *Corrective action/risk management process.*   Contingencies and corrective actions are based on remaining work, and are forward oriented. Contingencies are embedded in schedules to assure that should risks occur, contingencies have already been scheduled and budgeted.

- *Escalation system for decisions.*   Conflicts and differences within project process are reviewed regularly by top management to assure that decisions are not delayed.

Change Management System

- *Change order system.*   All changes to a scope of work are submitted by project team members or the sponsor/customer to assure that changes are reviewed and managed.

- *Change impact system.* Change impact statements are prepared for all substantial changes, with risk, schedule, cost, and quality impacts specified.

Program Evaluation System

- *Document lessons learned.* Close out includes lessons learned meeting and documentation of outcomes. The PMO is made responsible to assuring that lessons learned are integrated into future projects.
- *Financial auditing system.* A financial and program audit system is managed to assure accountability and internal control of all assets.

Limitations of Integration Systems

Again, systems don't integrate projects, people do. Even if the organization is able to design and install compatible systems to help integrate projects, they will not work if the people who manage the work don't use them. For instance, configuration management as an integrating function in product development between design and production cannot be effective if the configuration manager does not see both ends of that spectrum. Project managers who are obsessed with schedule and on time delivery at any price, and who do not care about costs simply because top management or the customer has not focused on costs, *will not succeed for the business as a whole.* The lesson is this: individual project success should not be at the expense of the business itself. To assure that this does not happen, company leadership must continuously work toward an integrative vision and process at all levels of the organization—they must daily walk the integrative talk.

In Sum

As we have seen, project integration occurs at several points in the project planning and implementation pipeline, from early integration of business plans with project selection, to development and implementation of the portfolio of projects, to final closeout. Integration is critical at several points in this process because each point, or "gateway," requires decisions to proceed. And those "gateway" decisions often involve trade-offs of many critical success factors, including quality, cost, schedule, customer satisfaction, and profitability.

Project Integration and Interface Points

We have also seen that integration is accomplished through effective interface management and strong product development processes in the testing, validation, and system integration stages.

Key points of interface and integration include the following phases:

Concept phase

Project planning phase

Product development process phase

Development of the project management system framework for product development phase

Project development phase

Program, multiproject management phase

Organizational and accountability phase

Project monitoring phase

Transition to marketing phase

Discussion of integration points

Concept phase

Integration of idea generation and evaluation, e.g., *ideation*.

The transition of concepts to projects requires the integration of the idea generation and evaluation process with early concept development and product identification. This is where innovative ideas about projects of all kinds, such as improvement projects, new product development ideas, and internal IT projects are filtered and refined for eventual documentation as a portfolio of candidate projects.

The figure that follows shows the integrated *portfolio pipeline*, the process through which businesses plan, select, and implement projects. The goal is to integrate projects with business strategies to assure that projects further business goals.

The process starts at the left with new concepts and project ideas as inputs to the pipeline. New ideas and project concepts are then analyzed for financial payoff, risk, and alignment with business strategy. Financial analysis requires that each project is projected out over 5 to 10 years to allow net income and net present value to be calculated. The pipeline shows project work breakdown structures (WBS) developed in the first year to enable the estimate of project costs. Payoffs are estimated from value produced by project deliverables.

A composite index is developed and projects are selected. High priority projects are selected for implementation in the second year.

Funding is accomplished through capital rationing, the process of allocating available business funds to business objectives that are weighted based on their relative importance to the business. Once objectives are funded, projects that support high priority objectives are funded first.

Project plans are developed in the second year, including goals and objectives, WBS, schedules, cost estimates and budgets, risk assessment, and team charter. At this point the technical processes, procedures, and life cycle phases tailored to the industry or product are outlined. As part of the scheduling, key decision trade-offs are identified and commercial value of alternative decision paths is calculated.

Once the project is kicked off, work is authorized and tasks are completed, monitoring progress through earned value analysis, such as schedule and cost variance. A risk audit is conducted during the first year of the project, examining 10 critical success factors for project success.

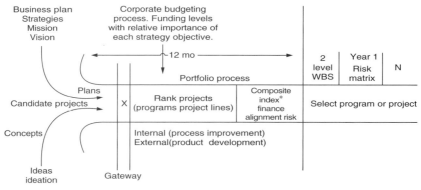

Integration of Customer Requirements and Project Scope of Work

At the same time that concepts transition to projects, potential customer and user expectations, needs, wants, and requirements are translated to draft scopes of work. Research and development, marketing, and sales participate in the generation of concepts and potential projects into statements of work.

Integrating customer expectations, needs, and requirements: a preliminary view

The integration of evolving customer expectations, needs, and requirements is managed during the concept phase. This process requires an iterative relationship with the customer, moving expectations to needs and needs to requirements that can be translated to product or deliverable specifications. The following figure shows the interrelationship of customer expectations, needs, and requirements.

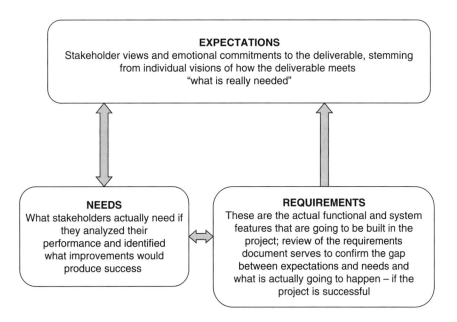

Achieving Alignment

Alignment is achieved when integration of business planning, e.g., strengths, weaknesses, opportunities, and threats, is integrated with project selection, based on financial viability, alignment with business purpose and strategy. This alignment phase integrates strategic objectives of a company with candidate projects. Alignment leads to project selection and funding based on the allocation of company funding to priority program areas.

The alignment tool, the weighted scoring model, scores projects against weighted strategic objectives as follows:

	Weighted/Scoring Model				
		Score		Index	
Strategy objective	Weight	Proj 1	Proj 2	Proj 1	Proj 2
Double total sales within the next decade	25	5	7	125	175
Develop and market new products based on the company's plastics experience	20	0	0	0	0
Reduce dependence on equipment suppliers	15	10	0	150	0
Be first or second, based on market share in any region	15	3	9	45	135
Attain a national presence in the container industry	15	0	5	0	75
Increase productivity	10	10	10	100	100
	100			420	485

Integrating Business Financial Goals with Project Selection

Projects are selected based on financial goals of the company, thus integrating the investment in project deliverables with the growth goals of the company. This is achieved through the use of net income projections and net present value calculations to allow comparison of project flows, as follows:

	Proj 1			Proj 2		
Year	Net income	NPV Factor (12% DR)	NPV	Net income	NPV Factor (12% DR)	NPV
0	−$2,475,000.00	1	−$2,475,000.00	−$2,550,000.00	1	−$2,550,000.00
1	$700,000.00	89.29%	$624,999.90	$550,000.00	89.29%	$491,071.35
2	$800,000.00	79.72%	$637,755.20	$600,000.00	79.72%	$478,316.40
3	$800,000.00	71.18%	$569,424.00	$900,000.00	71.18%	$640,602.00
4	$800,000.00	63.55%	$508,414.40	$1,150,000.00	63.55%	$730,845.70
5	$800,000.00	56.74%	$453,941.60	$1,300,000.00	56.74%	$737,655.10
			$319,535.10			$528,490.55

Project Planning Phase

Integration of scope of work with task definition and WBS

Once a project is successfully filtered through the concept definition phase and is made part of the program portfolio, further detailed planning takes place. This phase integrates the scope of work with a WBS and task definition.

The scope of work captures and documents key project functions, e.g., planning and design, that are identified in the WBS as high-level summary tasks at the top of the WBS. Each key function in the scope is represented in the WBS as a high-level task.

Below is an example of a WBS to the fourth level, which brings the high-level scope of work summary tasks down to work packages to be performed by small teams or individuals. Scheduling and cost estimating begin at the bottom of the WBS, with a task list, resource assignments, task durations, and linkages. Thus the WBS serves to integrate the scope of work into the schedule.

WBS: New Product Project

Below is a WBS to the fourth level, with one major component (plan) broken down.

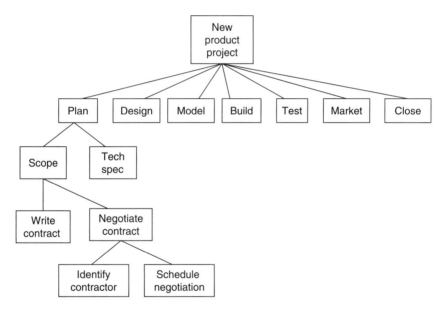

Integration of work scope with cost and schedule

Projects selected for the portfolio are based partially on net present value and are now transitioned into an integrated schedule and budget in Microsoft Project or equivalent software package.

Integration of quality, cost, risk, and schedule in single project planning

This is where quality and risk are integrated into the schedule. Risk is integrated by using the results of risk identification and completion of the risk matrix to calculate a risk-based schedule in MS Project through the use of the PERT tool.

Quality is integrated by assuring traceability to scope of work for each task and structuring task milestones to align with %complete determinations. When work is monitored for %complete, this ensures that progress reports can be matched directly to intermediate or final milestones, thus resulting in a qualitative control on monitoring progress through earned value.

Integration of the integrated master plan with the integrated master schedule

The high level, integrated master plan provides a structured method for outlining the required effort to be accomplished by identifying key project events, significant accomplishments, and the associated accomplishment criteria for closing out the accomplishments and associated project events. The master plan may be referred to as a high-level project plan.

The integrated master schedule is a subelement of the integrated master plan that is set in date format, and consists of tasks and subtasks that are typically networked by established predecessor and successor identities between the task and subtasks. Performance is evaluated and identified at this level based on a previously determined resource loading of the IMS that is directly tied to the control account plan either through manual input or electronic transfer through the established earned value system. The key to this integration, sometimes taken for granted in a Gantt chart view of the project, is that the tasks are interdependent and related to time and cost through an integrated software package such as Microsoft Project.

Integration of project schedules with generic WBS

As indicated in earlier chapters, the most effective way to assure quality in a multiproject, portfolio environment is to develop a generic WBS that describes the standard business processes, e.g., product development, service development, and then to describe each task in a "data dictionary" that serves as the basis for individual project schedules. This approach then provides a standard for each project in terms both of sequence, and task definition. Consistent task definitions guide better estimates of duration and linkage. In addition, the generic WBS would typically include project codes to provide for cost capture.

A standard WBS example of a generic WBS spreadsheet is as explained in Chap. 11.

Development of the Project Management System Framework with New Product Development

Integration of project management system with product development system

Perhaps the most critical integration especially in a new product development setting, is the problem of tailoring the project management system to the product development stages—ideation, business case, product testing and full development, and market launch. Each of these stages is managed as a distinct summary element in the project, which includes the entire spectrum of work from initial idea evaluation through to successful marketing, distribution, sales, and service. This holistic view of project management assumes that the job of the project manager does not stop when a deliverable is produced; it extends to the full production and marketing of the product.

This integration of project management with product development requires a broader perspective on projects. Projects are seen not simply as investments with costs and deliverables, but as opportunities for financial performance in the marketplace. The project manager would be accountable for making sure that the product is successful in producing revenues and customer value out in the target markets. This accountability stresses the importance of getting the deliverable to market, and minimizes the concentration simply on meeting project cost and schedule requirements.

Product development is a technical, market-driven process, focused on launching a product to market cycle. Managing the product development process requires a project management system that is aligned with this new product development process. This is essentially an integration of new product development and project management systems.

Here is the product development process:

Ideation.   Includes the generation of ideas and concepts in the business for potential development into projects; requires a filtering system and transition process for getting ideas for improvement, product development, service improvements, internal systems and technology, into firm documented concepts.

Project management during ideation includes the management of the ideation process, but not project planning. During this phase the focus is on customer requirements and demand for the new concept. This is done by a small team of new product development and marketing people in an informal team.

Concept definition.   Includes the development of concepts into project statements that include product definition, customer requirements, and general specifications.

Project management during concept definition.   Includes some early work breakdown development and initial review of schedule and cost parameters, but not final baseline scheduling.

Justify the project in business terms.   Here is where the case for the concept or product is made in business terms, such as financial, alignment with business strategy and competencies, and business risk assessment.

Project management during business case.   This is where the finished project plan is developed, including all elements of the package, customer requirements, specifications for the deliverable, WBS, task list, schedule, cost estimate, and risk matrix.

Also here is where the company selects the project or product and funds the process depending on the project cost estimate and the availability of funds in this program category.

Prototype Development.   This is the full development of the product, guided by a project plan and management system. Full development puts the product through design, testing, integration, and validation, and prepares it for launch.

Project management during full development controls the process through a baseline schedule, using earned value and Gate reviews as the product moves through the summary tasks involved in full development.

Market launch.   This is the final stage of product development, producing and distributing the product based on a comprehensive marketing plan that addresses brand, consumer demand, and price issues.

A key integration issue here is how to "fit" project management systems with the technical process of designing and producing the deliverable, by using project management to *guide and control* the process without diluting it.

Project/Product Development Phase

Integration of product design and configuration management

The freezing of a product design is a necessary part of developing the product for production. This process must be managed with a configuration process that preserves the product description, product breakdown, and parts list with production background from suppliers.

Integration of production scheduling with configuration management

Product scheduling is the process of scheduling the production of the new product into volume production, including inventory planning, product line tooling and improvement, and training of production assembly personnel.

Integration of marketing and distribution with production scheduling

The process of integrating marketing and sales planning with production requires the interface of very different functions and cultures. Marketing and sales are focused on customers, launching strategies, advertising, and consumer sales or user needs. Production is focused on production operations and management, unit's costs, quality control, and volume production planning.

Program, Multiproject Management Phase

Integration of several projects in parallel— multiproject portfolio management

The staging of projects into project implementation requires a grasp of the current project pipeline and current workforce needs and utilization. Once the program manager has an understanding of the current situation, new projects are "slotted" into the pipeline based on windows of opportunity as they develop.

Traceability

Vertical traceability occurs when all subelement tasks that support a summary element start and complete within the confines of the not to exceed schedule allotted for the summary element. In other words, vertical traceability occurs when the subtasks which "roll up" to a summary element are scheduled and actually complete within the total duration of the summary element. Vertical traceability simply confirms that the work was well planned and that work is on or ahead of schedule.

Horizontal traceability occurs when a stated milestone or event from one schedule is identified and used on another schedule, and shows the event and date as exactly the same on each schedule. In other words, when two or more projects are consolidated in one master portfolio schedule, key milestones such as final design, production complete, and market plan which are completed are all lined up on the same day. This facilitates interface management, the process of integrating functions and projects which are all at the same point.

Integration of manpower planning with portfolio implementation

A special integration challenge is the process of workforce and resource planning that will allow efficient phasing in of new projects as manpower becomes available. The first step in this process is building an accurate picture of how current resources are utilized, such as in person/hours, days, or weeks, using MS Project or another software package to document current project assignments by project and task. The second step is to determine the person/hours necessary to do the next project to be implemented from the portfolio. Then when there is a gap in current usage which will support the new project, the new project may be staged into the process. The challenge here is to determine what the capacity of the workforce really is when it is operating at maximum efficiency. In other words, if the workforce is not stretched by new projects coming into the system, current projects will *suffer because work expands according to the time available to do it*, especially when the workforce is under utilized.

Organizational and Accountability Phase

Integration of organizational structure and work breakdown structure

Alignment of the project team with task definition and accountability does not simply happen. It must be managed through a process of developing a responsibility assignment matrix (RAM). This matrix links departments and individuals with project tasks.

Integration of quality, cost, risk, and schedule through a control account manager

The control account manager (CAM) is an organizational concept that identifies an accountable manager who is incharge of work package or level of effort tasks. Sometimes called a task manager, the CAM is responsible for controlling task performance within his area of responsibility and makes sure that linkages and interfaces are made with other tasks consistent with the schedule.

Integration of project team with accounting and finance

The alignment of the project team with accounting and cost capture requires that the team and especially the CAM provides for capturing costs at the CAM level through electronic, project-coded time sheets, and other supply and fixed cost formats.

Integration of project team with procurement and acquisition

Integration of project work with procurement and acquisition allows the project manager to interface with purchasing and acquisition to assure that project supplies and equipment, and vendor contract activity, support project goals and objectives.

Integration of project team with human resources and training

The integration of project team management and leadership with HR involves developing and using personnel and supervisory tools, e.g., incentives and compensation, to further project goals.

Integration of individual work calendars with work package schedules

Successful project management always comes down to individual performance and the successful integration of individual and project team goals. While this is a complicated process, it begins with a system of calendar and time management tools that balances assignments and individual availability. In the end, the capacity of each project team member is different. This means that individual team members have a major role in the critical decisions on how much work they take on.

Integration of the project team with personnel competencies and skills

While time is a major issue in project team performance, the mix of talent and competencies with task assignments is critical as well. If the program or project manager cannot match task requirements with skilled professionals, the project is in jeopardy.

Project Monitoring Phase

Integration of actual technical performance with actual cost and schedule performance

The collection of actual cost data is a challenge for project managers because of two issues: (1) the difficulty in developing a system of cost capture *at the level where earned value is managed;* and (2) the typical delays in providing timely cost data to project managers so that they can make determinations of cost variance and appropriate corrective action.

Integrated project reviews

This discussion addresses the integrated quality project review, a scheduled, formal review which centers on project performance and quality metrics, and which raises broad issues for executive and customer attention.

The Project Management System Supports Integration

An enterprise project management system is the backdrop for an integrated project review. The project management system is a consistent approach and set of tools and techniques for planning and implementing task-oriented system development projects or professional services efforts with definable start and end points and distinct deliverables. Deliverables can include products as well as services. When implemented across the company, a project management system provides a corporate-wide way of thinking about the customer and about quality, and a set of professional tools and techniques for identifying and meeting customer requirements in a predictable way. Formats for planning, information exchange, project review, and decisions are governed by distinct project phases, reporting requirements, and schedule, cost, and quality controls. Project managers are trained and developed in a consistent way, both in technical project techniques and team leadership, and manage their projects using standard tools. Project teams are established as formal groups with charters in writing, with performance guidelines and criteria for evaluating team members. A project management manual is used to communicate policies, procedures, and support systems, and the system is continuously improved using business process reengineering tools. A common language governs communication about projects, both across the company and vertically through the hierarchy. Senior management is an integral part of the project management system, serving to create the conditions for success and using project information for business development.

In addressing project reviews, companies face common issues:

- *Find a balance in integrating project quality progress and information needs.* How can senior management arrive at an effective balance in reviewing for quality between increasingly excessive project task structures for reviewing complex projects and far-reaching, corporate quality information for senior managers?

- *Conduct effective project review meetings.* How can senior management obtain actionable quality information from project managers during project reviews without inhibiting the project management process?

- *Develop consistent application of project management tools and techniques.* How can senior management develop a disciplined project management system that project managers follow without creating expensive, time-consuming, and detailed reporting systems?

- *Build a project manager pool attentive to quality.* How can senior management identify core competencies and build a reliable project manager cadre?

- *Coordinate projects across functions.* How can senior management assure that projects are cross-functional and avoid insulated, company "silos"?

Senior management roles: creating the conditions for integration

In a firm committed to improving project success, senior managers are responsible for establishing and supporting a project management and professional services system that accomplishes corporate goals. However, projects are also a vehicle for building customer relationships and partnerships as well. The development of a professional services business relies on building relationships through successful projects. Project managers can identify new business development opportunities during the process if they are attuned to where the company is going and senior managers take interest in "actionable information." Actionable information is information that is produced during a project, product, or service development process, which helps senior management accomplish their key strategic and business development goals.

According to authors Englund and Graham, senior management is responsible for creating an environment for successful project quality through the following 10 roles:

1. Leading the transition to a fully project-based organization.
2. Aligning projects with the company's strategic business plan.
3. Understanding the impact of senior managers on the success of projects.
4. Developing a core project team process.
5. Assuring an effective project management organizational structure with clear lines of authority and responsibility.
6. Developing a project management information and project review system that produces "actionable information."
7. Developing a plan for identifying project manager core competencies and a selection and development process.
8. Developing a learning organization, stemming from project management documentation and processes.
9. Develop initiatives to improve the project management system.
10. Develop senior management's ability to manage project managers.

Here are more details on specific senior management actions to be taken:

1. Leading the transition to a fully integrated, project-based organization

   - Establish sense of urgency on project management success, connect to company's performance and individual compensation.
   - Create networks of project sponsors and support staff.
   - Communicate the changed vision, including the emphasis on professional services projects.
   - Empower project managers to perform.
   - Connect project management to strategic initiatives, such as professional services business development.

2. Integrating projects with the company's strategic business plan

   - Get involved early in project generation, planning, and approval and reflect movement toward professional services.
   - Make sure project managers understand the business plan.
   - Raise issues early on misaligned projects.

3. Understanding the impact of senior managers on the success of projects

   - Get feedback from project managers on effectiveness of project reviews and other senior manager involvement.
   - Communicate with other senior managers on impacts.
   - Listen to project managers.

4. Developing a core project team process

   ■ Encourage teams and teamwork.
   ■ Officially charter teams in writing.
   ■ Provide team incentives.

5. Assuring an effective project management structure

   ■ Delegate authority in writing.
   ■ Clarify reporting relationships.
   ■ Give authority with responsibility.
   ■ Build capacity to manage.
   ■ Focus on big picture.
   ■ Avoid conflicting messages on project detail and reporting needs.

6. Developing project management information system

   ■ Communicate project review information needs.
   ■ Benchmark good project review approaches.
   ■ Provide software and training.
   ■ Invest in project management information systems.
   ■ Control level of detail in project planning.

7. Developing core competencies

   ■ Identify what makes a good project manager.
   ■ Develop project manager profiles.
   ■ Publish core competencies.
   ■ Integrate into hiring.

8. Developing learning organization

   ■ Decide on documentation needs.
   ■ Create sense of urgency on lessons learned.
   ■ Identify costs of repeated mistakes.
   ■ Assign responsibility.

Integrated Project Review

A company is "ready" for integrated project review when:

■ The company is already embarked in an exercise to improve its project planning management, and documentation as part of a broad quality improvement program.

■ The company is heavily committed to education and training as a way to equip its people for project integration.

■ The company is moving in the direction of more standardization of products and processes, thus the consistency with a disciplined project management system.

- The company is going through change and transition and recognizes that employees at all levels need to know how to integrate their project work with the company's changing strategic direction.
- The company is developing a new product development process with gate reviews.

Integrating project management phases

What are the typical project management phases? Whether product or service oriented, project management processes should involve distinct, predictable phases. A standard approach to phasing allows all project and senior managers to be able to understand project progress in terms of progress through common phases, providing predictable "gateways" for communicating actionable information.

While there are always variations on the theme, there are four basic project management phases:

1. Concept
2. Project definition
3. Design and implementation (sometimes called production/operation)
4. Project close-out and follow-on

The following table shows the major activities in each phase of a typical project.

Phase 1 Concept	Phase 2 Project definition	Phase 3 Design and implementation	Phase 4 Close-out and follow-on
Identify and clarify customer requirements and quality objectives	Project definition Establish project team	Design concept	Financial performance
Planning and project selection	Detailed scope of work	Engineering studies	Project documentation
Generate new project concepts: Product and professional services	Project plan Quality plan Define WBS	Prototype and test	Lessons learned
Screen and rank-order project concepts	Develop task list with interdependencies	Installation plan	Obtain customer feedback
Broad Scoping	Develop critical path	Delivery of services	Close-out books
Establish and maintain potential project list	Develop responsibility matrix Enter baseline data Develop risk analysis	Earned value	Follow-on potentials

Phase 1—Concept: clarify customer requirements and generate and select projects

Introduction to Phase 1.   While senior managers must play in a role in all project phases, the senior management role in the concept and quality planning phases is critical. This is the point at which senior management can encourage project managers to think through the kind of project/product/professional services mix appropriate to each customer and market target. Here senior management sees that early project and professional services concepts are grounded in legitimate customer needs. The role here is to emphasize that projects will be selected on the basis of needs, pay-offs, and the company's strategy to develop a broad professional services practice.

Senior management keeps the project pipeline full through a process of encouraging new services and product concepts and designs to be developed to meet customer needs. A customer-oriented project firm will stress the development of a long-term planning process to assure that the highest pay-off projects are undertaken.

Identify and clarify requirements.   This step involves senior management focus on aligning projects so that they are consistent with corporate strategy and are grounded to meet customer requirements. This can be accomplished by requiring that proposed projects define customer requirements clearly upfront in the planning process. Concepts should include both product development and professional services.

Here is where the customer's quality policy and procedures are addressed, and if the customer does not have a quality policy, then one is developed for the projects under review.

Generate new project concepts.   A company that encourages continuous improvement, out-of-the-box thinking, and a strategic focus will generate new project and service concepts to generate the project selection process. Senior managers need to encourage a certain amount of "free-spirit" thinking to create the conditions for innovative, forward-thinking project formulation. They can accomplish this by establishing incentives and recognition programs for new project concepts that align with company strategy. Senior management is responsible for "inspiring" and generating breakthrough concepts by developing incentives, removing barriers, and encouraging project developers to challenge the current way of doing business—toward a mix of product and professional services.

Phase 2—Project definition

Generate new project concepts.   Approval of projects is a key senior management function, again assuring that projects are aligned with strategy. The process of rank ordering and selection should include formal presentations, preparation of proposals and justification material, and consistent criteria. These criteria will include pay-offs, revenue and business development potential, and contribution to the field.

Senior management must be careful to apply consistent guidelines to ranking and selecting project concepts, to avoid the appearance of "pet" projects and to assure that there are processes and incentives for proposing and justifying new project and product ideas. Ranking should be accomplished using corporate criteria, which are made clear company-wide.

Broad scoping.   Project managers should be encouraged to develop the capacity to broadly scope product and services projects in 1 or 2 page narrative formats that allow senior managers to make preliminary decisions to commit company resources. This is called "broad scoping" the project.

Establish and maintain potential project list.   Potential projects are kept alive through a listing of potential projects, which is updated frequently.

Senior management is responsible for choosing projects for implementation.

Introduction to Phase 2

This phase further defines the project, once approved, and "fine tunes" the concept, schedule, budget, and team. Here is where the company integrates the project into its project "pipeline" and schedules the work and resources required in detail. Typically, the budget process serves to facilitate project selection, but senior managers need to develop a way to transition from budget decisions to an "approved" listing of projects to be undertaken which is communicated widely.

Senior management's role here is to assure that product development and professional services projects are defined and costed out clearly in terms of work breakdown, deliverable specifications, schedule, budget, and quality requirements. A consistent approach to project definition, scheduling, and baseline data entry will assure that projects can be evaluated and reviewed effectively and that senior managers can concentrate on gleaning actionable information from projects rather than second-guessing project managers in their day-to-day project activities. Senior managers must be careful not to lay on reporting requirements that drive project managers into too much detail, at the same time expecting them to see the big picture as well.

Project definition and project scope statement.   The project scope statement is a brief description of the product deliverable or cost-reduction improvement. The statement includes the following information:

- Background customer information
- Description of work: what is to be done?
- Unique requirements
- Product and professional services information
- Special considerations and issues

Establish a formal project team.   Project teams should be formally established, authorized, and chartered in writing by senior management. The project manager is responsible for proposing the composition of the project team. The team will consist of the appropriate technical staff and representatives as approved by senior management. Establishment of a team indicates company commitment to the project.

Conduct kickoff meeting.   The project manager runs the kickoff meeting to communicate the requirements of the project and to discuss assignments, commitments, resource questions, and other issues relevant to completing the work.

Project plan.   The project plan is a package including project goals and objectives, customer requirements, general product specifications, quality policy and plan, schedule and budget, risk management plan, and team structure and roles.

Quality plan.   The quality plan includes the quality standards relevant to the project. Inputs include quality policy, scope statement, product description, standards and regulations, and other process outputs. Tools and techniques employed include benefit/cost analysis and net present value techniques, benchmarking, flowcharting, and design of experiments. Outputs include a quality management plan, operational definitions, checklists, and inputs of the quality process to other processes. (See appendix A for a full description of the quality planning process from the Project Management Institute Body of Knowledge).

Work breakdown and task list.   For complex projects, a summary work outline or breakdown structure, and a detailed task list unique to the project, is developed. The WBS is a top down outline of the steps in the project process. The breakdown will incorporate quality standards and testing in the definition of each task, as well as describe the quality planning, assurance, and control tasks. The task list, built from the work breakdown, indicates task name, duration, start and end dates, and interdependencies, or predecessors. No project should be detailed out in the WBS to more than 5 levels down.

Responsibility matrix.   The project manager and the team create a responsibility matrix or organization chart for the project, once all tasks are identified. This matrix is a formal assignment structure, which indicates workflows and unit responsibility for each task.

Develop schedule.   A detailed schedule is developed in consultation with appropriate stakeholders in the work, using the task list and project management software if available. Remember to include quality standards and task both as integral components of the tasks themselves as well as in quality planning, assurance, and control. The schedule is graphically displayed as a

Gantt chart. The critical path of the project is shown to indicate the combination of tasks, which, if delayed, would delay the overall project. A project baseline is established—a project schedule and budget, which is the point of departure for proceeding into work performance and monitoring.

Develop project budget.   A project budget is prepared indicating the total cost of doing the work and assuring the assigned profit margin. The budget is entered into the database system. Project budgets are built from the bottom-up, by costing out tasks and rolling them up, "loading" direct costs with appropriate indirect overhead and general and administrative costs.

Develop risk analysis.   During this phase, a risk analysis is prepared to anticipate the risk involved in the project and to prepare contingency plans. Risk analysis focuses on feasibility, technology, costs, quality problems, instability in customer requirements, and forecasting information that might impact the project.

Senior management must be attuned closely to risks in a project because project teams tend to become advocates of work initiated and sometimes lack the perspective to see increasing risks, which threaten project success.

Phase 3—Design and implementation

Introduction to Phase 3.   Phase 3 is the design and implementation of the project deliverable(s), including products and professional services. It includes execution of the project scope and schedule, and the utilization and consumption of project resources. Phase 3 involves monitoring actual performance against planned estimates for schedule and cost.

Design.   Design involves a detailed fleshing out of the outcomes desired and product and services design. Design includes a full description of the performance specifications for all products and systems, as well as a description of the kind of professional services that will meet customer requirements.

In prototyping and testing, designs are "dummied up" and tested with customers, and final testing is accomplished.

The installation plan is the detailed description of how a system is going to be installed in the customer's operating environment.

The senior management role in this phase is to be sure that the project manager is providing accurate performance data and information during design and testing of the product, and that the customer is satisfied that the design is appropriate.

Implementation.   Projects are implemented according to the schedule, sequencing tasks, and monitoring progress at convenient gateways in the schedule. Senior managers should focus on critical issues during this process, including:

- Accomplishments, what has been accomplished, especially unexpected gains
- Earned value, e.g., variations from schedule and cost estimates (see tools and techniques in next section)

- Customer feedback, what the actual client of the product or service is saying
- Performance feedback, e.g., team's data from testing and implementation in terms of performance to customer requirements
- Quality issues, e.g., product defects, service inadequacies, and process problems
- Other actionable information (see section given on project reviews for actionable information)

Phase 4—Project close-out and follow-up

Introduction to Phase 4.   Phase 4 should be seen as an opportunity to deliver the product and service and continue the relationship with the customer. Phase 4 should not be seen simply as "project close-out." Thus the key issue in phase 4 is finding follow-on business development potential from the project deliverable, documenting lessons learned, and moving to the next level of customer partnership.

Financial performance.   The project's financial performance is reviewed at this point, assuring that revenue and profit margin goals are going to be realized. Corrective action includes reestimating cost to complete and finding cost cutting measures if appropriate.

Document project.   Software is documented and a project history is prepared according to a template including:

- Project planning documents, scope, and the like
- Full files from each project phase
- Financial data
- Scheduling data
- Quality data
- Team performance information

Lessons learned.   The project manager is responsible for documenting lessons learned in a special database of information updated by the project management team.

- Unique lessons from this project
- Avoidable mistakes and failures
- Quality issues
- Communication problems
- Organizational issues
- Technology information

Obtain customer feedback.   A customer survey form is presented to the user or customer of the project. Senior management assures that customer feedback is obtained and routed to the appropriate senior and project managers for appropriate quality control and management action.

Explore follow-on potential.   Here is where the project manager and team are expected to explore follow-on opportunities with the customer. Senior managers should lead this process, focusing project managers on marketing targets and helping to build partnerships with customers to further professional services opportunities.

Integrating tools and techniques

From the senior manager's perspective, the key project planning management tools include the WBS, task list, Gantt chart, calendar plan, task usage chart, and earned value analysis. Senior managers should assure that project managers are trained in and can use these tools to manage their projects and report on them.

Because Microsoft Project is a useful and popular project management software program, illustrations of these tools in this manual are taken from that software. Below is a brief discussion of each tool and the senior management perspective on them. Care should be taken, however, with any project management software to avoid too much task detail and structure, simply because the software allows it.

A sample of each of these tools is shown following this discussion.

Work breakdown structure.   The WBS involves top down planning of the project, beginning with the product or services requirement. The WBS decomposes the project into greater and greater levels of detail. Roll up of the WBS completes the project, so its purpose is to plan down to 4 or 5 levels of detail in an "organization chart" of the project. Remember to keep your project managers focusing on integration of tasks horizontally and using the WBS to identify the "big chunks" of work at the top of the WBS early in the project that need to be completed and integrated before the project is successful.

Task list.   The task list shows the task of the project with durations, start and finish dates, predecessors, and resource names. The task list is the basis for preparing the Gantt chart. The task list is the basis for scheduling and resource allocation.

Gantt chart.   The Gantt chart is a bar chart showing each task, its dependencies, and its durations (both planning and actual) against an actual calendar, to permit scheduling and resource planning. The Gantt chart is a convenient way of showing senior managers, and the customer, the whole project and its key milestones, gateways, and interdependencies.

Calendar plan.   An actual weekly calendar showing project task activity.

Earned value analysis.   Earned value analysis is used to identify when the overall project is using resources at a greater or less than planned rate and when the project is ahead of or behind schedule. Because it is dangerous to look separately at schedule or budget for an indication of how things are going, earned value combines the two. Earned value is important to senior managers because use of the concept provides a simple indicator of *both* schedule and cost variance, using one measure—dollar value. From earned value indicators, senior managers can ask questions and assure themselves that the project manager knows how the project is going.

Some definitions:

- Budgeted cost for work scheduled (BCWS): the estimated cost of the project and each task.

- Budgeted cost for work performed (BCWP): the cost contained in the project budget for completed work, plus a proportional share of the budgeted cost of work partially completed. This is the actual earned value—it answers the question, "Of the work you have completed, how did its cost compare with your plans?" In effect, it is asking whether the project "earned" the budget devoted to the work completed or whether the work is actually behind schedule.

- Budgeted cost of work performed (BCWP): this is the actual expenditure to date.

The senior manager is interested in:

Cost variance (CV = BCWP – ACWP)

Schedule variance (SV = BCWP – BCWS)

Estimate at completion (EAC = ACWP/BCWP) times total budget

As an example, if a project is showing: BCWP = \$200K, BCWS = \$400K, and ACWP = \$400K, the project is badly behind because the value of work performed (BCWP) is far below what it should be (BCWS at this point in the project, but the project has spent project funds (ACWP) as if the work were on schedule.

See the earned value exercise at the end of this manual.

Narrative report and presentation.   Each project manager should be expected to report on accomplishments, issues, actionable information, and corrective plans in a consistent format across the company. Project reviews, however, do not have to consume large blocks of time and most review information can flow without the need for meetings.

Project reviews for actionable information

The purpose of this section is to place special emphasis on focusing on the right information—termed actionable information—for project reviews. Actionable information is information that creates opportunities for senior management action to develop technology and marketing concepts and accomplish corporate business development goals and objectives. Project reviews and reporting systems should focus on actionable information as follows:

Status of project, issues, and plans
  Overall progress compared to plan
  Accomplishments
  Issues
  Plans for corrective action
  Customer feedback
Quality issues
  Customer satisfaction and related quality issues
  Conformance to specifications
  Cost of quality
  Waste and rework
  Statistical process control information
  Effectiveness of quality policies and procedures
  Process performance
  Team performance
Marketing information
  Developing customer requirements
  Business process outsourcing potentials
  New product and market information
  Successful presentation approaches
  Key contacts at high levels in customer organization
Lessons learned in project management
  Organizational support issues
  Standard templates
  Tracking software successes
  Project management process improvements
  Financial and costing controls
  Successes in identifying customer requirements
  Successful communication and reporting strategies
  Change order management

Project performance

- Successful approaches to leading the project team
- Team performance feedback from customer and from team members

- Team core competency information, such as feedback from team composition and skill needs

Information on competitive challenges

- Intelligence on competitive developments in financial and insurance professional services
- Lessons learned by customers from competitors or stakeholders
- Financial and productivity data

Project team performance

- Successful approaches to generating excellent team performance
- Feedback on team interaction with the customer
- Insights on core competencies needed for project leadership and team membership
- Successful organizational approaches

Opportunities for customer partnering

- Shared interests with customer for alliances
- Business process outsourcing opportunities
- Opportunities for developing professional service relationships
- Joint project team opportunities

Earned value

- Tracking data showing major schedule problems and cost variances
- Cost to complete
- Plans for corrective action

Senior management is responsible for obtaining actionable information from project reviews, and avoiding costly project review sessions which sometimes second-guess project decisions without adequate information.

Breakthrough manufacturing or product development technology

Software innovations

New equipment test and performance information

Manufacturing opportunities

Transferability

Transition to Marketing Phase

Integration of market launch
with production scheduling

Market launch decisions require integration with product scheduling simply because launch requires specific volumes of product at distinct times and places for distribution.

New Concepts in Integration

Gary Chin's book *Agile Project Management* (Amacom, 2004) brings into stark contrast the "classic" project management and integrated, "agile" project management, the new, more flexible application of project tools to fast moving small business. Here are the salient points:

1. *Estimates of resources and work versus commitment.* While classic project management focuses on resources and time, agile project management focuses more on team commitment and key milestones. Less attention is paid to tight resource allocations, and more to ensuring that team members do whatever they need to do to get the whole project completed.

2. *Project manager takes an external perspective, not internal, and sees business risks.* Program and project managers are seen not simply as "task masters" over schedules and budgets, but rather representatives of the business and extensions of the business in the project environment. The external perspective places the project and program manager both in the world of translating, communicating, and negotiating with project sponsors, sensing market and global changes affecting the project deliverable, and adjusting to change.

3. *Achievements versus activities.* The emphasis is on the achievement of project objectives, with less attention on strict enforcement of work activities and tasks. In other words, team members are empowered to change the way work is conceived and done in the agile environment. This gives team members the challenge of owning the key deliverables and outcomes of the project and shifting job tasks and redefining and reinventing work processes to get the job done faster and better.

4. *Shorten the time horizons.* Because of the changes in project variables and competitive forces, the time horizon for planning becomes shorter and more focused. The 80-hour rule becomes the approach, while longer term planning and milestones are left more vague and undetermined. The assumption here is that project risk is increased if a project locks into a structured approach over the long term and cannot adjust when necessary. The focus is on "cost to complete" and remaining work, looking ahead to redefine and redirect the project work given the situation at any given project review point.

5. *Technical skills versus adaptability.*   Agile project management requires a stronger concentration on adaptability than technical skills. Team members are recruited and developed not simply to perform technical work but to be able to adjust and play a variety of roles across many technical interfaces; e.g., electrical engineers are expected to understand software engineering; mechanical engineers work with electrical and software engineers in "seamless" teams to integrate products and get them to market.

6. *Variances in external forces versus variance in plans.*   More attention to external influences, e.g., the price and quality of contract supplies, changes in market demand and customer requirements, and less attention to variance in plans, schedule, and cost. This does not mean that earned value and variance are no longer useful; but short-term shifts and variances are seen as indicators of the future rather than strict guidelines.

7. *Achieving business results versus managing schedule, scope, and resources.* Program and project managers are encouraged to look at business results, such as cash flow projections for marketing the project deliverable, profitability and cost reduction, and sponsor satisfaction. Team members are delegated more responsibility to manage day-to-day work schedules and variances with their eyes on the project outcome.

8. *Achievement-based networks rather than Gantt charts.*   Track network diagrams and "project paths and interdependencies," rather than standard Gantt chart schedules. Achievements are seen as key "gateways" or milestones that must be reached.

9. *Look at decisions rather than activities.*   There is more emphasis on decisions made in a project and less on activities per se. This trend has more project managers looking at decision *trees* and key options at various project crossroads, rather than assuming project tasks are settled and pose no decision challenges. In other words, if a project manager must make a decision to deal with a future risk and there are important implications for taking one or another decision path, those decision paths are mapped into the schedule and team members contribute to the decision-making process.

10. *Successful product versus successful project.*   More emphasis on the outcomes and products of the project than the project itself. Projects that meet schedule and cost goals but do not produce marketable and profitable deliverables are not considered successful projects.

11. *Integrating the project and the business.*   Rather than seeing projects as separate from the business, agile project managers *consider themselves the business.* In practice this means that project managers are aware of business considerations—market share, product cost and pricing, competition, quality and customer satisfaction, and reflect them in project decisions.

12. *Build contingencies into schedules and plans.*   This approach gives more priority to looking at key risk decisions and options and building contingencies

into the baseline schedule rather than keeping them outside the project circle until needed.

13. *Alternative pathways to deliverable versus shortest path.*   Program and project managers encourage team members and support staff, including the project management office, to identify shorter pathways to task and project outcomes, loosening up the WBS and schedule and "authorizing" different ways of accomplishing the work.

14. *Expect versus discourage change.*   Project changes are encouraged as the project team and the customer learn from the project, and change management practices and procedures take on more significance. The built-in bias against change is transformed into a "learning environment" that adjusts to change and new insights especially in new product development.

15. *Reinventing project boundaries versus enforcing them.*   Boundaries between functional and project managers are blurred as team members cross technical and project boundaries to get the job done, e.g., professional engineers help technicians understand and compete testing requirements; purchasing agents spend time with team members to understand supply and equipment needs and issues to allow them to serve the project team more effectively.

16. *Risk-based infrastructure for the agile company.*   The agile project management company builds a supporting culture for risk based scheduling and decision making. Support systems encourage tight short-term management but provide for analysis of future options in project reviews.

17. *Balance innovation and process.*   Barriers to innovation and creativity are removed in the project planning and execution process; premium is placed on finding better ways to get the work done and to redefining the work with "workarounds" and "out-of-the-box" thinking.

18. *Emphasis on the execution stage versus emphasis on the planning stage.* Risk and uncertainty encourages more focus on execution, corrective action, and agility, and less on long-term planning. Rather than spending 20% of the project life cycle on planning and getting to a baseline, work is initiated with skeletal scheduling (5%) and cost information. More emphasis is placed on midstream adjustments and realignments of tasks to new forces which surface during project execution.

Integrating project management and product development

Integrating risk into the product development process.   The product development process produces designs and prototype products for manufacture, marketing, and sale. Product requirements are translated into engineering design specifications, drawings, and the like through the product development process. The process is oriented to develop, control, verify, and validate the design as it progresses to completion. Design risk in the product development process is created by the potential for failure in validating the design. In other words, one kind of product development risk is risk that the design does not do what it is supposed to do.

Product development faces two major risks; that a product prototype will not align with the specifications for the product; and that even if there is alignment with specifications, the product will not work in a user setting. Product development involves these key risk concepts that underlie the project risk management process, verification, and validation. Verification is the process of ensuring that a product design meets the specification for the product—that the design will do what the specification would have it do. Validation is testing the product in a user setting to ensure that the product meets customer needs.

Each of these risk strategies is integrated into the product development process in order to yield useful data on both risks. Thus product development is a good example of the integration of risk into the project process.

Each product follows the development process defined herein and follows the following general stages:

Stage 1: Requirements definition

Stage 2: Detailed design

Stage 3: Prototype development (design verification)

Stage 4: Design validation

Stage 5: Production transition

Each of the stages has distinct entry and exit criteria and risk exposures; however, each of the stages will overlap in time and the entry/exit criteria can be satisfied incrementally (at subsystem levels) in order to provide for an expeditious development cycle. For example, detailed design activity can and will begin on certain parts of the product before all the requirements are known and defined. Likewise, hardware validation activities can and will begin prior to the completion of software design/development.

Design and development plans are prepared and updated as the design evolves. These plans guide the design process, are the basis for defining all design tasks, and establish program schedules for each design activity. Department managers are responsible for staffing each program with competent, adequately trained personnel, and providing necessary resources. Other personnel may be called upon, on an as-needed basis, to perform specialized analyses or to act as consultants.

Design reviews in new product development

The term review is used to describe program events scheduled for each program and/or project at well defined stages and to describe an integrating process by which engineering documentation is reviewed for accuracy and compliance to requirements.

Design reviews, conducted by program and technical personnel, are held during each stage of the product development cycle in order to ensure adherence to requirements defined within the product development policies and procedures as well as to the requirements of the product in development. The results of these reviews, including all action items, are documented and retained for future reference.

The reviews that are included in the development process are as follows:

System requirements review (SRR)

Task level (subassembly) requirements review (TLRR)

Task level (subassembly) design review (TLDR)

Test readiness review (TRR)

Production transition review (PTR)

The development process is depicted in Figs. 13.1 and 13.2. Figure 13.3 depicts the policy/procedure documentation structure that supports the development process.

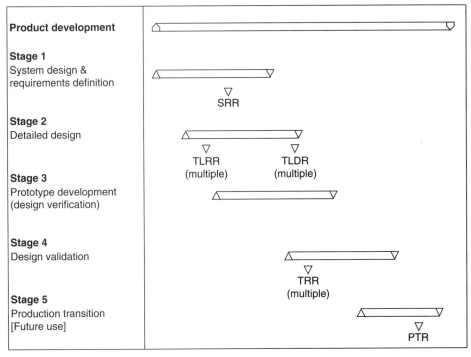

Figure 13.1   Product development process stages.

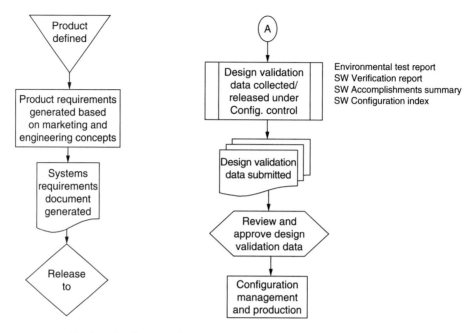

Figure 13.2   Product development flow.

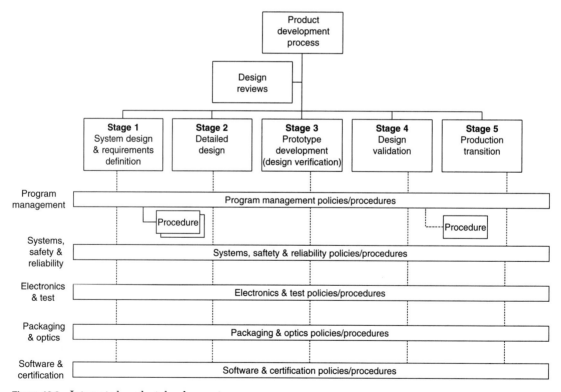

Figure 13.3   Integrated product development.

Product requirements definition

The purpose of product design is to define

Functional requirements

Product architecture

Hardware requirements

Software requirements

Design validation requirements

Test equipment requirements

The overall process integrates customer need, performance requirements, and design.

Each program and/or project develops product requirement specifications based on performance requirements. Customer-driven product requirement specifications are converted to individual subsystem design and performance specifications.

The "release" of a system or product design means the integration of requirements and design.

Detailed design

Detailed design translates product requirements into digital drawings used to produce the product. Subsystem design follows overall integration of system and subsystem such as electrical or software.

Design documents allow the product to be manufactured through use of a configuration management system that documents product and subsystem components. Release reviews confirm readiness for the next phase.

Prototype development

Prototype development ensures that the detailed designs produced in Stage 2 result in a product that meets the product requirements and results in a product that is ready for validation.

Prototype development includes all the following steps to complete testing:

- Procurement of material for the prototype product under development

- Manufacture of prototype product(s)

- Test and integration (hardware and software) of the prototype products

- Special development tests

- Development of the acceptance test procedure

Procurement of prototype material and manufacture of prototype products are performed by the purchasing and manufacturing departments. Engineering provides definition of the material to be ordered and the product to be manufactured through drawings generated as part of the detail design process.

To ensure that design meets requirements, prototypes are verified. Design verification is accomplished by testing and evaluating and reviewing products in gate reviews. Integrating reviews occur prior to the release of design output documentation to ensure that all requirements are addressed. Design changes resulting from this process are incorporated and documented prior to final production design release. The risk in this process is that the product performance will not validate against design input, or specification.

Design validation

Design validations ensure that the system meets all the requirements imposed by the specifications. Hardware and software validation of a production product are governed by the appropriate industry standards. The requirements for a given product are captured in requirement documents.

Production planning

The purpose of production planning is to facilitate a smooth transition from the development of the product to production. The production planning stage ensures that:

1. Configuration management provides all documentation required to produce the product in a production environment.

2. All test equipment are tested and available as scheduled.

3. Special manufacturing test needs are defined.

4. Production personnel have a working knowledge of the equipment and test methods used to test/troubleshoot the equipment.

The production planning stage concludes with a production integration review, culminating in a meeting involving engineering, manufacturing, and project team members.

Organizational and Technical Interfaces

Program teams have individual and team responsibilities, task assignments, and technical competencies to assure timely and complete transmittal of information among team elements, as well as to and from outside functional organizations supporting the team.

Design changes

A change control system is anchored in configuration management which controls the design change process through engineering change orders.

Design review and risk

There is inherent risk in design review because of the potential for design flaws that will impact on performance and testing, and therefore on schedule and cost. Design risk is addressed in design reviews; risk is why design reviews are completed.

Risk Reviews

The following technical risk reviews are planned and facilitated by program management at the appropriate stage of product development.

Preliminary design risk review (PDRR)

Critical design risk review (CDRR)

Production readiness risk review (PRRR)

System design risk review (SDRR)

Test readiness risk review (TRRR)

Task level requirements risk review (TLRRR)

Task level design risk review (TLDRR)

Risk analysis can be conducted on three levels of program management: project, system, or task level, as follows:

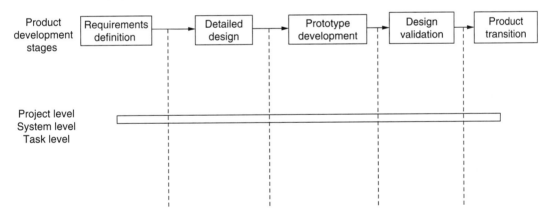

Preliminary design risk review

A preliminary risk review occurs early in the detailed design stage. Its purpose is to uncover risk in design, hardware, and production.

Critical design risk review

A critical design review ensures that critical performance requirements are met by the design. This review integrates the company's functional departments and the project team and "authorizes" advancement to production readiness.

Production planning risk review

This review includes identification of high risk/low yield manufacturing processes. This is when actual production flow is analyzed in terms of the product design.

System design risk review

The system review checks for integration of the product itself with "conditions of use" and necessary interfaces.

Test readiness risk review

If testing is scheduled to be outsourced, this review integrates the contractor's testing processes with the sponsor company processes.

Task level requirements risk review

"Task level" review goes to the fourth or fifth level of the WBS to assure clear definition of requirements.

Task level design risk review

This review focuses on design to ensure completeness.

General Responsibilities

Project or phase level/stage level/task level reviews

Program management is responsible for assessing the necessity of project or phase level reviews but they are typically performed unless conceled in a high performance, project integration system. They are integrated into the baseline schedule.

Program management is responsible for ensuring that all parties to the product development process participate. Program management coordinates the attendance of customers, subcontractors and vendors.

Program management is responsible for integrating reviews into the project schedule and authorizing personnel to charge time in attendance to project budgets.

Detailed Requirements

Preliminary design risk review

General. In the detailed design stage and integrated with gate reviews, PDRs shall be conducted, at the discretion of program management, for each configuration item under development. PDRs are normally conducted after a design approach has been formulated.

Review items.   Items reviewed include:

Overall design status
Design Requirements
   Quality of design documents
   Performance requirements
   Design standards
   Configuration
   Standardization
   Design trade studies
   Design to cost goals
   Design for growth capabilities
   Layout drawings and preliminary drawings/BOMs
Regulatory requirements
   Applicable regulations
   Verification plan
Producibility and manufacturing
   Manufacturing process requirements
   Design challenges
   Tooling requirements
Testability requirements.
   Preliminary production test procedure
   Specific subassembly requirements to support production test
Reliability/maintainability/availability (R/M/A) requirements.
   Reliability issues with past designs
   Preliminary assessment of high risk, long-lead items
Technical risk
   Risk impacts and probabilities
   Preliminary risk mitigation plan

Critical Design Gate Review

When detailed design is complete the design is again checked to ensure that it supports all performance requirements.

Review items.   In the critical design gate review, the following items are reviewed.

All engineering documents (layout files, schematics, and drawings)

Adequacy of the detailed design in satisfying requirements of the specification. The detailed design shall be assessed in the following areas:

Software design

Hardware design

Reliability and maintainability

Quality assurance provisions

Design provisions for inspection

Identification of critical integration issues

System design risk review

At the systems level, the allocation of requirements to design characteristics is evaluated.

Review items.

System or product

Functional analysis

Requirements allocation

Regulatory requirements

Subassembly synthesis

Standardization

Analytic studies

Functional allocation between hardware, software, and firmware
Cost versus performance
Design versus manufacturing consideration
Common versus unique support equipment
Size and weight

Test readiness risk review

General.

Test procedures to test integration

Support equipment requirements

Configuration of the unit under test

Configuration of support equipment

Task level requirements review

At the task level (fourth or fifth WBS level) requirement reviews are focused in individual or team design issues related to specific subsystems or components:

Review items.

Key design tasks related to requirements

Subcomponents

Regulatory and industry requirements

Producibility and manufacturing assembly issues

Testability requirements

Quality assurance provisions

Reliability/maintainability/availability (R/M/A) requirements.

Task level design risk review

General.   The design review at the task level ensures that the detailed design satisfies all requirements.

Review items.

Detailed engineering documents

1. Component design
   a. Functional/performance requirements compliance
   b. Power requirements and estimates
   c. Detailed schematics
2. Mechanical Design
   a. Mechanical assembly methodology
   b. Regulatory design requirements
3. Reliability and Maintainability

Software Development "Points of Risk": A Function of Complexity

Software integration and risk go hand in hand. This is because there are so many "points of risk" in the software design process, so many detailed decision, steps, and coding actions that can go wrong. This relationship between software and risk can be illustrated with reference to the "law of requisite variety," a seminal part of systems theory, indicating that the job of system design and control becomes more and more difficult as the complexity of the system and its interrelated parts increases. Risk can be said to be a function of complexity and control, the more the system can be controlled the less risk it generates.

The software development presents unique risks and challenges associated not only with the design and development process, but also with the potential gap between functionality of the product and customer or user needs, requirements, and expectations. Add to this system the natural creativity of software design and development, and you have a process inherently risky.

This is why software design and development often includes embedded quality assurance and control in order to reduce risk at every key "point of risk."

While a software development engineer is typically responsible for developing software, creating documentation to meet or exceed a requirement, and assuring that each software development process step is accomplished, a so-called "certification" engineer is also responsible for reviewing and verifying software development artifacts to assure that requirements are testable and certifiable. Thus risk management and integration in the software business are expensive and time consuming. The certification engineer is also responsible for developing and implementing cases and procedures that test code and requirements to specified levels, for capturing the test procedures and results in accordance with company procedures, and for assuring that each verification process step is accomplished. In addition, a software quality assurance engineer is often responsible for monitoring the software life cycle process to assure that it meets or exceeds the intent of this document.

Integrating Risk Mitigation

While it is almost axiomatic in the project management literature that risk management involves separate analytic processes and special efforts during the project process, the most effective risk mitigation actions are integrated into the process, closer to quality assurance to risk management per se as described in the PMBOK. Anticipated risk and contingency is built into the process.

Quality and Risk in Software Development

Quality requires the integration of risk with customer requirements. The risks inherent in conformance are different from the risks inherent in customer satisfaction. Conformance involves design, verification, and validation that is planning the product around system requirements, verifying that the design is consistent with the specification, and validating that the system performs accordingly. Customer or user satisfaction risk is generated when the client's expectations are not met by the system, even though it conforms to specification. Real risk in this situation is a function of the large gap in any creative process between what is stated as the goal—the system requirement—and what the client really needs and/or expects. And further complicating the process, the client alters expectations the more the process itself provides visible and tangible products. The syndrome is captured by the statement, "I don't know exactly what I want, but I will tell you when you produce it." Ironically, the more the client is involved in the process, the more the risk that the controlled environment of conformance will be disrupted by scope and specification creep, and the more the client's original needs and/or expectations will change.

Integrated Project Management—An Introduction

All appendices provide organized slide material based on the topics covered in the book. Appendix 1 addresses the basics of project integration management.

Introduction

- Project management tools—schedule, cost, and quality.
- Requirements, features, and scope of work.
- Project life cycle controls key process gateways.
- Work Breakdown Structure (WBS) defines product deliverable and work to be performed.
- Schedule defines work sequence/interdependency.
- Resources, cost estimates, and risk management.
- Tracking, monitoring, and change management.
- The project team and organization.
- MS Project information support.

Requirements and Features

- Customer requirements captured in requirements document; performance versus design.
- Freeze requirements in baseline project WBS; baseline schedule against frozen requirements.
- Appreciate that change is expected dynamically in product development as learning occurs.

- Accommodate change as development proceeds.
- Exercise: Identify user requirements.

Scope of Work

- Scope is a general statement of the work to be performed whichreferences product requirements.
- Scope is written into contract or agreement.
- Scope is frozen at baseline.
- Monitor for scope creep, change management process, and ensure orderly review and approval of change.
- Exercise: Write a scope of work.

Project Life Cycle

- Concept: early customer requirements.
- Project planning: objectives, WBS, schedule, and budget.
- Design: preliminary product design.
- Development: Develop prototype.
- Production: Produce prototype.
- Close out: Close out project.
- Gateways at each entry point to the next phase.
- Exercise: Define life cycle phases and illustrate with a real product.

Work Breakdown Structure

- Defines all work to be performed in outline or organization chart form.
- Controls process and deliverable.
- Generic WBS assures that schedules include all necessary work in the product development process.
- Exercise: Develop a WBS.

Scheduling

- WBS.
- Task list, duration estimates, and calendar.
- Key linkages between tasks.
- Use linkages to generate concurrent work to accelerate process.

- Use MS Project, Gantt chart, and resource usage table as baseline reference.
- Exercise: Enter tasks and durations into MS Project.

Resources and Costs

- Identify teams and resource needs.
- Assign resources to tasks with percentage of total time.
- Add resource costs.
- Add fixed and variable costs.
- Reports will product budget and cash flows.
- Resolve resource conflicts.
- Exercise: Enter resource assignments and costs.

Risk Planning and Management

- Risk planning: Prepare for risk management.
- Risk identification: Identify high risks.
- Risk assessment: Assess risk qualitatively and quantitatively.
- Contingency management.
- Risk management: Manage and monitor risk.
- Exercise: Prepare risk matrix (risk description, probability, impact, severity, and contingency).

Monitoring and Tracking

- Kick off project; use baseline as the point of departure for monitoring variance.
- Monitor for earned value, schedule, and cost variance.
- Project reviews, schedule, cost, and quality.
- Engineering and design reviews.
- Estimate of %complete.
- Capture actual costs.
- Exercise: Interpret earned value results and take corrective action.

Change Management Process

- Configuration-management (CM) approach to product (bill of material).
- Engineering prototype defined early.
- Change accommodated through CM process.
- Exercise: Develop change request and approval format.

The Project Team and Organizational Structures

- Team is defined by work to be done.
- Team is chartered.
- Project manager is appointed.
- Team meetings and agendas.
- Project reviews, data, and information.
- Alternative project organizations; matrix, pure project, and functional.
- Exercise: Prepare agenda for team meeting.

Microsoft Project

- Well suited to product development.
- Gantt chart and optional tables useful in documenting schedules, resources, and the like.
- Varied report formats.
- Earned value calculations.
- Risk-based schedule calculations.
- Communication in team through MS Project.
- Exercise: Practice MS Project applications.

Contract Management Issues

- Structure contract to share risk.
- Procurement process.
- Preparing the request for proposal (RFP).
- Contractor bidding.
- Contractor selection.
- Contractor management.
- Contract project reviews.

Nine Elements of Integrated Project Management

- A uniform project life cycle. This consists of a definition of phases, deliverables, key milestones, and success criteria for each group involved in the project. This is sometimes referred to as a methodology.

- Project requirements, objectives, and scope must be documented. It is also essential that a system be in place to ensure that the project requirements and scope are stabilized as early in the life cycle as possible.

- A work authorization and change control system. A frequent source of problems on projects involves the expansion of the scope of work without adding value to the overall project. Change control must include formal systems for reviewing, evaluating, and authorizing changes to scope, once the project has begun.

- Defined roles for project team members and functional supervisors must be identified and documented. Similarly a system of communication between the project participants must be established.

- A planning system must be in place that allows for the creation of plans based on organizational capability, not on wishful thinking. The planning system allows for the creation of the scope, WBS, schedule and budget plans.

- Quality metrics and systems to ensure quality must be in place in the organization. These systems must include identified metrics for each element of the WBS as well as the procedures for assessing quality.

- Tracking and variance analyses are vital functions for controlling the project. Projects are managed through an exception process in which deviations from plans are reported and acted upon. An effective project management process requires regular reports and meetings of the project team to identify when things are off target. Schedule slips, cost overruns, open issues, new risks, and identified problems must be dealt at the earliest.

■ An escalation process is a set of procedures that defines how problems, open issues, and risks should be addressed in a timely manner. Issues and problems are inevitable in projects. A good escalation procedure requires problems and issues to be addressed by the lowest level of management first. If the lowest level cannot resolve the problem, then it is escalated to higher levels until a resolution occurs.

■ Corrective action decisions are necessary when variations from the plan are detected. In some cases trade-offs must be made. Systems and procedures must be in place to address how corrective action decisions will be made.

Integrated Program Management Tools

The following are the basic "tools" of integrated program management.

- Organization-wide project management system
- Program/portfolio planning and development system
- Resource management system
- Program information technology system
- Product/service development process
- Interface management
- Portfolio management
- Program monitoring and control system
- Change management system
- Program evaluation system

Organization-Wide Project Management System

- Project management culture
- WBS
- Scheduling system
- Resource assignment
- Task linkages and interdependency
- Steering group
- Matrix team structure

Program Management System

- Business planning system and strategic objectives
- Decision process
- Budgeting system
- Risk management system
- Program definition
  - Portfolio pipeline system
  - Criteria
  - Selection process

Resource Management System

- Workforce planning
- Workforce utilization system
- Staffing
- Financial control
  - Earned value
  - Industry standards
  - Facilities and equipment management
  - Resource pool system

Program Information Technology System

- Network system
- Accessibility to key information
- Reliability
- Flexible formats
- Workforce training
- Web-based communication and reporting system

Product/Service Development Process

- Key process definition for development of products and services
- Assigned functions in matrix organization structure
- Industry standards
- Technology support and testing
- Technically training workforce
- Uniform work breakdown structure

Interface Management

- Matrix organization
- Program review meeting formats
- Assignment of support functions
- Control "gates"

Portfolio Management

- Top management visibility of programs and projects
- Uniform project management system
- Pipeline management
  - Generation of projects
  - Evaluation of projects
  - Selection of projects

Program Monitoring and Control System

- Project management office
- Corrective-action procedures
- Reporting system
- Escalation process

Change Management System

- Change order system
- Change impact analysis
- Risk management assessment

Program Evaluation and Audit

- Document lessons learned
- Close out system
- Audit system
- Corrective action follow up

Project Manager Challenges in Integration

- Scope creep
- Resource/budget/funding
- Client management
- Risk management
- Control reports and processes; clear reports
- Communication
- Vendor management
- Access to right tools
- Juggling too many projects, not enough resources; diversity
- Documentation and right software
- Changing requirements
- Schedule
- Contractors
- Office space
- Accountability without responsibility/authority
- Lack of functional support
- Lack of senior management support
- Lack of correct skills on team
- Changes in management
- Inadequate planning tools
- Scope, deliverables, and so forth, not well defined

- Scheduling team meetings
- No process to resolve and escalate issues
- No model for costing and budgeting
- No method for archiving project materials
- General workload pressures and time management
- Training
- Red tape
- Team members' conflicts
- Communicating urgency
- Getting buy-in
- Coordinating cross-functional group availability
- Managing remote contractor
- Unrealistic dates determined without team input
- Long projects; keeping everyone engaged
- Taking corrective action
- Unclear roles of participants

Graphs on Earned Value
and Integration

Earned Value Analysis

- BCWS = Budgeted cost of work scheduled

- ACWP = Actual cost of work performed

- BCWP = Budgeted cost of work performed

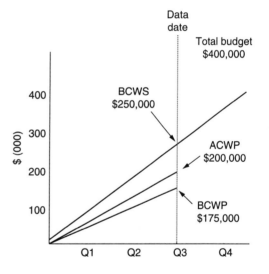

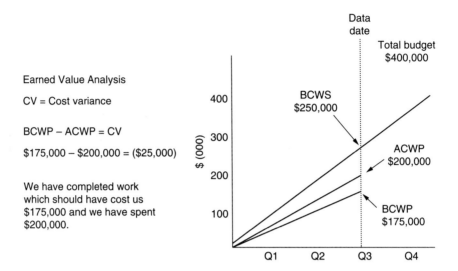

Earned Value Analysis

CV = Cost variance

BCWP – ACWP = CV

$175,000 – $200,000 = ($25,000)

We have completed work
which should have cost us
$175,000 and we have spent
$200,000.

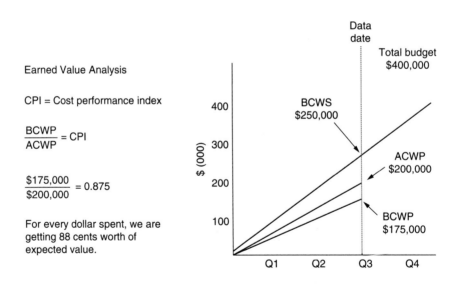

Earned Value Analysis

CPI = Cost performance index

$$\frac{BCWP}{ACWP} = CPI$$

$$\frac{\$175,000}{\$200,000} = 0.875$$

For every dollar spent, we are
getting 88 cents worth of
expected value.

Earned Value Analysis

SV = Schedule variance

BCWP – BCWS = SV

$175,000 – $250,000 = ($75,000)

We expected to complete $250,000 worth of work but have completed only $175,000 worth.

We would need to spend (accomplish) $75,000 worth of work today to catch up.

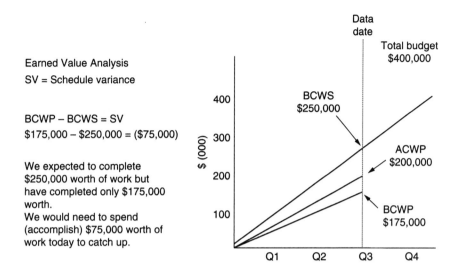

Earned Value Analysis

SPI = Schedule performance index

$$\frac{BCWP}{BCWS} = SPI$$

$$\frac{\$175,000}{\$250,000} = 0.70$$

We are 70% effective in maintaining our schedule.

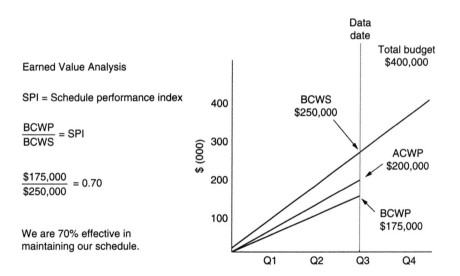

Estimate at Completion (EAC)

Cost performance index = 0.875
I have 200,000 left in my budget.
If current trend continues, it will
cost $200,000/0.875 or $228,571.

This means the project will cost
$428,571 instead of the original
$400,000.

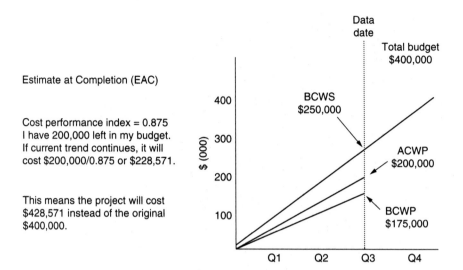

6

Notes on Project Integration

How to Fail in Project Management Without Really Trying

- Ignore the project environment (stakeholders).
- Push a new technology to market too quickly.
- Don't bother building in fallback options.
- When problems occur, shoot the most visible.
- Let new ideas starve to death from inertia.
- Don't bother conducting feasibility studies.
- Never admit a project is a failure.
- Overmanage project managers and their teams.
- Never conduct post failure reviews.
- Never bother to understand project trade-offs.
- Allow political expediency and infighting to dictate crucial project decisions.
- Make sure the project is run by a weak leader.

What You Don't Know About Making Decisions

- Decisions as process: two approaches—advocacy or inquiry.
- Constructive conflict: cognitive and affective.
- Leaders pay attention to:
  - Way issues are framed.
  - Step back and avoid established coalitions.
  - Shift people out of their "groves."
  - Ask key participants to gather new data and information.

- Leaders can structure the debate: Point-counterpoint versus intellectual watchdog.
- Closure
  - Deciding too early
  - Deciding too late

Bringing Discipline to Project Management

- Goldratt; theory of constraints.
- Focus on constraints.
- Projects as a whole.
- Measurements should induce parts to do what is good for the whole.
- Managing projects as a portfolio.
- Putting flexibility where it counts.
- Finding the ultimate constraint.
- Critical chain schedule.
  - Protects critical chain from non-critical task variation—feeding buffer.
  - Protects due date from critical chain variation—project buffer.

Theory of Constraints Dictionary

- Buffer: Time or budget allowance used to protect scheduled throughput, delivery dates, or cost estimates on a project.
- Drum: Bottleneck workstation; the most highly used resource; one that is not easy to elevate.
- Rope: The information flow from the drum to the front of the line which controls project.

What You Don't Know

- Multiple alternatives
- Assumptions testing
- Well-defined criteria
- Dissent and debate
- Perceived fairness

Learning From Projects

- Postmortem—a process and document
- Professional, factual, brief

- Postmortem meeting
  - Length
  - Room
  - Who should sttend
  - Facilitator
  - Recorder
- Preparing
- Running
  - Opening
  - Timeline
  - What went poorly
  - What went well
  - Recommendations
- Postmortem summary document
- Next steps

The Successful Integrated Project

- Support environment
- Enterprise environment
- Business environment
- Success factors, user involvement, clear requirements, proper planning, competent staff, clear vision and objectives, and hard working staff
- Teams, balanced problem solving, decision making, conflict management, and skills

Selecting and Developing PMs

- Sense of ownership
- Political awareness
- Relationship development
- Strategic influence
- Interpersonal assessment
- Action orientation

Synergistic Team Relations

- Teams and productivity—related?
- Lessons
  - Communicate
  - Manage themselves
  - Facilitation

Criteria for Competent PMs

- Enthusiasm
- Tolerance for ambiguity
- Team building skills
- Customer focus
- Business orientation

Leadership

- Strongman
- Transactor
- Visionary
- Superleader

Leadership Impacts

- Overpowering
- Powerless
- Power building
- Empowerment

Developing Core Teams

- Continuous membership on team through project cycle
  - Reduce cycle time
  - Increase quality
  - Better plans
  - Overcome organizational problems
  - Encourage creativity
  - Technical expertise

Project Team Competence

- Team efficiency
- Matrix
- Disorganized
- Coresponsibility
- Customer focus
- Self managed
- Balance team and self recognition

Assessing Team Competence

- Goals
- Deliverables
- Skills
- Tools
- Discipline
- Cohesion
- Effective leadership
- Structure
- Integrate diversity
- Achieve desired results
- Work with customers
- Chutzpah

Motivation

- Theory X/Y
- Maslow
- Hertzberg Hygiene theory
- Locke: Goal setting
- Understanding value and risk

Total Manager

- True leadership: substance, humanity, and morality
- Leadership
    - Show the way
    - Have a compass
    - Give credit
    - Take risks
    - Keep faith
- Act the part
- Delegate
- Be enthusiastic
- Be competent
- Thrive on change
- Don't ignore company culture

Communication

- Active listening
- Silence
- Perception checking
- Giving feedback
- Receiving feedback
- Nonverbal communication

Presentations

- Define objective
- Define audience
- Define approach
- Develop presentation
- Prepare and rehearse
- Deliver
- Critique the presentation

Motivation and Leadership

- Needs differ
- Management style affects motivation
- Satisfaction versus dissatisfaction factors
- Job satisfaction
- Leaders establish vision
- Challenge beliefs
- Take risks
- Leaders are honest
- Competency
- Align individual and project missions
- Get people involved
- Active
- Encourage contrary opinions
- Doable goals
- Recognize performers
- Make it fun

Project Management and Conflict

- Conflict is not a state, but a process
- Conflict is perceptual
- Sources
  - Reward
  - Scarce resources
  - Uncertainty
  - Differentiation

Steps in Conflict

- Frustration
- Conceptualization
- Orientation
- Interaction
- Outcome

Getting Unstuck

- Unclear goals
- Attitudes
- Missing skills
- Membership changes
- Lack of discipline
- Outsider intervention

Negotiating

- Negotiate with people
- Shape project quality
- Defeat the problem
- Deal with the problem
- Planning
- Goals, options
- Negotiation session

Conflicts

- Objectives
- Conflict environment
- Managing conflict
- Conflict intensity
  - Schedules
  - Priorities
  - Manpower
  - Technical issues
  - Administration
  - Personalities
  - Cost

Meeting Skills

- Listening
- Meeting necessary?
- Who should attend
- Where and when
- How long
- Best room
- Present ideas
- Visuals
- Stimulate, inspire, productivity

Personal Effectiveness

- Set long term goals.
- Establish strategies and short term goals.
- Personal strategies and "to do" lists.
- Expect the unexpected.
- Confront procrastination.
- Delegate.
- Paperwork management.
- Controlling interruptions.

Why Project Risk Management and Integration?

Introduction

- Risk is inherent in business; competitive edge comes from overcoming risks better, faster, and cheaper than competition.
- Projects imply risk; deliverable is new.
- Project uniqueness implies risk and opportunity; integrates challenge and potential opportunity.
- Advanced technology and complexity.
- More project-based companies.
- Good risk management skills make you more marketable as a project manager.

Purpose of Project Risk Management

- Planning and control tool.
- Understand project complexity and value.
- Identify key success or failure factors that will impact project success at the earliest.
- Assess and rank.
- Quantify probability.
- Mitigate (control) risks through risk management plan.
- Monitor change in the nature and impact of risks.

Risk and Decision Making

- Why take risk?
- Difference between "taking risks" (implies lack of plan) and risk management.
- Nature of business itself—serving customers is risk management.
- What will be gained if you control risk—opportunities.
- What could be lost—if risk occurs, it could jeopardize project success.
- Chances of success and failure?

Risk Elements

- Frequency of loss
- Information available
- Severity of loss
- Manageability of risk
- Potential for publicity
- Measure consequences
- Source of finances

Rewards of Taking Risks

- Achieving project success with minimum cost and time.
- Cost of risk management increases the later it is undertaken.
- Advance state of the art—make real contribution to field.
- Enhanced profitability—competitive edge.
- Improve market position—market share.
- Ensuring customer satisfaction—customer shares risk in financing project.

Potential Project Risk Factors

- Lack of top management commitment
- Failure to get user commitment
- Misunderstanding requirements
- Inadequate user involvement
- Changes in scope
- Lack of personal and professional skills
- New technology

- Staffing, conflicts
- Inadequate processes and procedures

Project Management Body of Knowledge (PMBOK)

- PMBOK is a standard for approaching project risk management.
- Process approach: describes project risk management as "inputs/tools/outputs."
- Course organization is consistent with PMBOK.
- Note that PMBOK was updated in 2001 to include a new risk management process—risk planning.
- Following are more details on each process:

PMBOK Section 11: Risk Management Processes

- Risk management planning
- Risk identification
- Qualitative risk analysis
- Quantitative risk analysis
- Risk response planning
- Risk monitoring and control

Risk management planning: inputs

- Decide how to approach and plan the risk management activities for a project.
- Project charter.
- Organization's risk management policies.
- Defined roles and responsibilities.
- Stakeholder risk tolerances.
- Template for risk management plan.

Risk management planning: tools

- Planning meetings
- Agendas
- Review data
- Variances
- Special reports

Risk management planning: outputs

- Risk management plan
- Methodology
- Roles
- Budget
- Timing
- Scoring
- Thresholds
- Reporting and tracking

Risk identification: inputs

- Risk management plan
- Project planning outputs
- Risk categories
- Historical information

Risk identification: tools

- Documentation reviews
- Information gathering techniques
- Checklists
- Assumptions analysis
- Diagramming techniques

Risk identification: outputs

- Risks
- Triggers
- Inputs to other processes

Qualitative risk analysis: inputs

- Risk management plan
- Identified risks
- Project status
- Project type
- Data precision

- Scales of probability and impact
- Assumptions

Qualitative risk analysis: tools

- Risk probability and impact
- Probability/impact risk rating matrix
- Project assumptions testing
- Data precision ranking

Qualitative risk analysis: outputs

- Overall risk ranking for project
- List of prioritized risks
- List of risks for additional analysis and management
- Trends in qualitative risk analysis results

Quantitative risk analysis: inputs

- Risk management plan
- Identified risks
- List of prioritized risks
- List risks for additional analysis and management
- Historical information
- Expert judgment
- Other planning outputs

Quantitative risk analysis: tools

- Interviewing
- Sensitivity analysis
- Decision tree analysis
- Simulation

Quantitative risk analysis: outputs

- Prioritized list of quantified risks
- Probabilistic analysis of project
- Probability of achieving the cost and time objectives
- Trends in quantitative risk analysis results

Risk response planning: inputs

- Risk management plan
- List of prioritized risks
- Risk ranking of project
- Probabilistic analysis of project
- Probability of achieving the cost and time objectives
- List of potential responses
- Risk thresholds
- Risk owners
- Common risk causes
- Trends in qualitative and quantitative risk analysis results

Risk response planning: tools

- Avoidance
- Transference
- Mitigation
- Acceptance

Risk response planning: outputs

- Risk response plan
- Residual risks
- Secondary risks
- Contractual agreements
- Contingency reserve amounts needed
- Inputs to other processes
- Inputs to revised project plan

Risk monitoring and control: inputs

- Risk management plan
- Risk response plan
- Project communication
- Additional risk identification and analysis
- Scope changes

Risk monitoring and control: tools

- Project risk response audits
- Periodic project risk reviews
- Earned value analysis
- Technical performance measurement
- Additional risk response planning

Risk monitoring and control: outputs

- Workaround plans
- Corrective action
- Project change requests
- Updates to the risk response plan
- Risk database
- Updates to risk identification checklists

Integrated Risk Planning

Introduction

- This process prepares for good project risk management.
- Plans approach, support, and standards.
- Establishes risk management policies.
- Roles and responsibilities.
- Provides template for risk management plan used in the course project.
- Sets culture for risk management, defining it as integral to project management.

Risk Planning: Inputs

- Decide how to approach and plan the risk management activities for a project.
- Project charter.
- Organization's risk management policies.
- Defined roles and responsibilities.
- Stakeholder risk tolerances.
- Template for risk management plan.

Risk Planning: Tools

- Planning meetings
- Agendas
- Review data

- Variances
- Special reports

Risk Planning: Outputs

- Risk management plan
- Methodology
- Roles
- Budget
- Timing
- Scoring
- Thresholds
- Reporting and tracking

Risk Planning: Setting Up Company for Risk Management

- Policies and procedures set up risk management processes.
- Company leadership establishes risk as an integral part of planning and control.
- Information databases.
- Templates for risk planning documents.
- Project histories and lessons learned.

Issues in Risk Planning

- Scope of work risks
- Resource risks
- Quality risks
- Cost risks
- Time/schedule risks
- Technology risks
- Project information: What data is needed on risks

Scope Risks

- Nonconformance of customer needs and expectations with requirements, leads to "scope creep."
- Scope does not adequately describe deliverable.

- No process to manage scope creep.
- No project process to trace from scope to requirements to deliverable.

Resource Risks

- Resources scheduled for work not the right ones; bad match of competence and task.
- Resources not available when scheduled.
- Resources leave company.
- Key resource acts as bottleneck and cannot be managed.
- Resources not trained adequately.

Quality Risks

- Quality processes not in place.
- Quality assurance upfront in process is not effective.
- Quality control, inspections for conformance, and so forth not effective.
- Definitions of quality differ between customer and team.

Cost Risks

- Cost estimates inaccurate.
- Unit cost information not up-to-date.
- Cost controls not in place, leading to inaccurate cost capture systems.
- Hidden costs not uncovered in project plan and budget.
- Cost variance indicates lag in capturing and registering costs in earned value analysis.

Time/Schedule Risks

- Schedule structure not adequate, leading to unscheduled tasks and costs.
- Schedule durations wrong.
- Schedule linkages not accurate.
- Customer schedule and timing requirement for deliverable is not feasible.
- No schedule review and update process.

Technology Risks

- Project equipment does not perform as planned.
- Unproven tooling or project techniques.
- Key contractor technology not available; no in-house competence.
- Hidden technology issues do not surface early enough to address and respond.

Risk Information

- Information on past risks in similar projects not available
- Risk information templates, e.g risk matrix formats, not available
- Lessons learned not captured
- Spreadsheet formulas for calculating probabilities not available

Risk Intensity in Project Life Cycle Phases

- Phase 1 (concept): Low amount at stake; opportunity to discover and manage risk before impacts
- Phase 2 (development): Higher amount at risk; impacts begin to occur
- Phase 3 (implementation): Highest risk impacts; highest amount at stake; sunk costs
- Phase 4 (termination): Too late

Integrated Risk-Based Scheduling Using Microsoft Project

Introduction

- Once risks are identified, categorized, and assessed, begin identifying optional scenarios.
- Focuses on three scenarios—expected, pessimistic, and optimistic.
- This week's focus is on impacts of three scenarios on schedule.
- Microsoft Project (PERT tool) helps document options, assumptions, and calculates probable durations for tasks.

Choose Risks for Three-Scenario Analysis

- Risk assessment has helped you identify and rank tasks with the highest risks considering impact, severity, and probability.
- Choose the five highest-risk tasks for analysis.
- Generate three scenarios for these tasks and review schedule impacts.

Generating Scenarios

- Generating scenarios involves thinking through the extent of the risk for each task.
- For each task, identify the impact of the task risk on task duration.
- Tailor the duration to the anticipated impact on schedule of that scenario.
- Example: A 2-week (expected) software review becomes 5 weeks in the pessimistic scenario.

Scenario 1: Expected

- Expected scenario is the option that, given all the risks and issues inherent in that task, they will likely occur.
- Expected scenario is generated by consensus, drawing on team members and assigned resource, to determine *normal* delays.
- Expected scenario would be the baseline schedule under normal circumstances.

Scenario 2: Pessimistic

- Pessimistic scenario is the task duration that results from the worst case.
- Worst case implies that all risks inherent in the task *all go wrong*.
- Worst case (pessimistic) implies Murphies Law if something *can* go wrong it *will* go wrong.

Scenario 3: Optimistic

- Optimistic scenario results when all risks are controlled—everything goes right.
- All task risks are managed effectively so that there is no delay in any task.
- No unanticipated risk impacts.
- Can imply some tasks are finished early, allowing some float.

Microsoft Project PERT Tool

- PERT analysis tool barprovides buttons to perform PERT analysis.
- PERT entry box allows entry of duration for three scenarios.
- PERT weights box allows entry of weight to be given to that scenario—judge weight on best estimate of *severity* of impact.
- Pert entry sheet schedule calculates and presents the three schedules, which result from entries, in one Gantt chart.

PERT Is "What If" Analysis

- PERT analysis gives project manager a way of establishing the outer bounds of "what if" scenarios.
- Working with team, project manager identifies highest risk tasks and brainstorms possible "what if" discussions.
- Task managers participate to assure that their best estimates of outcomes is reflected.
- Process itself helps task managers plan for the unexpected.

Index

Accessibility to key information, 216
Accountability, 23, 179–180
Accounting:
    financial/internal control interface with, 217
    project team integration with, 230
    as support system, 42
Accounting control, 216
Actionable information, 243–244
Active listening, 145
Activity schedules, 99
Actual cost of work performed (ACWP), 180
ACWP (actual cost of work performed), 180
Administrative closure procedure, 25,
        30, 31
Affinity diagram, 157
Affordability requirements, 96–97
Agenda, meeting, 150
Agile Project Management (Gary Chin), 245
Alignment, 60, 223–224
American Association of Laboratory
        Accreditation, 196
Approved change requests, 24–25
Approved corrective actions, 24
Approved defect repair, 25
Approved preventive actions, 24
Arrow diagrams, 87
Audit:
    program, 267
    support systems, 42–43
Auditing system, financial, 219

Balanced score card, xix
Baldrige criteria, xvi–xvii
Baselining, 77–79, 101
BCWP (*see* Budgeted cost of work performed)
BCWS (*see* Budgeted cost of work scheduled)
Benefit measurement methods, 18
Body movement, 162
Bottom-up planning, 101

Brainstorming, 153–157
    affinity diagram technique of, 157
    methods of, 155–156
    nominal group technique of, 156
    rules for, 154–155
Breakthrough manufacturing, 244
Budgeted cost of work performed (BCWP),
        101, 180, 242
Budgeted cost of work scheduled (BCWS), 180,
        242
Budgeting, 85, 181
Budgeting system, 215
Buffers, xviii, 276
BuildIt, Inc. (case study), 63–65
Built-in test assessment, 214
Business case, 227
Business culture, 173
Business financial goals, 224
Business need, 15
Business plan/planning:
    of ITS case study, 40
    product development/production integration
        with, 111–114
    of QuickTech Building Systems case, 48
    system for, 215
Business strategy, 174
Business-to-business, 93

CAD (computer-aided design), 122
CAE (computer-aided engineering), 122
Calendar plan, 242
CALS (computer-aided acquisition and
        logistics support), 123
CAM (*see* Control account manager)
CAM (computer-aided manufacturing), 122
CAM (cost account manager), 180
Capital rationing, 43
Cash flow analysis, 5
CE (*see* Concurrent engineering)

Celebrations, 142
Change(s):
  design, 252
  managed, 69
  tracking, 168–169
Change control system, 22–23
Change control tools, 105–106
Change impact system, 219
Change intervention, 44
Change management process, 261
Change management system, 218–219, 267
Change order system, 218
Charter (*see* Project charter development)
Chin, Gary, 245
CIM (computer integrated manufacturing),
  122
Cleland, David I., 130
Close-out, 240–241
Close project process, 30–32
Closeout, 82
Closure procedure:
  administrative, 25, 30, 31
  contract, 30, 31
Collaboration, 68–69, 171
Collective self-led organizations, 138
Commitment:
  generating, 131–132
  to mission, 187, 193
Communication, 280
  of strategic plan, 186
  team, 143–144
Communication program, 202
Community (as stakeholders), 187
Community Internet system, 95
Company scale of integration, 57
Competitive challenges, 244
Computer-aided acquisition and logistics
  support (CALS), 123
Computer-aided design (CAD), 122
Computer-aided engineering (CAE), 122
Computer-aided manufacturing (CAM), 122
Computer integrated manufacturing (CIM),
  122
Computer systems, MRPII, 122
Concept phase, 120, 130, 131, 227, 236
Concurrent engineering (CE), 118–119
Configuration management:
  product design integration with, 228
  production scheduling integration with, 228
  and project management plan, 22
  as support system, 42
Conflict(s), 282
  and project management, 281
  steps in, 281

Conflict management, 139–141
Conformance costs, 121
Constraints, theory of, 276
Contingency plan development, 102–103
Contract(s):
  closure procedure for, 30, 31
  documentation of, 30–31
  goals of, 94
  integration of, 107–110
  objectives of, 94–95
  and project charter development, 15
Contract management, 262
Contracting (as support system), 42
Contractor integration, 93
Control (of project work), 26–27
Control account, 85
Control account manager (CAM), 84–85, 230
Cooperation, 152
Coordination, 48
COPQ (*see* Cost of poor quality)
Core competencies, 193
Core team development, 278
Corrective action, 98, 218
Cost(s), 261
  of conformance/nonconformance, 121
  control account manager for integration of,
    230
  integration of, 59–60
  in MS Project, 205–207
  risks with, 293
  scope of work integration with, 225
  in single project planning, 225–226
Cost account manager (CAM), 180
Cost constraint, 127
Cost control, 2, 30
Cost of poor quality (COPQ), 118,
  121–122
Cost performance, 231
Cost performance index (CPI), 272
Cost schedule integration, 85
Cost variance (CV), 113, 272
CPI (cost performance index), 272
CPM (critical path method), 107
Critical chain management, 87
Critical chain theory, xviii–xix
Critical design gate review,
  255–256
Critical design risk review, 253
Critical path, 88
Critical path method (CPM), 107
Culture:
  business, 173
  differences in market/customer, 44
  integrated project management, 213

Customer(s):
  awareness/satisfaction of, 188, 195–197
  integrating with, 10
  interface with, 44
  risk tolerance in, 178
  as stakeholders, 187
  voice of, 118
Customer-directed teams, 166
Customer-driven project management,
  124–125, 132
Customer-driven teams, 169
Customer-integrated project management, 125
Customer reporting, 88, 112
Customer requirements:
  meeting, 67
  scope of work integration with, 223
CV (*see* Cost variance)

DAI (Development Associates, Inc.), 91
Data incorporation, 87
Decision making, 275–276
Decision process, 215
Definition phase, 130, 236–239
Deliverables, 24, 25, 51
Demonstration phase, 131
Department managers, 71
Department of Defense (DoD), 123, 124, 126,
  130
Design, detailed, 251
Design changes, 252
Design of experiments (DOE), traditional, 120
Design phase, 239
Design reviews, 248–250, 253
Design risk reviews, 253, 254
Design validation, 252
Detailed design, 251
Development Associates, Inc. (DAI), 91
Direct and manage project execution process,
  23–26
Directive organizations, 138
Discipline, 276
Disintegration, xviii–xix
Dissatisfaction, team, 139
Distribution, 228
Divestment phase, 130
Documentation:
  of contracts, 30–31
  of formal acceptance, 31–32
  of lessons learned, 219
  of project closure, 32
DoD (*see* Department of Defense)
DOE (traditional design of experiments), 120
Drum, 276
Durations, 107, 205–208

EAC (*see* Estimate at completion)
Early start analysis, 55–56
Earned value (EV):
  application of, 82–83
  criteria for, 84
  definition of, 82
  graphs on, 271–274
  and monitor/control project work, 27
  in MS Project, 208, 209
  performance analysis integration
    with, 113
  in project management integration, 101
  on project reviews, 244
  in resource management, 216
  standards used in, 84
  for task list prioritization, 53–54
Earned value analysis, 242, 271–274
Earned value control, 61
Earned value management system (EVMS),
  179
Eastern Company strategic integration (case
  study), 185–203
  acquisition interruption in, 202
  commitment/partnership in, 187
  communication program in, 202
  customer-awareness/satisfaction strategy in,
    195–197
  economically-priced-power strategy in, 194
  environmental-impact strategy in, 200–201
  and global/international projects, 202–203
  key strategies in, 188–189
  resources-at-reasonable costs strategy in,
    194–195
  responsible/knowledgeable-workforce
    strategy in, 197–199
  results of, 202
  risks/goals identified in, 185–186
  safe-working-environment strategy in, 197
  stakeholder relations in, 187
  strategic plan in, 192–193
  SWOT in, 189–192
  technology/equipment-improvement strategy
    in, 199–200
  waste/cost-reduction strategy in, 201–202
Effectiveness, personal, 282
Electronic procurement (eProcurement),
  xix–xx, 6, 42
Employees (as stakeholders), 187
Empowered organizations, 138
Empowerment, 133, 138
Engineering environment, 110
Enron, 8
Enterprise environmental factors, 16
Environmental impact, 189, 200–201

Environmental scanning (*see* Business plan/planning)
eProcurement (*see* Electronic procurement)
Equipment improvement, 189, 199–200
Escalation system for decisions, 218, 264
Estimate at completion (EAC), 180, 274
Ethics, 8, 170
EV (*see* Earned value)
Evaluation:
    in-plant quality, 123–124
    program, 219, 267
    project, 218
    (*See also* Program evaluation and review technique)
EVM measurement techniques, 86
EVMS (earned value management system), 179
Expert judgment, 18
External factors integration, 108
External integration, 3
Extrinsic rewards, 141, 142
Eye contact, 162

Failure in project management, 275
Failure modes and effects analysis (FMEA), 214
Federal Aviation Administration, 167
Federal government model of contract integration, 107–110
Feedback, 241
FHA (functional hazard analysis), 214
Final product/service/result, 31
Finance:
    accounting/internal control interface with, 217
    project team integration with, 230
Financial auditing system, 219
Financial control, 216
Financial goals, 224
Financial reporting, xix, 42
Fire suppression systems, 95
Fixed costs, 205, 207
Flexible organizations, 166
Flipcharts, 160
FMEA (failure modes and effects analysis), 214
Focus setting, 145–147
    goals in, 147
    mission in, 146–147
    steps of, 147
    vision in, 146
Focus statement, 149–150
Follow-up, 240–241
Force field analysis, 158

Forecasts, 27
Formal acceptance documentation, 31–32
Forward integration, 2, 3, 33, 110
Free-wheeling, 155–156
Friedman, Thomas, 39, 57
Functional hazard analysis (FHA), 214
Functional integration, 108–109
Functional support, 42
Functional teams, 134
Future value indicator, 168

Gantt chart, 56, 73–75, 99, 206–208, 241
Gateway decisions, 12, 33, 217
Gestures, 162
"Getting unstuck," 281
Global interface, 39
Global projects, 202–203
Global scale of integration, 57
Global teams, 41–42
Goal setting, 147
Government acquisition, 107–110
Groupthink, 140

Handouts, 160
Hardware integration, 46
Hiegel, James, xx
Historical information, 32
Horizontal integration, 4, 101
Horizontal traceability, 180–181
Human resources (HR):
    interface with, 218
    project team integration with, 230
    as support system, 42

Ideation, 227
Images of Organization (Gareth Morgan), 58, 171
IMP (*see* Integrated master plan)
Impact statement, 49–50
Implementation phase, 239–240
Implemented change requests, 25
Implemented corrective actions, 25
Implemented defect repairs, 25
Implemented preventive actions, 25
IMS (*see* Integrated master schedule)
In-plant quality evaluation (IQUE), 123–124
Incentive awards, 94
Individual involvement, 132–134
Individual work ethic, 165–166
Industry scale of integration, 57
Industry standards, 216
Information technology:
    program, 216–217, 266
    as support system, 43

Initiator, 14
Integrated change control, 27–30
Integrated cost control, 2
Integrated Logistics Support Handbook
    (James V. Jones), 130
Integrated master plan (IMP):
    as Gantt type, 99
    and IMS, 110–111, 226
    as schedule structure, 106
Integrated master schedule (IMS):
    as Gantt type, 99
    and IMP, 110–111, 226
    in MS Project, 210
Integrated matrix organization, 127–128
Integrated monitoring, 57–58
Integrated product development (IPD), 88, 89
Integrated product teams (IPTs), 88–89
Integrated program schedule, 113
Integrated project management, 259–262
    change management process, 261
    contract management issues, 262
    elements of, 263–264
    monitoring/tracking, 261
    MS Project, 262
    project life cycle, 260
    project team/organizational structures, 262
    requirements/features of, 259–260
    resources/costs, 261
    risk planning/management, 261
    scheduling, 260–261
    scope of work, 260
    tools for, 265–267
    WBS, 260
Integrated project management culture, 213
Integrated project teams, 131–132
Integrated risk planning, 291–294
    company setup for, 292
    for costs, 293
    issues in, 292
    life cycles in, 294
    for quality, 293
    for resources, 293
    and risk information, 294
    for scope, 292–293
    for technology, 293
    for time/schedule, 293
Integrated Transportation System (case
    study), 33–46
    business planning (gateway 2) of, 40
    chassis/mechanical/electronics
        design/development (gateway 10) of, 46
    global interface (gateway 1) of, 39
    global team composition/development
        (gateway 4) of, 41–42

Integrated Transportation System (case study)
    (Cont.):
    market/customer interface (gateway 7) of, 44
    organizational development (gateway 3) of,
        40–41
    portfolio development/management
        (gateway 6) of, 43
    project integration management (gateway 8)
        of, 44–45
    schedule of, 33–39
    software design/development (gateway 11)
        of, 46
    software/hardware integration (gateway 13)
        of, 46
    support systems audit (gateway 5) of, 42–43
    systems safety/reliability (gateway 9) of, 45
    test equipment/testing (gateway 12) of, 46
Integration, xv–xx, 1–32
    and balanced score card, xix
    change control process of, 27–30
    characteristics of, 3–4
    close project process of, 30–32
    concept of, 3
    critical chain theory in, xviii–xix
    direct/manage project execution process of,
        23–26
    eProcurement, xix–xx, 6
    and ethics, 8
    indicators of, 2
    leadership function of, xvii
    model of, 8–9
    monitor/control project work process of,
        26–27
    organizational issues with, 9–12
    PMBOK standard on, xviii, 6–7, 11
    PMI OPM 3 maturity model of, xix
    preliminary project scope statement
        development process of, 19–21
    processes of, 12, 13
    project charter development process of, 12,
        14–19
    project management plan development
        process of, 21–23
    project/program managers' roles in, xv–xvi
    and project selection, 5
    quality standards for, xvii–xviii
    steps in process of, 60–61
    and strategic planning, 7–8
    vertical/horizontal, 4–5
Integration skills:
    developing, 10
    of program/project managers, 61
Integration support systems, 3
Integration systems, limitations of, 219

Integration thinking, 3
Integrative capacity, 41
Interface management, 60, 217–218, 267
Internal control, 217
Internal control management, 170
Internal integration, 3
International partnering, 39
Internet, 167–168
Internet system, community, 95
Intrinsic rewards, 141, 142
Introduction to Quality Engineering (Taguchi), 120
IPD (*see* Integrated product development)
IPTs (*see* Integrated product teams)
IQUE (*see* In-plant quality evaluation)
ISO 9000, 196, 202

Job assignments, 68
Jones, James V., 130
Just-in-time method, 122

Kerzner, Harold, 130

Late start analysis, 55–56
LCL (lower control limit), 121
Lead time, 99
Leadership, 278
  impacts of, 278
  integration as function of, xvi
  and motivation, 280
Leased land under public ownership, 92
Lessons learned, 82
  documentation of, 219
  process of using, 276–277
  questions to examine, 171–172
  risk integration in, 179
Life cycle:
  project, 260
  risk intensity in project, 294
  system development, 108, 109
Line of balance, 99, 100
Listening, 144–145, 151–152
Loss, 120
Lower control limit (LCL), 121

Management approach, 96
Management reserve, 181
Management skills, 61
Manual:
  program management (*see* Program management manual)
  project, 177
Manufacturing, breakthrough, 244
Manufacturing resource planning (MRPII), 122–125
  CAD/CAE/CAM in, 122
  CALS in, 123

CIM in, 122
computer systems in, 122
customer-driven project management in, 124–125
DoD system development/improvement methodologies in, 123
IQUE in, 123–124
R&M 2000 approach in, 124
TIL in, 123
VE in, 124
Market interface, 44
Market launch, 228, 245
Marketing:
  production scheduling integration with, 228
  and sales interface, 218
Marketing transition, 245
MARTA (*see* Metropolitan Atlanta Rapid Transit Authority)
Material resource planning (MRP), 112
Mathematical models, 18
Matrix organization, 127–128, 217
Matrix team structure, 214
Mean time between failure, 45
Measurement of integration success, 10
Meetings:
  program review, 217
  skills for, 282
  teams (*see* Team meetings)
Metropolitan Atlanta Rapid Transit Authority (MARTA), 64, 65
Microsoft (MS) Project, 205–211, 262, 295–296
  integrating projects in, 209–211
  PERT/risk matrix terminology in, 105
  WBS/task outline in, 205–209
Milestones, 99
Mission:
  of Eastern Company (case), 193
  team, 136–137, 146–147
Mission statement, 137
Mitigation, 87, 98
Monitoring, 231, 261
  customer reporting interface with, 112
  of project work, 26–27
Monte Carlo analysis, 182
Morgan, Gareth, 58, 171
Motivation, 279
  and leadership, 280
  team, 141–142
  of workforce, 94
MRP (material resource planning), 112
MRPII (*see* Manufacturing resource planning)
MS Project (*see* Microsoft Project)
Multifunctional teams, 134
Multiproject integration, 93
Multiproject management, 62–63, 229

Narrative report, 242
National Baldrige Quality Award criteria, xvi–xvii
Need, business, 15
Negotiating, 281
Net present value (NPV), 5
Network logic diagrams, 54–55, 99, 100
Network management of schedules, 79
Network scheduling, 87–88
Network system, 216
Networks, 106–107
New Orleans, rebuilding (see Rebuilding New Orleans (case study))
New Orleans Community Development District, 91
New product development, 226–228, 248–250
New Vision, Inc., 91, 94, 96, 97
Nominal group technique, 156
Non-value-added costs, 188, 201–202
Nonconformance costs, 121
NPV (net present value), 5

Operations phase, 130
Organization, 230–231
    preparing, 9–10
    risk management setup in, 292
Organization-wide project management system, 213–215, 265
Organizational development, 40–41
Organizational integration, 39
Organizational interfaces, 252–253
Organizational process assets:
    at closure, 31–32
    for conducting work, 17
    and project charter development, 16–18
    for storing/retrieving information, 17–18
Organizational Project Management 3 (OPM 3), xix
Organizational quality, 165–172
    and change tracking/midstream corrections, 168–169
    and embedded/integrated quality, 166–167
    and ethics/internal control management, 170
    factors affecting, 165
    and flexibility, 166
    and full cycle customer involvement, 166
    and individual work ethic, 165–166
    and Internet, 167–168
    and lessons learned, 171–172
    and projectized teams, 170
    and traditional project teams, 169–170
    and vertical integration, 171
Organizational structures, 230, 262
Orientation, team, 139
Overhead transparencies, 160
Owners (as stakeholders), 187

Parallel multiproject management, 229
Parameter design, 120
Participative organizations, 138
Partnering opportunities, 244
Partnership, 193
Payment milestones, 96
PCAS (Project Cost Accounting Systems), 65
Performance analysis:
    earned value integration with, 113
    from status, 102
Performance assessment, accuracy of, 98
Performance constraint, 127
Performance prediction, reliability of, 98
Personal effectiveness, 282
PERT (see Program evaluation and review technique)
Peters, Tom, 132
Pipeline management, 218
Planning:
    bottom-up, 101
    business, 40, 48, 215
    integrated risk, 291–294
    manufacturing resource, 122–125
    material resource, 112
    production, 252
    and program administrator/planner, 71–75
    in program management manual, 85–86
    project, 224–225
    reliability, 217
    resource, 79–80
    risk, 182, 261, 291–294
    risk management, 182, 285–286
    staffing, 216
    strategic, 7–8, 48
    workforce, 216, 229
Planning package, 86, 181
Planning process group, 12
PMBOK (see Project Management Body of Knowledge)
PMI (Project Management Institute), 1
PMI OPM 3 maturity model, xix
PMIS (project management information system), 18
PMO (see Project management office)
PMO (program management office), 70
PMP certification (see Project Management Professional certification)
PMs (see Project managers)
Portfolio:
    development/management of, 43, 49–50
    implementation of, 229
Portfolio management, 218, 267
Portfolio pipeline, 215, 222
Portfolio planning and development system, 215
Power costs, 188, 194
Preconcept phase, 131
Preliminary design risk review, 253–255
Preliminary project scope statement, 21

Preliminary project scope statement development, 19–21
Presentation(s), 157–163, 242, 280
    arranging for, 161
    developing materials for, 158
    example of, 158–159
    follow-up to, 163
    giving, 161–163
    outline of, 159
    practicing, 161
    preparing materials for, 159–160
    producing materials for, 160–161
    steps of, 157–158
    steps of preparing, 158
Presenters, 161–162
    delivery of, 162
    preparation of, 161–162
    style of, 162
Process groups, 12
Process improvement standards, xvi–xvii
Process improvement target(s), 213–219
    change management system as, 218–219
    interface management as, 217–218
    organization-wide project management system as, 213–215
    portfolio management as, 218
    product/service development process as, 217
    program evaluation system as, 219
    program information technology system as, 216–217
    program monitoring/control system as, 218
    program/portfolio planning/development system as, 215
    resource management system as, 216
Process teams, 88
Procurement:
    electronic, xix–xx, 6, 42
    interface with, 217
    project team integration with, 230
    timely, 69
Product design, 228
Product development, 228
    design reviews in, 248–250
    as process, 217, 266
    and production, 111–114
    project management system integration with, 226–228, 247–248
    risk integration in, 178, 247–248
    technology for, 244
Product lines, 215
Product requirements definition, 251
Product teams, 88
Production, team, 139
Production capability, 193
Production phase, 130

Production planning, 252
Production planning risk review, 254
Production scheduling:
    configuration management integration with, 228
    marketing/distribution integration with, 228, 245
Program administrator, 71–75
Program definition, 215
Program evaluation and audit, 267
Program evaluation and review technique (PERT), 65, 105, 207, 296
Program evaluation system, 219
Program information technology system, 216–217, 266
Program management:
    integration skills of, 61
    as multiproject management, 62–63
    principles of, 67–69
    (See also Integrated project management)
Program management manual, 67–89
    budgeting/planning/resource loading in, 85–86
    closeout/lessons learned described in, 82
    control account manager described in, 84–85
    customer reporting described in, 88
    data incorporation described in, 87
    earned value described in, 82–84
    integrated product teams described in, 88–89
    integrated schedule fundamentals in, 87
    network scheduling in, 87–88
    principles of program management in, 67–69
    product/process teams described in, 88
    resource planning/control described in, 79–80
    risk management scheduling in, 86–87
    roles/responsibilities described in, 69–75
    scheduling process described in, 75–79
    tracking/review described in, 80
    transitions described in, 88
    update procedures scheduling in, 80–81
    variance analysis in, 81–82
Program management office (PMO), 70
Program management system, 266
Program management tools, 5
Program managers:
    integration roles of, xv–xvi
    roles/responsibilities of, 70
Program monitoring and control system, 218, 267
Program networks, 88, 106–107
Program planner, 71–75
Program planning and development system, 215
Program review, 80
Program review meeting formats, 217
Program scale of integration, 57
Program structure, 63–65
Project charter, 18–19

Project charter development, 12, 14–19
    inputs to, 15–18
    outputs from, 18–19
    tools/techniques for, 18
Project closure documentation, 32
Project contract integration, 107–110
Project Cost Accounting Systems (PCAS), 65
Project definition, 236–239
Project development, 228
Project evaluation, 218
Project files, 32
Project generation, 218
Project integration:
    assessing team competence in, 279
    communication in, 280
    conflict in, 281, 282
    core team development in, 278
    decision making in, 275–276
    discipline in, 276
    failure in, 275
    "getting unstuck" in, 281
    and interface points, 221–222
    leadership impacts in, 278
    leadership in, 278
    lessons learned from, 276–277
    meeting skills in, 282
    motivation in, 279
    motivation/leadership in, 280
    negotiating in, 281
    in New Orleans project, 94
    personal effectiveness in, 282
    PM criteria, 278
    PM selection/development in, 277
    presentations in, 280
    project team competence in, 278
    successful, 277
    team relations in, 277
    theory of constraints in, 276
    total managers in, 279
    unknowns in, 276
Project integration management, 117–134
    activities of, 11–12
    concurrent engineering in, 118–119
    cost of poor quality in, 121–122
    customer as source of, 118
    cycles of, 129–131
    definition of, 126
    history of, 125–126
    individual involvement in, 132–134
    of ITS case study, 44–45
    just-in-time method in, 122
    manufacturing resource planning in, 122–125
    matrix organization in, 127–128
    organizational issues with, 9–11

Project integration management (Cont.):
    processes of, 12, 13
    quality function deployment in, 119–120
    robust design in, 120–121
    statistical process control in, 121
    steps for, 9, 10
    team commitment in, 131–132
    teams in (see Team(s))
    time/cost/performance trade-offs in, 127
    total production maintenance in, 122
Project integration management plan, 6–7
Project life cycle, 260, 294
Project management, 235–244
    close-out/follow-up phase of, 240–241
    concept phase of, 236
    customer-driven, 124–125
    definition of, 126
    definition phase of, 236–239
    design/implementation phase of, 239–240
    methodology for, 18
    multi-, 62–63
    phases of, 130, 235
    philosophy of, 128–129
    principles of, 129
    product development integration with, 247–248
    single, 61–62
    tools/techniques for, 241–244
    uniqueness of, 126–127
Project Management, Strategic Design, and
        Implementation (David I. Cleland), 130
Project Management (Harold Kerzner), 130
Project Management Body of Knowledge (PMBOK),
        xviii, 1, 6–7, 11, 285–289
Project management information system (PMIS), 18
Project Management Institute (PMI), 1
Project management integration activities, 101–106
Project management office (PMO), 42, 43, 218
Project management plan, 6, 23, 24, 26,
        214–215
Project management plan development, 21–23
Project Management Professional (PMP) certification,
        xviii, 1
Project management system:
    framework for, 226–228
    integration supported by, 231–234
    organization-wide, 213–215
    uniform, 218
Project managers (PMs):
    criteria for competent, 278
    identification/assignment of, 12, 14
    integration challenges for, 269–270
    integration roles of, xv–xvi
    integration skills of, 61, 62
    risk integration roles of, 180–181

Project managers (PMs) (*Cont.*):
  selection/development of, 277
  teams and selection of, 42
Project manual, 177
Project performance, 243–244
Project plan, 174–175
Project planning, 224–225
Project reporting requirements, 96
Project reviews, 231
  for actionable information, 243–244
  readiness of company for, 234–235
Project scale of integration, 57
Project selection, 5, 218
  business financial goals integration with, 224
  methods of, 18
  risk integration in, 174
Project team, 262
  accounting/finance integration with, 230
  HR/training integration with, 230
  performance of, 244
  personal competencies/skill integration with, 231
  procurement/acquisition integration
    with, 230
Prototype development, 46, 228, 251–252
Public-private community policy, 92–93

QFD (*see* Quality function deployment)
QS 9000 certification, 196, 202
QS 14000 certification, 196, 202
Qualitative risk analysis, 286–287
Quality:
  control account manager for integration of, 230
  embedded/integrated, 166–167
  risks with, 293
  in single project planning, 225–226
  in software development, 258
Quality function deployment (QFD), 117–120
Quality integration, 59–60
Quality optimization, 120
Quality standards, xvi–xvii
Quantitative risk analysis, 287
Q.U.E.S.T. teams, 201, 202
QuickTech Building Systems (case application),
    48–63
  cost/schedule/risk/quality integration in,
    59–60
  early/late start analysis in, 55–56
  earned-value task list in, 53–54
  Gantt chart in, 56
  integrated monitoring in, 57–58
  integration process steps in, 60–61
  management skills integration in, 61
  multiproject management in, 62–63
  network diagram in, 54–55

QuickTech Building Systems (case application) (*Cont.*):
  portfolio development/management of, 49–50
  "reading" project as whole in, 58–59
  resource integration in, 56
  scale/integration in, 57
  single project management in, 61–62
  WBS of, 51–53

Rainbow team, 132
RAM (*see* Responsibility assignment matrix)
"reading" project as integrated whole, 58–59
Rebuilding New Orleans (case study), 91–100
  accurate performance assessment in, 98
  affordability requirements in, 96–97
  community Internet system in, 95
  contract goals in, 94
  contract objectives in, 94–95
  fire suppression systems in, 95
  integration challenge in, 92–94
  leased-land-under-public ownership in, 92
  management approach in, 96
  New Vision program in, 97–98
  project reporting requirements in, 96
  reliable prediction of future performance in, 98
  security systems in, 95
  stage gate process/payment milestones in, 96
  structures in, 95
  timely management action in, 98–100
  transportation in, 95–96
Recognizing integration success, 10
Recommended corrective actions, 27
Recommended defect repair, 27
Recommended preventive actions, 27
Recovery plan development, 102–103
Recurring schedule status, 101
Regulators (as stakeholders), 187
Rejected change requests, 26
Reliability, 45
Reliability and maintainability (R&M) 2000
    approach, 124
Reliability planning, 217
Reports/reporting:
  customer, 88, 112
  financial, xix, 42
  narrative, 242
  requirements for, 96
  schedule, 102
Requested changes, 25, 27
Resolution, team, 139
Resource assignment, 214
Resource integration, 56
Resource loading, 85–86
Resource management, 71–75
Resource management system, 216, 266

Resource planning and control, 79–80
Resources, 261
    cost of, 188, 194–195
    risks with, 293
Responsibility assignment matrix (RAM),
        179–180
Review(s):
    program, 80
    progress, 69
Review meetings, 217
Rewards, 141–142
Risk(s), 173–183
    control account manager for integration of,
        230
    and decision making, 284
    elements of, 284
    potential factors of project, 284–285
    product development integration of, 247–248
    ranking of, 86
    rewards of taking, 284
    in single project planning, 225–226
    in software development, 258
Risk analysis, 86, 182
Risk assessment and management, 5
Risk-based scheduling, 86, 103, 104
Risk identification, 182, 286
Risk information, 294
Risk integration:
    budgeting issues in, 181
    checklist for, 173–179
    earned value as indicator of, 179
    and Monte Carlo analysis, 182
    project manager roles in, 180–181
    of QuickTech Building Systems case, 59–60
    rationale for, 181–182
    and sensitivity analysis, 182
    in software development, 183
    and unaccountability, 179–180
Risk management, 261, 283–289
    decision making in, 284
    elements of risk in, 284
    identification of risks in, 286
    monitoring/control in, 288–289
    planning in, 285–286
    PMBOK on, 285–289
    and potential project risk factors, 284–285
    processes of, 175–177, 218, 285–289
    purpose of, 181, 283
    qualitative/quantitative risk analysis in,
        286–287
    response planning in, 288
    and rewards of taking risks, 284
    scheduling, 86–87
Risk management planning, 182, 285–286

Risk management system, 215
Risk matrix, 102–105, 115
Risk mitigation, 258
Risk monitoring and control, 288–289
Risk planning, 261
    integrated, 291–294
    and mitigation, 182
Risk process, 86
Risk ranking, 104
Risk response planning, 288
Risk reviews, 253–254
Risk tools, 86
Risk tracking, 182
R&M (reliability and maintainability) 2000
        approach, 124
Robust design, 118, 120–121
Rolling wave, 86, 181
Rope, 276
Round robin, 155

Safe working environment, 188–189, 197
Sales, 218
Sarbanes-Oxley Act, xix, 8, 23, 32, 96, 170, 215
Scale of integration, 57
Scenarios, 295–296
Schedule(s):
    baselining of, 77–79
    categories of, 99–100
    control account manager for integration of,
        230
    elements of, 70
    generic WBS integration with, 226
    network management of, 79
    risks with, 293
    scope of work integration with, 225
    in single project planning, 225–226
Schedule control, 77
Schedule-driven work, 69
Schedule integration, 59–60
Schedule linkages, 107
Schedule performance, 231
Schedule performance index (SPI), 273
Schedule reporting, 102
Schedule variance (SV), 113, 208, 209, 273
Scheduling, 260–261
    elements of, 98–99
    five-step process of, 75–77
    fundamentals of integrated, 87
    of individuals and work packages, 230–231
    in New Orleans case, 97–98
    and program administrator/planner, 71–75
    risk-based, 86
Scheduling system, 214
Scope description, 16

Scope of work, 260
    cost/schedule integration with, 225
    customer requirements integration with, 223
    defining/communicating, 68
    task definition/WBS integration with, 224–225
Scope risks, 292–293
Scrubbing, 103
Security systems, 95
Self-esteem, 142
Sensitivity analysis, 182
Service development process, 217, 266
Single project management, 61–62, 225–226
Slack, 55
Slip, 156
Software:
    integration of, 46
    for project management, 73
Software development:
    complexity in, 257–258
    in ITS case study, 46
    quality/risk in, 258
    risk integration in, 183
    risk mitigation in, 258
SOW (statement of work), 15
SPC (see Statistical process control)
Speaking (at meetings), 151
SPI (schedule performance index), 273
Sponsor, 14
SRS (see System requirements specification)
Staffing planning, 216
Stage gate process, 96, 114–115
Stakeholder relations, 187
Standards, industry, 216
Statement of work (SOW), 15
Statistical process control (SPC), 117, 118, 121
Strategic objectives development, 40, 215
Strategic plan/planning, 7–8
    of Eastern Company case, 186–187
    of QuickTech Building Systems case, 48
    on SOW, 16
Strengths, weaknesses, opportunities, and threats (SWOT) analysis:
    of Eastern Company case, 189–192
    of QuickTech Building Systems case, 48
Structures (New Orleans), 95
Subcontractors, 93
Subtasks, 51
Summary tasks, 51
Supplier data integration, 106
Supplier management, 87
Supplier quality management, 6

Supplier schedules, 87
Suppliers (as stakeholders), 187
Supply chain management, 6
Support systems audit, 42–43
SV (see Schedule variance)
SWOT analysis (see Strengths, weaknesses, opportunities, and threats analysis)
System design risk review, 254, 256
System integration, 117–125
    concurrent engineering in, 118–119
    cost of poor quality in, 121–122
    customer as source of, 118
    just-in-time method in, 122
    manufacturing resource planning in, 122–125
    quality function deployment in, 119–120
    robust design in, 120–121
    statistical process control in, 121
    total production maintenance in, 122
System requirements specification (SRS), 67, 72
Systems design, 120
Systems of integration, developing, 10
Systems safety/reliability, 45
Systems theory, 3

Taguchi approach, 120
Task definition, 224–225
Task level design risk review, 254, 257
Task level requirements risk review, 254, 257
Task linkages and interdependency, 214
Task list, 241
    earned-value prioritization of, 53–54
    in MS Project, 205–209
Tasks, 107
Team(s), 134–163, 262
    assessing competence of, 279
    brainstorming by, 153–157
    communication on, 143–144
    competence of, 278
    conflict management on, 139–141
    critique of teamwork by, 143
    definition of, 134
    dynamics of, 138–139
    effective teamwork in, 134–136
    focus setting by, 145–147
    generating commitment/purpose in, 131–132
    global, 41–42
    importance of, 168
    integrated program/project/process, 113–114
    and listening, 144–145

Team(s) (*Cont.*):
   meetings of, 147–153
   member roles/responsibilities on, 137–138
   mission identification for, 136–137
   motivation of, 141–142
   presentations by, 157–163
   product/process, 88
   and self-esteem, 142
   traditional vs. customer-driven, 169–170
   types of, 134
Team integration, 108–109
Team meetings, 147–153
   in action, 150–154
   critiques of, 152–153
   effective, 147–148
   focus statement for, 149–150
   roles/responsibilities/relationships in, 149
   rules of conduct for, 148–149
Team relationships, 109–110, 277
Teamwork, 134–136
   benefits of, 135
   building, 136
   critiques of, 143
   in engineering environment, 110
   principles of, 135–136
   as program management principle, 68
Technical interfaces, 252–253
Technical performance, 231
Technical process development, 178
Technical support, 42
Technology:
   improvement of, 189, 199–200
   risks with, 293
   support/testing of, 217
Test equipment, 46
Test readiness risk review, 254, 256
Testing:
   of ITS case study, 46
   of technology, 217
Theory of constraints, 276
Third-party certification, 183
TIL (total integrated logistics), 123
Time-based network diagram, 54–55
Time constraint, 127
Time risks, 293
Tolerance design, 121
Tools, 103–115
   change control, 105–106
   contract integration, 107–110
   CPM, 107
   network, 106–107
   risk matrix, 102–105
   supplier data integration, 106
   WBS/IMP, 106

Top-down integration, 101, 102
Top management:
   roles of, 232–234
   visibility of programs/projects with, 218
Total integrated logistics (TIL), 123
Total managers, 279
Total production maintenance (TPM), 122
Total quality management (TQM), 120
TPM (total production maintenance), 122
TQM (total quality management), 120
Traceability, 180–181, 229
Tracking, 261
   integrated, 80
   of progress, 69
Trade-off management, 61
Traditional design of experiments (DOE), 120
Traditional project teams, 169–170
Training:
   project team integration with, 230
   workforce, 217
Transitions, programmatic, 88
Transportation, 95–96
Transportation system (case study) (*see*
   Integrated Transportation System)
Trust, 133

UCL (upper control limit), 121
Undistributed budget, 85, 181
Uniform project management system, 218
U.S. Army Audit Agency, 96
Universal Avionics, Inc., 167
"Unstuck, getting," 281
Update procedures, scheduling, 80–81
Upper control limit (UCL), 121

Validated defect repair, 25
Validation, design, 252
Validation phase, 131
Value engineering (VE), 124
Variance analysis, 81–82, 86
VE (value engineering), 124
Verification process, 183
Vertical integration, 4–5, 101, 171
Vertical traceability, 180
Virtual teams, 41
Vision, 146
Voice of customer, 118

Waste reduction, 188, 201–202
WBS (*see* Work breakdown structure)
WBS dictionary, 213
Weighted scoring model, 5, 43
WIP (work in progress), 101
Work and task planning, 59–60

Work authorization system, 214
Work breakdown structure (WBS), 51–53, 106,
    241, 260
  deliverables (level 1) of, 51
  generic, 51, 213–214, 226
  integration issues of, 52–53
  in MS Project, 205–209
  for new product project, 225–226
  organizational structure integration with,
    230
  scope of work integration with task
    definition and, 224–225
  standard, 68

Work breakdown structure (WBS) (*Cont.*):
  subtasks (level 3) of, 51
  summary tasks (level 2) of, 51
  workpackage (level 4) of, 52
Work ethic, 165–166
Work in progress (WIP), 101
Work package, 52, 85–86, 181
Work performance information, 24–26
Workforce, 189, 197–199
Workforce planning, 216, 229
Workforce training, 217
The World is Flat (Thomas Friedman),
    39, 57